AN INDEX TO
SKITS AND STUNTS

By

NORMA OLIN IRELAND

BOSTON

THE F. W. FAXON COMPANY, INC.

1958

TO

THE BORNS: EVA, HARLAN FRED, MARGARET

AND THE MEMORY OF

HARLAN, SR.

WHO ALWAYS BELIEVED IN MY "IDEAS"

"Old Friends Are Best" — John Selden

FOREWORD

The idea for this index was born many years ago when the compiler was in college! Assigned to find skits and stunts for a weekly group-presentation, we found it a real problem to locate suitable material in libraries. Even today we have learned that libraries do not always have sufficient books to meet the demand, either in book or pamphlet form. It is our purpose in this little volume, therefore, not only to index a representative collection of sources, but also to emphasize the fact that there is much good material that can be acquired easily and at small cost. While most of the books we have indexed are worth cataloging for the permanent collection, some of the small and inexpensive titles may be added, in duplicate, to the pamphlet file.

Arrangement and Scope

We have indexed 148 collections by author, title and subject. As in all indexes of this type, the main entry is the title because the title is most frequently remembered and requested. In these collections authors of individual skits and stunts are not always given but we have listed them when available. Subjects are vitally important, of course, as many users want material appropriate for a particular occasion or subject.

Our policy for inclusion has been most generous. We have indexed not only "skits and stunts", literally speaking, but many other entertainments of related interest and usability. Altho we have endeavored not to duplicate material indexed elsewhere, we have included some entertainment forms when they were recent and especially usable. For instance, we have included small sections of *Monologs* and *Dialogs* which we feel will be supplementary to our own previously-published index.[1] This is also true of *Games, Parties* and a few other types, or forms, which we have included, altho sparingly. In addition to the

---

[1] An Index to Monologs and Dialogs. Faxon, 1949.

vii

above we have also indexed the following supplementary materials: *Blackouts, Burlesques, Chalk-talks, Chorus, Jokes, Minstrels, Musical, Pantomimes, Parodies, Poetical, Puppet plays, Shadow plays,* etc.

The number of characters is given only for dialogs and skits of two or more *speaking* parts. These are indicated by asterisks, and the number of characters is given in parenthesis following the title. The reasons for this are threefold: first, because most stunts, pantomimes, etc. are flexible, and the number of characters can be added or substracted at will; secondly, because the compilers of collections, themselves, were not always consistent in giving this information; and thirdly, for the sake of uniformity in our own index, we felt that only such specific information should be given, as specified above.

When the same title appears in two or more different collections the number is indicated in parenthesis, e.g. (2), (3), etc. following the title, and the separate information on author, number of characters and key to collections and page is given. An exception, however, is in the case of a skit and stunt of the same title, which, because of their form, are listed separately. We have alphabetized according to library procedure, primarily, except for foreign words such as el, la, etc. which are herein considered as words because of the humorous value of their titles.

Subject Headings

We have included over 800 different subjects in this book, exclusive of "see" references. We have endeavored to index only the most usable subjects, many of which were used in our "Index to Monologs and Dialogs".[2] Some others were taken from our "Pamphlet File"[3] while a goodly number were new with this index. While we have included some "old" subjects, for historical or humorous purposes, we have added many new ones, such as *Atomic Energy,* etc.

We have added many cross-references, for the convenience of the user. Some headings are necessarily inclusive, such as

---

[2] *Ibid.*

[3] The Pamphlet File. Faxon, 1954.

Radio, which includes skits and stunts about Radio as well as those selections suitable for radio use. Some overlapping of subjects is unavoidable, such as Pantomimes and Shadow Plays; Tableaux and Living Statues. But we felt there is a slight difference which justifies the using of two headings.

Few "Athletic" stunts have been indexed because we felt that gymnastics were more readily found elsewhere. We excluded one good stunt book because it was primarily athletic. But again, we included a few *Races, Relays* and representative sports, to be used in camps, school and outdoor entertainments.

As to the listing of titles under subjects, we have not included selections beginning with the subject-word because we felt it was obvious by its title and could be easily found adjacent to the subject. For instance "Christmas belle minstrels" would not be indexed under the subject *Christmas* because of its obvious subject word starting the title and its adjacent place following the subject.

Acknowledgments

This work makes no claim for completeness altho we do feel that 148 collections indexed is probably more that the usual number found in the average, medium-sized library. We did not always index the latest editions, however, because of the unavailability of books in local libraries.

We are very grateful to the play-publishers who most generously and kindly loaned us their books, insofar as possible, and wish to acknowledge and thank them at this time:

Baker's Plays (Walter H. Baker Co.), 569 Boylston St., Boston 16, Mass.

Denison, T.S. & Co., 321 Fifth Ave., South, Minneapolis 15, Minn.

Eldridge Publishing Co., Franklin, Ohio

French, Samuel, Inc., 7623 Sunset Blvd., Hollywood 46, Calif.

National Recreation Association, 8 West Eighth St., N.Y. 11, N.Y.

Northwestern Press, 315 Fifth Ave., So., Minneapolis 15, Minn.

N. O. I.

TABLE OF CONTENTS

xi

LIST OF ABBREVIATIONS, ETC.

*—dialog, or skit, with no. of characters given

b—boy

char.—characters

f—female

g—girl

m—male

no.—number

Ved August 1966

LIST OF COLLECTIONS ANALYZED IN THIS WORK
AND KEY TO SYMBOLS USED

ABELL—PEP
> Abell, Marietta and Agnes J. Anderson. Pep meeting stunts. Minneapolis, Northwestern press, 1937. 127p.

ABELL—STUNTS
> Abell, Marietta and Agnes J. Anderson. Stunts for every occasion. Minneapolis, Northwestern press, 1939. 96p.

BAKER'S GAY
> Baker's gay nineties scrapbook. Boston, Baker's plays, 1941. 60p.

BARBEE
> Barbee, Lindsey. Assembly skits. A collection of short novelty skits aimed to promote an educational idea. Minneapolis, Northwestern press, 1941. 95p.

BERLE
> Berle, Milton. Laughingly yours. Edited by S. Sylvan Simon. N.Y., French, 1939. 74p.

BREEZY
> Breezy stunts and diversions, by various authors. Franklin, Ohio, Eldridge pub. co., n.d. 103p.

BRIDGE
> Bridge, Margaret. Snappy stunts for social gatherings. Franklin, Ohio, Eldridge pub. co., n.d. 86p.

BRINGS—MASTER
> Brings, Lawrence M. The master stunt book. Minneapolis, Denison, 1956. 431p.

BUCHANAN
> Buchanan, M. C. Chalk talks for farm audiences and other groups. Minneapolis, Denison, 1950. 112p.

BUGBEE

Bugbee, Willis N. and others. Catchy programs, games and stunts, for school and community. Syracuse, N.Y., Willis N. Bugbee co., 1928 111p.

BUGBEE—GOOFY

Bugbee, Willis N. Goofy stunts. Syracuse, N.Y., Willis N. Bugbee co., 1936. 117p.

BUGBEE—LIVE WIRE

Bugbee, Willis N. and others. The live wire stunt book. Franklin, Ohio, Eldridge pub. co., n.d. 144p.

BUGBEE—LIVELY

Bugbee, Willis N. Lively dialogs. Minneapolis, Denison, 1937. 127p.

BUGBEE—NUTTY

Bugbee, Willis N., Grace Keith Samuelson, Arthur Kaser, Karin Sundelofasbrand, and others. Nutty stunts; one of the Bugbee famous stunt series. Syracuse, N.Y., Willis N. Bugbee co., 1937. 116p.

CANOPY—BURL.

Canopy, Willard M. Burlesque debates. Minneapolis, Northwestern press, 1932. 117p.

CANOPY—HIGH

Canopy, Williard B. The high school stunt show and carnival. Minneapolis, Denison, 1929. 115p.

CASEY

Casey, Arten. Intermission specialties. Vaudeville specialties for presentation between the acts of full-evening plays. Minneapolis, The Northwestern press, 1933. 126p.

CASEY—PEPPY

Casey, Beatrice M., Alta M. Toepp, Cressy M. Weaver, Grace Keith Samuelson, Beatrice Plumb, Gladys Lloyd, Mabel Tuttle Craig, and others. Peppy stunts and games. Franklin, Ohio, Eldridge pub. co., n.d. 120p.

CHAPLIN

Chaplin, Alice Williams. Six rehearsal-less entertainments. Boston, Baker, 1921. 88p.

DRUMMOND—STUNT FUN
    Drummond, Richard. Stunt fun. A collection of brief stunts for all occasions. Minneapolis, Northwestern press, 1939. 117p.

DRUMMOND—THREE
    Drummond, Richard. Three-minute blackouts. Minneapolis, Northwestern press, 1935. 94p.

EASY—BLACKOUTS
    Easy blackouts. By various authors. Boston, Baker's plays, 1934. 93p.

EASY—ENTERTAIN.
    Easy entertainments with music. By various authors. Boston, Baker's plays, 1935. 96p.

EASY—IMPR.
    Easy impromptus. Twenty blackouts by various authors. Boston, Baker's plays, 1936. 125p.

EASY—SKITS
    Easy skits, blackouts, and pantomimes. Chicago, Dramatic pub. co., 1939. 112p.

EASY—STUNTS
    Easy stunts and skits N.Y., National recreation assoc., n.d. 32p.

EDGERTON
    Edgerton, Alice Craig. Selections and plays for juveniles. Boston, Baker, 1931. 151p.

EISENBERG—FUN
    Eisenberg, Helen and Larry. Fun with skits, stunts and stories. N.Y., Association press, 1955. 256p.

EISENBERG—HAND.
    Eisenberg, Helen and Larry. The handbook of skits and stunts. N.Y., Association press, 1953. 254p.

ENTERTAIN—STUNTS
    Entertainment stunts. N.Y., National recreation association, n.d. 6p.

793
F41p

FERRIS

Ferris, Helen. Producing amateur entertainments. N.Y., Dutton, 1921. 266p.

FRICK—FALL

Frick, Flora M. Stunts for fall. Chicago, Dramatic publishing co., 1929. 80p.

FRICK—SUMMER

Frick, Flora M. Stunts for summer. Chicago, Dramatic publishing co., 1930. 94p.

FUNNY

Funny stunts with music. Franklin, Ohio, Eldridge pub. co., n.d. 68p.

793
G27n

GEISTER—NEW

Geister, Edna. The new ice-breakers. N.Y., Harper, 1942. 153p.

GEORGE—TEN

George, Charles. Ten novelty skits, a collection of novelty entertainments. Minneapolis, Northwestern press, 1933. 47p.

GEORGE—TWELVE

George, Charles. Twelve novelty skits. Minneapolis, Northwestern press, 1935. 57p.

GITHENS

Githens, Harry and others. Hilarious stunts. Franklin, Ohio, Eldridge pub. co., 1946. 131p.

GODDARD—CHILDREN'S

Goddard, Richard. The children's entertainment book. Minneapolis, Denison, n.d. 120p.

792.9
H19

HANLEY—STUNTS

Hanley, Elizabeth Hines. Stunts of fun and fancy. N.Y., French, 1925. 36p.

HOPE

Hope, Courtney. Fun for the footlights. London, Frederick Muller, 1936. 86p.

HOXIE
Hoxie, Evelyn. Seven dialogues for adults. Boston, Baker, 1925. 75p.

HUBER
Huber, Louis J. Short, short plays. A collection of ten-minute plays. Minneapolis, Northwestern press, 1940. 91p.

HUBER—ALL
Huber, Louis J. All in fun. Minneapolis, Northwestern press, 1948. 123p.

HUBER—ARENA
Huber, Louis J. Easy arena plays. Minneapolis, North-western press, 1951. 120p.

HUBER—CHAR.
Huber, Louis J. Character sketches. Minneapolis, North-western press, 1949. 128p.

HUBER—EASY
Huber, Louis J. Easy initiations. A collection of practical initiation stunts, for the club, lodge and fraternity. Min-neapolis, The Northwestern press, 1937. 95p.

HUBER—FOUR
Huber, Louis J. Four minutes of fun. Minneapolis, North-western press, 1949. 159p.

HUBER—GIANT
Huber, Louis J. The giant pep book. Minneapolis, North-western press, 1946. 160p.

HUBER—NO
Huber, Louis J. No rehearsals required. Minneapolis, North-western press, 1945. 95p.

HUBER—NO SCENE
Huber, Louis J. No scenery required. Minneapolis, North-western press, 1950. 118p. 124p.

HUBER—PRACT.
Huber, Louis J. Practical pantomimes. A collection of hum-orous sketches in pantomime. Minneapolis, Northwestern press, 1937. 91p.

HUBER—SIX
> Huber, Louis J. Six minute sketches. Minneapolis, Northwestern press, 1950. 126p.

792
H86e   HUBER—TV
> Huber, Louis J. Easy television plays. Minneapolis, Northwestern press, 1952. 106p.

HUBER—THREE
> Huber, Louis J. "Three minutes of fun". A collection of snappy blackouts. Minneapolis, Northwestern press, 1935. 96p.

HUBER—VAUD.
> Huber, Louis J. Vaudeville skits. Minneapolis, Northwestern press, 1941. 107p.

IRISH—CATCHY
> Irish, Marie. Catchy comic dialogues. Minneapolis, Denison, 1933. 119p.

IRISH—CHILDREN'S
> Irish, Marie. Children's comic dialogues. (A collection of humorous dialogues for little folks, particularly adapted for school entertainments. For children from six to eleven years of age.) Minneapolis, Denison, 1933. 102p.

JOHNSON—BAKER'S
> Johnson, Theodore. Baker's stunt and game book. Boston, Baker, 1928. 104p.

JOHNSON—EASY
> Easy-to-do novelty entertainments. Boston, Baker's plays, 1946. 128p.

JOLLY
> Jolly stunts and pastimes, by various authors. Syracuse, N.Y., The Willis N. Bugbee co., 1939. 106p.

KASER—ACTS
> Kaser, Arthur L. (Jest fun), or, Acts for actin' up. Boston, Baker's plays, 1950. 96p.

KASER—AMATEURS'
Kaser, Arthur L. The amateurs' entertainment book. Minneapolis, Northwestern press, 1945. 72p.

KASER—BUSHEL
Kaser, Arthur L. A bushel of fun. Minneapolis, Denison, 1950. 115p.

KASER—BUTTON
Kaser, Arthur L. Button busters. Boston, Baker's plays, 1949. 112p.

KASER—FUNNY
Kaser, Arthur L. Funny skits for amateurs. Minneapolis, Northwestern press, 1948. 120p.

KASER—GAY
Kaser, Arthur L. Gay nineties fun. Minneapolis, Denison, 1945. 24p.

KASER—HALF
Kaser, Arthur L. Half a dozen mock trials. Boston, Baker, 1933. 75p.

KASER—MERRY
Kaser, Arthur L. Merry mocks, a collection of mock trials and mock weddings. Franklin, Ohio, Eldridge pub. co., n.d. 95p.

KASER—SURE
Kaser, Arthur L. Sure-fire acts for amateur vaudeville. Boston, Baker, 1929. 127p.

KASER—TEN
Kaser, Arthur L. Ten easy acts for women. Chicago, Dramatic publishing co., 1930. 108p.

KASER—TOP
Kaser, Arthur L. Top-liner acts for amateurs. Minneapolis, Northwestern press, 1932. 97p.

KAUFMAN—HIGHLOWBROW
Kaufman, S. Jay. Highlowbrow. N.Y., French, 1943. 171p.

KELLEY
> KELLEY, OWEN. Stunt plays, for your club night. N.Y., French, 1930. 78p.

KEMMERER—GAMES
> Kemmerer, James W. Games and parties and social occasions. Minneapolis, Northwestern press, 1939. 129p.

KENT—ONE
> Kent, Mark. One-rehearsal novelty programs. Boston, Baker's plays, 1946. 112p.

KERR
> Kerr, Walter F. Denison's variety revue. Minneapolis, Northwestern press, 1935. 107p.

LAMKIN & FLORENCE
> Lamkin, Nina B. and Edna Keith Florence. Class day programs (All through the year series). N.Y., French, 1937. 123p.

LAUFE—EASY
> Laufe, A. L. Easy swing time novelties. Boston, Baker's plays, 1945. 78p.

LEVIS—TEN
> Levis, Marjorie Rice. Ten snappy revue sketches. N.Y., French, 1936. 56p.

LLOYD
> Lloyd, Gladys. Easy parodies for popular singing. Boston, Baker's plays, 1939. 80p.

LYONS
> Lyons, Jimmy. Encyclopedia of stage material. Boston, Baker, 1925. 157p.

McCOY—HOLIDAY
> McCoy, Paul S. Holiday chuckles. Minneapolis, Northwestern press, 1938. 104p.

McCOY—SIXTEEN
> McCoy, Paul S. Sixteen short skits. A collection of ten-minute sketches for amateur productions. Minneapolis, Northwestern press, 1935. 95p.

MacDonald

MacDonald, Dora Mary. "Novelty stunts". A collection of skits and stunts. Minneapolis, Northwestern press, 1932. 126p.

MacDonald—Carnival

MacDonald, Dora Mary. Carnival capers for schools. Minneapolis, Northwestern press, 1932. 85p.

Malcolm

Malcolm, Doris N. Easy specialties for women and girls. Boston, Baker's plays, 1938. 128p.

Miksch—Curtain

Miksch, W. F. Curtain raisers, a collection of skits and plays for boys and girls of teen age. Minneapolis, Northwestern press, 1948. 148p.

Miksch—Teen

Miksch, W. F. Teen-age sketches. Minneapolis, Northwestern press, 1947. 134p.

Miller—Broadway

Miller, Norman H. Broadway in revune. Modern blackouts. N.Y., French, 1935. 87p.

Miller—Lands

Miller, Catharine Atkinson. Stunts of all lands. N.Y., Richard R. Smith, 1930. 198p.

Miller—Stunt

Miller, Catherine Atkinson. Stunt night tonight! Garden City, Doubleday, Doran, 1928. 200p.

Parsons

Parson, Margaret. Almost rehearsal-less plays. Boston, Baker, 1931. 109p.

Parties

Parties plus. Stunts and entertainments, by Ethel Bowers, ed. N. Y., National recreation assoc., n.d. 62p.

PRESTON
> Preston, Effa E., Beatrice Plumb and Harry W. Githens. The modern stunt book. A collection of stunts and skits for teen ages, adults and grammar grades. Minneapolis, Denison, 1945. 102p.

PRESTON—FUN
> Preston, Effa E. Fun with stunts. Minneapolis, Denison, 1950. 175p.

PRESTON—PANTOM.
> Preston, Effa E. Modern pantomime entertainments. Minneapolis, Denison, 1938. 180p.

PROVENCE—EASY
> Provence, Jean. "Easy stunt plays from literature". Dramatizations from literature. Minneapolis, Northwestern press, 1938. 95p.

PROVENCE—FLASH
> Provence, Jean. "Flash farces". A collection of short blackouts. Minneapolis, Northwestern press, 1938. 96p.

PROVENCE — KNOCKOUT
> Provence, Jean. Knockout blackouts. Franklin, Ohio, Eldridge pub. co., n.d. 50p.

PROVENCE—LIGHT
> Provence, Jean. Lightning laughs. Minneapolis, Northwestern press, 1949. 124p.

PROVENCE—VAUD.
> Provence, Jean. "The vaudeville stunt book". Minneapolis, Northwestern press, 1937. 90p.

QUICK
> "Quickies". Rehearsal-less entertainments. Black outs in playing time of one to three minutes. Boston, Baker, 1941. 126p.

QUICK COM.
> Quick comedies, a collection of short comedy sketches. By various authors. Boston, Baker's plays, 1935. 122p.

REACH—QUICK

Reach, James. Quick tricks. Sixteen playlets for the club or school stage. N.Y., French, 1936. 107p.

ROGERS—PLAYS

Rogers, Ethel. Plays and stunts for 4-H clubs. Minneapolis, Northwestern press, 1945. 95p.

ROHRBOUGH

Rohrbough, Katherine Ferris. Successful stunts. N.Y., Richard R. Smith, 1929. 184p.

RYAN

Ryan, Reynolds. Easy shorts. Boton, Baker's plays, 1937. 114p.

SHANNON

Shannon, Molly, comp. Easy Novelty numbers. Boston, Baker's plays, 1937. 128p.

792
Sh4

SHELDON

Sheldon, George E. Rehearsal-less skits for stunt night fun. Minneapolis, Northwestern press, 1941. 94p.

SHELDON—GIANT QUIZ

Sheldon, George E. The giant quiz book. Minneapolis, Northwestern press, 1941. 98p.

SIX-MORE

Six more dramatic stunts. N.Y., National recreation assoc., n.d. 36p.

SIX—NEW

Six new dramatic stunts. N.Y., National recreation assoc., n.d. 32p.

SNAPPY

Snappy blackouts, by Len D. Hollister, Edwin Scribner, Jay Tobias, Walter F. Kerr, Earl J. Gilbert, Paul S. McCoy and Robert L. Sherman. Minneapolis, Denison, 1935. 158p.

TARBELL—CHALK STUNTS
Tarbell, Harlan. Chalk talk stunts. Minneapolis, Denison, 1926. 100p.

TARBELL—COMEDY
Tarbell, Harlan. Comedy stunts for laughing purposes. Minneapolis, Denison, 1944. 95p.

TARBELL—CRAZY
Tarbell, Harlan. Crazy stunts for comedy occasions. Minneapolis, Denison, 1929. 102p.

TARBELL—FUN
Tarbell, Harlan. Fun with chalk talk. Minneapolis, Denison, 1931. 106p.

TARBELL—SUNDAY
Tarbell, Harlan. Chalk talks for Sunday schools. Minneapolis, Denison, 1928. 152p.

"THAT GOOD"
"That good" stunt book, one of the Bugbee famous stunt series, by various authors. Syracuse, N.Y., The Willis N. Bugbee co., 1941. 94p.

THREE STUNTS
Three stunts for recreation programs. N.Y., National recreation assoc., n.d. 4p.

TOPOLKA
Topolka, Nelda S. Radio skits for high school. Minneapolis, 1941. 112p.

VAN DERVEER—ANY
Van DerVeer, Lettie C. Any-day entertainments. Boston, Baker, 1922. 92p.

WEATHERS
Weathers, Winston. Adventures in radio. Minneapolis, Northwestern press, 1947. 170p.

WEATHERS—MYSTERIES
Weathers, Winston. Mysteries for radio. Franklin, Ohio, Eldridge pub. co., 1946. 115p.

WILLIAMS

Williams, Bertha. Hail! Stunt night. Fifty new stunts for camp frolics or social gatherings. Franklin, Ohio, Eldridge pub. co., n.d.   48p.

YOUNG—GAMES

Young, William P. and Horace J. Gardner. Games and stunts for all occasions. Phila., J. B. Lippincott co., 1935. 118p.

AN INDEX TO
SKITS AND STUNTS

AUTHOR, TITLE AND SUBJECT LIST

*À la "Al Jolson". DEPEW p260.

*À la carte. (3m, 4f, children) KELLEY p46-48.

*À la Eugene O'Neill. (1m, 1f) EASY—BLACKOUTS p24-28.

À la Spike Jones. EISENBERG—HAND p118-119.

*An abandoned baby. (1m, 4f) IRISH—CATCHY p100-103.

Abie and Cutie. ROHRBOUGH p169-170.

*About time, by Jean Provence. (2m) BRINGS—MASTER p200-201; PROVENCE—LIGHT p75-76.

Abrams, Joe
Silence, please

Absence is a pleasure. FUNNY p29.

*Absent-minded, by Charles George. (1m, 1f) BRINGS—MASTER p231-234.

Accident. FRICK—SUMMER p61.

Accidents
See also Automobile accidents
*Byron's accident
*The fatal pickle
*How horrible!
*Hurry, doctor

*Accuracy. (1m, 1f) PROVENCE—KNOCKOUT p49.

*A-courting we will go (21m, 2f, extras) KERR p16-32.

The acrobatic violinist. BRINGS-MASTER p386.

"Across the plains"—"The Texas rangers". FERRIS p76.

Acting
See also Actors and actresses; Moving pictures; Theatre
*Curtain time
Dashing dramatics
*The first rehearsal
I'm going to be an actress

1

"Movies"
*Mystery of the green room
*Opportunity
 A playlet—The drama department
*The revenge and repentance of grandpa
 Screen test game
*Spirit of peace
*Spirits on parade
*Their first play
Acting out rhymes. EISENBERG—HAND. p36-39.
Acting proverbs. DEPEW p301-302.
The actor. CORMACK p32-33.
Actors and actresses
 *The big stunt
 *Congratulations, my dear
  The Elberta: a peach of a tea room in Georgia
  Finding the stars
 *The ham what am
  Hasty Harry
  A Hollywood chance
 *A Hollywood romance"
  "It's colossal"
  Movie stars
  Oh! To be an actoress!
  Screen stars
The ad contest. MACDONALD—CARNIVAL p78-80.
Ad writing, by Alta Toepp. CASEY—PEPPY p95.
*Adam, Eve and apples. (4b, 4g) IRISH—CHILDREN'S p93-95.
Adams, Jane
 *Hull House
Add a man. HUBER—GIANT p135-136.
Adjectives
Adding adjectives. RYAN p102.
*Addition. (1m, 2f) HUBER—FOUR p26-29.
Additional shadow picture ideas. BRIDGE p23-24.
An address. BRINGS—MASTER p396.
Adjectives
 Adding adjectives
 Fiction
Adjectives. YOUNG—GAMES p65.

*Adopting the baby, by Mabel Tuttle Craig. (2m, 1f) "THAT GOOD" p18-19.
*Adventure after midnight. (2m, 2f) HUBER—ARENA p116-120.
Advertisers. GEISTER—NEW p115.

Advertising
See also Commercials, Singing
Ad writing
A broadcasting fantasy
Chuckle ads
A commercial relay
Famous advertisements you see everyday
*99 and 44/100% pure
Scooping the scoop
*This is the night
*Three o'clock in the morning
Who reads the ads
Advertising favors. DEPEW p211.
Advertising minstrels. FERRIS p124-125.
Advertising slogans. EISENBERG—HAND. p125.

Advice
*Assert yourself
*Blank check
Hartenhome problems
*Taking Maw's advice
*Advice aplenty. (6f) MALCOLM p59-62.
Advice to draftees, by Vance Clifford. BRINGS—MASTER p327-328.
*Advice to students (1m, 4b, 4g) STARR—RADIO p27-30.
Aeroplane ride. JOHNSON—BAKER'S p97-98.
*Affair in the park. (3m, 1f) MIKSCH—TEEN p113-123.
*A-fishing I have been, by Arthur L. Kaser. (2m) BRINGS—MASTER p278-279.

Africa
*With General Wow in darkest Africa"
*African aria. (2m, 2f) SULLIVAN—MORE p44-51.
*The African explorer. (1m, 2f) STAHL—MORE p58-61.
After-dinner speeches, by Willis N. Bugbee. BREEZY p100-102.
After-dinner stories. "THAT GOOD" p90.
After midnight. HUBER—PRACT. p64-69.
*After the ball (3m, 5f, extras) DEASON—SKIT p32-40.

After the bawl is over. RYAN p93.

*After the history test. (4b) BARBEE p47-49.

*Afternoon at Central Station. (5m, 2f, extras) MIKSCH—CURTAIN p30-45.

*Afternoon of October twentieth. (12m, 3f, or 15m) PRESTON—FUN p5-19.

*Agatha's errands. (1m, 2f) SIX—MORE p22-26.

Age
> See also Old age
> How old was Bill?
> Tell my age

Age and telephone number. DEPEW p353.

Agents. See Salesmen and salesmanship

Ah! The Hour! RYAN p103.

Aim for the basket. YOUNG—GAMES p81.

Ain't it a shame? WILLIAMS p8,9.

Air Corps. See United States—Armed forces

Air power. GEISTER—NEW p92-93.

Airplanes
> Aeroplane ride

Alabama attaboy minstrels. KASER—SURE p107-114.

*Aladdin and the vamp. (4m, 3f) LAUFF—EASY p60-78.

The alarm. DEPEW p148.

An alarming time, by Gladys Lloyd. JOLLY p96.

Alaska
> *Partners

Albright, Helen
> Aunt Samanthy's photygraft album

Aldrich, Mrs. Mabel
> And the lamp went out

Alexander the Great
> *The beginning of knowledge

Alice in Wonderland. FRICK—SUMMER p21-26.

Alice-in-wonderland tea dance. FERRIS p40-41.

All aboard! By Beatrice Plumb. BRINGS—MASTER p424.

*All aboard for Washington! (speaker, 3b, 4g) BARBEE p93-95.

*All ashore. CHAPLIN p70-79.

All blowed to pieces. KASER—SURE p96-101.

*All due to chemistry (3b, 2g) BARBEE p70-72.

All Fool's day social or party. BUGBEE—CATCHY p41-43.

All fours relay. DEPEW p331.

All in a day's work. PARTIES p31-32.

*All men are stupid. (1m, 4f) HUBER—SIX p69-76.

All on for da Beega show. BUGBEE—NUTTY p71.

*All one-sided, by Robert L. Sherman. (announcer, 2m, 1f) SNAPPY p155-158.

All participating. BRIDGE p3-8.

*All who enter. (1m, 2f) HUBER—NO p57-62.

All wound round. GEISTER—NEW p41.

All you et. DEPEW p276.

All's swell that ends swell, by Harry W. Githens. GITHENS p102-107.

Allison, Agnes
   Out of the garret

Alliterative applications. DRUMMOND—STUNT FUN p96-103.

*Almost the last day of school. (1m, 1f, 4b, 4g) KASER— FUNNY p83-88.

"Aloha-oe". FERRIS p75.

*"Along the straight and narrow". (3m, 1f) STAHL—BITS p15-17.

Alphabet
   Alliterative applications
   *The 4-H quintuplets
   The orator

Alphabet game. GEISTER—NEW p43-44.

The alphabet is queen. STARR—JR. p25-26.

Alphabet meal. YOUNG—GAMES p55.

Alphabet play. BRIDGE p27-28.

Alphabet skits. EISENBERG—HAND. p33-36.

Alphabetic faces. BUCHANAN p20-26.

Alternate choice. EISENBERG—FUN p91-92.

Alumni
   *Chip off the old block
   *The old fight

Always a gentleman; or, Sunday morning with Crusoe and his girl Friday. (2m, 1f, extras). PRESTON—PANTOM. p31-40.

*"Always bragging". (2m, 1f) HUBER—THREE p33-34.

The amateur half-hour. MACDONALD—CARNIVAL p58-59.

Amateur hours
  Major Blows' amateur hour
  Majoress Bow-wow's amateur hour
"The amateur magician". DRUMMOND—STUNT p25-40.
Amateur night. FERRIS p142-143.
*The ambulance always. (3m, 3f) TOPOLKA p25-32.
Ambush. GEISTER—NEW p50.
The amen corner. BUGBEE—GOOFY p39.
America
  *Gods country
  *This brave new world
America. JOHNSON—BAKER'S p55.
*America begins (11m, 1b) STAHL—LAND. p75-90.
America first, by Grace Keith Samuelson. "THAT GOOD" p48.
America, the beautiful. HANLEY—STUNTS p34-35.
American literature
  *The magic wand
Americans all. PARTIES p13.
Ammons, Edna C. and Beatrice H. McNeil
  The home town minstrel show
Amnesia. YOUNG—GAMES p39.
Anatomy
  Essay on anatomy
  Twelve parts of the body
The ancient festival (Thanksgiving). PRESTON—PANTOM.
    p227-230.
*And he never came back. (2m, 1f) DRUMMOND—THREE p41-
    44.
*And so it goes. (1m, 1f) KASER—SURE p56-65.
*And so the new minister arrives. (1m, 7f) EASY—STUNTS
    p 29-32.
*"And spooking of ghosts". (1m, 3f, 6g) KASER—ACTS p37-44.
And the lamp went out. DEPEW p34-37.
*And the villain still pursued her, by Agnes Dubbs Hays. (2m,
    2f) SHANNON p76-80.
*And the willin still pursueder. (2m, 2f) KASER—SURE p75-82.
And then. HUBER—GIANT p149-150.
*"And they get paid," by Selden M. Loring. (5m, 2f) EASY
    IMPR. p76-83.
*Androcles and the lion. (5m, 1f, extras) CONNOR p41-49.

Androcles and the lion. (A shadow play with reading). PRESTON—PANTOM. p205-212.

*"Angel child". (1m, 2f, 1b) STAHL—HEARTY p40-42.

Angleworm relay. DEPEW p332.

Animal carnival. FRICK—FALL p52-53.

Animal crackers
  Four animal cracker ideas

Animal hunt (2) DEPEW p183; FRICK—SUMMER p19-20.

Animal pageant. DRUMMOND—STUNT p60-61.

Animal sextette. BUGBEE—NUTTY p99.

The animal show. MACDONALD—CARNIVAL p11-17.

Animals
  See also Circus; Zoos; names of animals, e.g. Dogs
  Barnyard melody
  *The bear (bare) dance
  Cat fight
  Cooperative artists
  Feed the animals
  Haunts of the jungle
  Lion act
  Magic animals
  Noah's Ark charades
  Popular pets; a revival of old time favorites
  Silent menagerie
  Solomon's seals
  Trained animals
  Zoological garden

Animals, by Beatrice Plumb. BRINGS—MASTER p415.

*Animals in the circus. (4b) IRISH—CHILDREN'S p57-58.

Animals that didn't win at the fair. BUCHANAN p29-32.

*Animated freight. (2m) "THAT GOOD" p75-76.

The animated newspaper. BUGBEE—LIVE WIRE p85-88.

*Animated scarecrows, by Harry W. Githens. (7b) GITHENS p105-107.

Anniversaries
  See also Weddings, golden
  *Dog tricks
  *"That beautiful woman"

Announcing an entertainer. BRINGS—MASTER p387-388.

Annual meeting of the X.Y.Z. DRUMMOND—STUNT FUN p47.

Annuals. *See* School annuals

Another egg trick. DRUMMOND—STUNT p35.

Another prophecy. LAMKIN & FLORENCE p29.

The answer is "Yes", a pantomime by Mary Holmes. SHANNON p91-95.

The ant and the grasshopper. PRESTON—PANTOM. p175-182.

An antique auction. HANLEY—STUNTS p20-22.

Antique, mystical, Egyptian order of night owls. CORMACK p12-14.

Antiques

  See also Junk shops

  *"Markheim"

Antonio: The dare-devil trapeze performer. FERRIS p36.

*"Annuder lankwich". (3m) STAHL—HEARTY p70-72.

*Anxious moments, by Norman Bridge Eaton. (2m, 1f) EASY SKITS p48-60.

*Anybody's gift (3m, 3f) MIKSCH—CURTAIN p104-119.

*"Anything to get votes". (6f) DRUMMOND—FUNNY p81-89.

*An apartment for rent, by Paul S. McCoy. (1m, 3f, announcer) SNAPPY p118-126.

Apartments

  *The flat below

*"An apple a day". (1m, 2f) PROVENCE—VAUD. p57-59.

Apple-eating contest. DEPEW p320-321.

Apple pass. CASEY—PEPPY p86.

The apples. DEPEW p340.

*An April Fool joke. (1m, 4b) IRISH—CATCHY p74-76.

April Fool party. KEMMERER—GAMES p16.

April Fool's Day

  All Fool's day social or party

  *At the Court of King April Fool

  *Backfire

  Backward party

  A backward party for April Fool's day

  Crossword puzzle

  Endless thread

  Fake peanut hunt

  *The love lyric of letters

  *No trading today

April Fool's day. YOUNG—GAMES p106.

Arabian Nights
  *One Arabian night was stunt night
Arbor Day
  *Birds, trees and flowers
  *The planters
Arcades. GEISTER—NEW p47-48.
Archibald. LLOYD p38-39.
Arctic regions
  *As the Byrd flies
Are you an elk? YOUNG—GAMES p28-29.
Are you from the country? DEPEW p173.
Are you nutty? BUGBEE—NUTTY p7.
Argument. BRINGS—MASTER p387.
Aristotle
  *The beginning of knowledge
Arizona
  Lily of the alley
Armistice day
  The flag
  In Flanders field
Armistice day stunt. ABELL—STUNTS p91.
Armistice, 1918. DEPEW p182.
Army. *See* United States—Armed forces
Arnold, Mrs. J. Y.
  The Elberta: a peach of a tea room in Georgia
Around America in song. PARTIES p13.
Around America in stunts. PARTIES p13.
Around the corner. DEPEW p287-288.
Around the world. PARTIES p13.
*Around the world in bed (4m, 8f) CHAPLIN p7-16.
Around the world quiz, by Willis N. Bugbee. JOLLY p5-12.
Arranging and adding. DEPEW p366.
*Arrival in person. (2m, 2f) McCoy—SIXTEEN p83-89.
*"The arrival of Columbus". (4m) DRUMMOND—STUNT p22-
  24.
*'Arry and 'Arriet, by Kurtz Gordon. (1m, 2f) QUICK—COM.
  p66-69.
Art
  See also Artists
  Chalk talks, or tableaux—the art department

Each for his own art
I just love paintings
*The modernist
The two messages
Art (three versions), by Vance Clifford. BRINGS—MASTER
    p403-405.
Art contest. DEPEW p182.
*Art is a wonderful thing. (3f) McCOY—SIXTEEN p57-60.
Art on the installment plan. YOUNG—GAMES p37-38.
Artists
  *Art is a wonderful thing
  Cooperative artists
  *One timetable
  A preposterous painter; or, a coolheaded cartoonist of con-
    siderable concentration
  Two benches in the park
  *Watch this
  "When artists frolic"—"Mind-the-paint girls"
The artist's model. HUBER—PRACT. p70-74.
As it might have been, by Harry Githens. GITHENS p7-8.
As it used to be. JOHNSON—BAKER's p57-58.
*As the Byrd flies, by Norman L. Zeno, Jr. (5m, 1f) MILLER—
    BROADWAY p63-68.
As we see the movies (2) ENTERTAIN—STUNTS p5-6; PARTIES
    p28.
As you were! March music. GEISTER—NEW p12-13.
Asbjornsen, P. J.
  *The squire's bride—Sweden
Asbrand, Karin
  Song parodies
  When Johnny joined the Army
Ask and ye shall know. BUGBEE—NUTTY p9-11.
*Ask me another. (2b and others) JOHNSON—BAKER's p32-37.
*"Asking father". (1m, 1b, 1g) PROVENCE—VAUD. p79-80.
*Asleep in the deep, by Leroy Stahl (2) (1m, 2f) BRINGS—
    MASTER p206-207; STAHL—HEARTY p30-31.
Asleep with the sheets. TARBELL—COMEDY p40-41.
Assembly. GEISTER—NEW p22-23, 116.
"Assembly song stunt". DRUMMOND—STUNT p90.
*Assert yourself. (2m, 2f) HUBER—SIX p40-47.

Assessors. *See* Tax assessors

*Assorted nuts (8m) TAGGART—MEN p43-56.

Astaire, June

    Fashion show from Hollywood

Astrology

    "Personal" readings from the signs of the zodiac

    Your horror-scope

Astronomical observatory. CONNOR p53-54.

Astronomy

    See also Planets; names of planets

   *The earth and the sky

    The eclipse

    The interstellar league

    Mars views the earth

   *Seeing stars

   *Singing stars

    Stars of the gay nineties

*At a railway station. (1m, 1f) HOPE p18-20.

At both ends of a rope. TARBELL—CRAZY p30,31.

*At Eagle Bend. (1m, 1f, child) STAHL—MORE p52-54.

At home with the range. SHELDON p84-87.

At King Goofers' court. BUGBEE—GOOFY p7-12.

"At the ball"—"Love's dream after the ball"—"Love's dream-
    land". FERRIS p71.

At the broadcasting station. BUGBEE—LIVE WIRE p97-102.

*"At the corner drugstore". (10m, 10f) DRUMMOND—IMPR.
    p37-49.

"At the country club". FERRIS p67.

*At the court of King April Fool. (any no.) DEASON—SKIT
    p64-72.

*At the day nursery. (2f) BUGBEE—NUTTY p18-20.

*At the gates, by Jean Provence. (2m, extras). QUICK—COM.
    p116-122.

At the movies. (3) EISENBERG—FUN p78-79; FERRIS p49-50;
    JOHNSON—BAKER's p101.

*At the music counter, a singing act. (5f) KASER—TEN p87-91.

*At the photographer's. (5m, 10f) IRISH—CATCCY p112-119.

*At the river. (2m, 1f) HUBER—FOUR p152-155.

*At the school ball game, by Katherine Ferguson. (1m, 3b)
    SIX—NEW p25-28.

*At the ticket office, by Minnie L. Petersen. (2m, 2f) ROHR-
   BOUGH p31-32.
At the union station, by Harry Githens. GITHENS p8-9.
*At the zoo. (2) (2f) BUGBEE—LIVE WIRE p42; REACH—QUICK
   p57-61
At what intervals? DEPEW p361.
*At your service, by J. P. Heald. (2m, 1f) SHANNON p110-122.
*Atavism or Women are so brave, by Jay Tobias. (2m, 3f)
   EASY—IMPR. p45-50.
The athletes. MACDONALD—CARNIVAL p17-18.
Athletic meeting. DEPEW p184.
Athletic minstrels. FERRIS p121-122.
Athletic tableaux. DEPEW p92.
Athletics
   See also Olympics; Quizzes—Athletics;; names of individual
      sports, e.g. Football
   Our team—the athletic department
   Physical feats and tricks
   Professional encounters
   A talk on athletics
   *Then—and now
Athletics of other days. FERRIS p35.
Atomic energy
   *Twenty-first century
*Atomic energy, by Willis N. Bugbee. (2m) BREEZY p39-41.
Attendance
   Bedroom suite
   Chart committee report
   Ima Rotarian
   Matching them off
   Names in the bulletin
   Round table luncheon
   Special recognition
   Talks on attendance
Attendance chart committee. DEPEW p244.
Attendance committee. DEPEW p242.
Attendance contest. DEPEW p244.
Attendance letters. DEPEW p242-243.
Attendance prizes. DEPEW p241-242.
Attendance stunts. BUGBEE—GOOFY p77.

*Au revoir. (2m) DEPEW p110.

Auction. JOHNSON—BAKER'S p100.

An auction sale. JOLLY p86.

Auctioning the kid pictures. BUGBEE—GOOFY p43-44.

  An antique auction

  *"A box of trouble"

  Chinese auction

  A Dutch auction

  The escaped prisoner

*Audition (2m, 3f) KASER—AMATEUR'S p28-34.

Auctions

*Aunt Emma brings Dickie by Vance Clifford. (2). (1m, 2f)
      BRINGS—MASTER p177-179; DRUMMOND—THREE p37-40.

*Aunt Mehitabel's beaux. (4m, 2f) BUGBEE—CATCHY p83-88.

Aunt Samanthy's photygraft album, by Helen Albright. JOLLY
  p54-62.

Aunt Sophie's household hints. KASER—BUSHEL p113-115.

Aunts

  *The will and the way

*Aunty Cheerful's visit. (4f) IRISH—CATCHY p90-94.

*Aunty Hodge's Thanksgiving dinner. (4b) BUGBEE—LIVELY
  p48-50.

Authors

  *Call me dear

  *The eyes have it

Auto show, by Gladys Lloyd. JOLLY p95.

*Auto suggestion, by LeRoy Stahl. (2) (1m, 1b, 1g) BRINGS—
  MASTER p204-205; STAHL—HEARTY p38-39.

The automat lunch. FERRIS p55.

Automobile. GEISTER—NEW p48-49.

Automobile Accidents

  *The bent fender

  *Hospitality

  Rumblings from wrecks

  *"Snakes"

Automoblie trouble. CANOPY—HIGH p81-83.

Automobiles

  See also Automobile accidents; Buses; Taxicabs

  Auto show

  *Calling all cars!

*The driver's test
The driving lesson (2)
The end of a perfect Jay
"A ford feud"
Gasoleen mavourneen
Hickville comes to conference
*Is it worth the sacrifice?
*It's her or the car
Joy riding
Motor trouble
The old flivver ride
Over the pavement and through the towns
Portrait of a man thinking aloud
Teaching them to drive
*Through traffic
Unwarranted speed
Women drivers (2)
Autumn party. YOUNG—GAMES p109-110.

Aviators
*The heroine's husband
*The awful fate of a fibber, by Catherine Miller Balm. (3m,
1f) EISENBERG—HAND. p210-212.
See also *A thrill from Japan

Babies
*An abandoned baby
*At the day nursery
*"Bundles from heaven"
*Don't cry baby
Drawing for the babies
The nursery quartette
*Where's the baby? (2)
The babies. DEPEW p245-246.
The baby. EISENBERG—FUN p79.
The baby bottle. DEPEW p247.
*Baby hands. (3m, 1f) HUBER—CHAR. p12-20.
Baby Lon. ABELL—STUNTS p28-30.
Baby pictures. GEISTER—NEW p63-64.
Baby quartet. DEPEW p257.

The baby show. (3) Bugbee—Live Wire p112-114; Canopy
—High p109,111,112-113; Ferris p143.
*"The baby show". (8m, 7f) MacDonald p57-66.
*The baby sitter. (2m, 2f) Huber—All p33-38.
Baby sitters
  *Sitting tonight
The baby sitters. Eisenberg—Hand. p125.
Baby sitting. Goddard—Children's p35-39.
Baby stuff (2). Brings—Master p378; Drummond—Stunt
  Fun p50.
Baby's cradle. Eisenberg—Fun p27.
*Baby's first word, by Jay Tobias (2m, 2f and baby) Snappy
  p42-47.
*Bachelor Hall medley. (5m, 5f) Bugbee—Lively p84-87.
*Bachelor husbands, by Richard Drummond. (5m) Brings—
  Master p113-118.
The bachelor's dream. Chaplin p17-27.
Bachelor's quartet Depew p257.
Back seat driving. (3) Easy—Stunts p3; Parties p29; by
  Nancy Beach. Rohrbough p54.
Back to back race. Drummond—Stunt Fun p106.
*A back-yard build-up. (6f) Kaser—Acts p59-64.
The back yard concert. Bugbee—Live Wire p56.
*Backfire. (2m, 3f) McCoy—Holiday p31-37.
Backgammon. Depew p295.
Backward and forward sisters. Williams p32,33.
*The backward helper, by Bob Royce (2m) Brings—Master
  p265-266.
Backward luncheon. Depew p182.
*A backward march of time, by Kurtz Gordon. (1m, 2f)
  Baker's Gay p11-12.
Backward party. Johnson—Baker's p98.
A backward party for April Fool's Day, by Ruth Putnam
  Kimball. Johnson—Easy p102.
Backward program. Depew p213.
*Bad boy. (3f) Taggart—Five p75-82.
*A bad luck sign, by Arthur LeRoy Kaser. (2m, 1f) Bugbee—
  Live Wire p134-136.
Badge place cards. Depew p209.
Baffle, Wilmer

*Bound to please
*Mrs. Murphy isn't home
Paul Revere's ride
Bag and baggage. PRESTON—FUN p98-100.
A bag of tricks, by Katherine Ferguson. ROHRBOUGH p167-168.
The bag relay. DEPEW p197.
Baik. EISENBERG—FUN p34-35.
Baker, Mrs. Camilla Athenasio
  A day in Seville
Balance sheet, by Grace Keith Samuelson. "THAT GOOD" p46.
The balancing act. DRUMMOND—STUNT FUN p16.
Balancing egg on pencil. DEPEW p195.
Balentine, Warren
  *Cream puffs
Ball game deluxe, by Harry Githens. GITHENS p59.
Ballads
  Baby Lon
  The delectable ballad of the Waller lot
  The fatal ride
  The laidly worm
  St. George and the dragon
Ballet
  *The sign on the door
Balloon balance, by Beatrice Plumb. BRINGS—MASTER p413.
Balloon battle. GEISTER—NEW p94.
Balloon dance. GEISTER—NEW p118-119.
Balloon yell. BUGBEE—LIVE WIRE p30.
Balloons
  I'm forever blowing bubbles
  Passing the balloon
Balloons. (2) DEPEW p150; GEISTER—NEW p101.
"Balloons! Balloons! Who said balloons?" FERRIS p68.
*Ballyhoo, by Selden M. Loring. (8m, 2f) SHANNON p81-85.
Balm, Catherine Miller
  *The awful fate of a fibber
  *The generous fisherman
  The ogre of Rashamon
  The proud princess (2)
*Balm of life. (3m) HUBER—VAUD. p53-57.
Baltimore. PRESTON—PANTOM. p255-256.

*Never kick a man's shin
Personal service to boys
Presenting the grand piano
Self-introduction
A toast to the banquet
Toasts for the class banquet
Volstead quartette
Where did you meet him?
Bantam fight. DRUMMOND—SPOT p73.
The barber shop. McCORMACK p29.
Barbers
  *Blackout in black
  *The gay nineties barber shop
  Ladies before gents
  Lather harmony
  *Pop's tonsorial parlor
  *Shining example
  U.R. next
The bare facts. ABELL—STUNTS p46.
*Bargain present. (2m, 2f) McCOY—HOLIDAY p88-95.
Barley Bright. FRICK—SUMMER p19.
The barnyard clock. STARR—JR. p73-75.
Barnyard geography. EISENBERG—FUN p95.
Barnyard melody. YOUNG—GAMES p31-32.
The barnyard quiz. SHELDON—GIANT QUIZ p28-35.
Barrel-hoop relay. DEPEW p334.
Barrel-organs
  "Tony"
The barrel parade. BUGBEE—LIVE WIRE p53.
*The barrel parade. (4m, 3f) BUGBEE—NUTTY p35.
Barrels of fun. BUGBEE—LIVE WIRE p28.
Barrooms
  *The lady known as Lou
  *Ten barrooms in one night
The Barrys. EISENBERG—HAND. p96.
Barton, Clara
  "How the Red Cross began"
The base quartet. EISENBERG—FUN p192.
Baseball
  See also Chorus, Baseball

*At the school ball game
*Captain of the ball nine
*Fit as a fiddle
Home run Bill
*Kill the ump
Kiwanis baseball game
Opening the world series
A preliminary baseball game
A resolution
*Three strikes
The world series.
Baseball minstrels. FERRIS p120-121.
Bashful lover. EISENBERG—FUN p121-122.
Basket ball (2b) DRUMMOND—STUNT FUN p12.
Basketball
Ball game deluxe
*"Come to the basket ball game"
Come to the game
Extra! Extra!
*The fatal pickle
Impersonations
*It's a silly game
*Just basketball
The life of a basketball player
Living basketball statuary
*Making a note of it
Meet the team
The quintuplets
The rules of the game
The speed kids vs. lightning flashes
*Stay awake
The tournament
Who's who is basketball
Bass quartet. (2) EASY—STUNTS p7; PARTIES p32-33.
Bat kicking for distance. DEPEW p323.
Bathing beauties. EISENBERG—HAND. p56.
The bathing beauty. BUGBEE—NUTTY p13-14.
The bathroom door, by Emily Seaber Parcher. JOHNSON—
    EASY p103-106.
Batter up! A sports quiz show. SHELDON—GIANT QUIZ p9-19.

The battered cyclist, by Robert N. McGregor. BREEZY p67.

The Battle of spaghetti. BUGBEE—LIVE WIRE p68.

Bavis, Chester S.

Heaven's gate

Bawl game. EISENBERG—FUN p106.

Bazaar, Hallowe'en. FRICK—FALL p33-37.

Bazaars

See also Carnivals; Fairs

*School bazaar

The shadowgraph

The witches' cauldron

*Be careful, judge. (3m, 3f) HUBER—ALL p83-91.

*"Be kind to animals" (1m, 2f) STAHL—HEARTY p45-47.

Be kind to insects. KASER—ACTS p82-84.

Beach, Nancy

Back-seat driving

*The wasted tip

Beach

Help! Help!

*There are life guards and life guards

Bean bag baseball. DEPEW p313.

Bean bag boards. DEPEW p313.

Bean bag gold. DEPEW p312-313.

Bean bag grab. DEPEW p313.

Bean bag shuffleboard. DEPEW p314.

Bean bag snatch. DEPEW p312.

Bean-passing relay. DEPEW p332.

*The bear (bare) dance. (3m) BUGBEE—NUTTY p98,99.

The bearded lady. CONNOR p40.

Beards

*Bound to please

Bears

Bruin, the tame bear

The three bears

The three modern bears

The beater. GEISTER—NEW p99-100.

Beatrix Fairfax—her column. BRIDGE p27.

Beautiful but dumb, by Beatrice Plumb. JOLLY p87-88.

The beautiful silk hanky. DRUMMOND—STUNT FUN p13.

A beautiful view. Crowley p90,91.

Beauty and the clock. Eisenberg—Fun p176-180.

Beauty contests
 *Be careful, judge

*"A beauty gets the bird". (3m) Stahl—Amat. p92-94.

Beauty parade. Johnson—Baker's p87-89.

Beauty parlor confessions, by Grace Keith Samuelson. "That
 Good" p53-54.

*The beauty parlor. (1m, 3f) Hope p40-42

Beauty Shops
   The beauty specialist
   Fore and aft beauty shop
   *"The monster"
   *The Venus beauty factory

The beauty specialist. Bugbee—Goofy p44-46.

Becky Sharp. (1g) Goddard—Children's p16-18.

Bedroom suite. Depew p151.

Bed-time hour (for adults) Connor p62-65.

Bedtime story. Geister—New p65-66.

*Befo' de wah". (4m, 4f) MacDonald p111-115.

Beggars
   *"Help the blind" (2)
   *"Kind-hearted people"

Beggars not wanted. Bugbee—Live Wire p50.

*The beginning of knowledge. (7m, 1f) Stahl—Land. p11-23.

Behind the eight ball, by Grace Keith Samuelson. "That
 Good" p45.

Behind the scenes. Funny p17.

Being generous. Drummond—Stunt p30-31.

*Being poor is no disgrace. (1m, 2f) Drummond—Three p79-
 82.

Believe it or not famous catches, by Beatrice Plumb. Breezy
 p62,63.

Believe it or not, it's true, by Beatrice Plumb, Breezy p62.

Believe me, if all those fictitious young charms. Lloyd p7-8.

Belinda, the gem of creation. Lloyd p43-44.

Bell, Alexander Graham
   *Speech through wires

Bell backs. Eisenberg—Fun p190.

Bell pass. GEISTER—NEW p45.

Bell ringers. GEISTER—NEW p42.

"Belle and Bill" or "The rewards of virtue". MacDONALD p117-126.

Belles we have met. BREEZY p87-90.

Bells, by Beatrice M. Casey. CASEY—PEPPY p38-42.

Benefits. *See* Bazaars; Carnivals; Fairs

The bent bosom. (2) BRINGS—MASTER p382; DRUMMOND— STUNT FUN p52.

*The bent fender. (2m, 2f) HUBER—CHAR. p21-28.

Berle, Milton
  *Berle meets a girl in Central Park.
  *Hotel Hokum
  *You can't try an insane man

*Berle meets a girl in Central Park. (2m, 1f) BERLE p31-33.

The berth of an upper or Howareya? EISENBERG—FUN p89-91.

Bessie of Bar X ranch. PARSONS p51-61.

The best joke. HUBER—GIANT p134-135.

*The best laid plans. (5m, 1f) HUBER p16-25.

*The best people. (2m, 3f) HUBER p5-15.

Best spring romances, by Beatrice Plumb. "THAT GOOD" p39-40.

"Betsy speaks a piece for the caller". FERRIS p20-21.

*Better not be bettor. (2m) BRINGS—MASTER p397-398.

Betty at the telephone. GODDARD—CHILDREN'S p18-20.

Betty's misfortunes. TARBELL—SUNDAY p39-46.

Beverages. YOUNG—GAMES p98-101.

*Bewildering popularity. (12f) MALCOLM p63-73.

Biblical
  See also Quizzes—Biblical; Religion
  Scripture spelling match

A Biblical quiz. SHELDON—GIANT QUIZ p80-86.

A Biblical tug-o'-war, by Willis N. Bugbee. JOLLY p12-15.

Bicycles
  *Danger, fate at work
  *A daring bicycler

The big bad wolf or How Popeye saved Betty Boop Ba Doop, by Annetta Eldridge. GITHENS p9-11.

*The big bribe. (4m) HUBER—NO SCENE p109-118.

*"Big business", by Selden M. Loring. (4m) EASY—IMP. p7-13.

*Big businessman. (2m, 1f) McCoy—SIXTEEN p61-67.
*Big moments in history (The landing of the Pilgrims—as it wasn't). (8b, 8g) PRESTON p33-36.
A big mouth. DRUMMOND—STUNT p40.
Big mystery. EISENBERG—HAND. p94-95.
*The big stunt, by McElbert Moore (5m, 1f) QUICK p94-103.
"Big things". HUBER—EASY p76-78.
The Biggs' family skelton. WILLIAMS p16-18.
"Bill and Mabel". FERRIS p43-44.
Bill Tell. DEPEW p28-29.
*Bill, the matchmaker, (2m, 2f) by Bob Royce. BRINGS—MASTER p35-41; DRUMMOND—IMPR. p62-68.
A billion. RYAN p101-102.
Bills lost. EISENBERG—FUN p118-119.
Biographies, by Mabel Tuttle Craig. CASEY—PEPPY p82.

Biography
    See also Historical; Quizzes—Biography; names of special groups, e.g. Artists
    In the limelight
    Prof. Dauber's art gallery
    Statuesque de silly
    Who was who?
Biography. YOUNG—GAMES p47-48.
Biological contests. DRUMMOND—STUNT FUN p59-60.
"Bird blood". HUBER—EASY p42-44.
Bird competition. YOUNG—GAMES p43-44.
*A bird in the hand. (4f) SULLIVAN—MORE p30-36.
The bird with the big bill. CROWLEY p47-48.

Birds
    *Aunt Emma brings Dickie
    *Birds, trees and flowers
    How's this for romance?
    The penguin family
*Birds and blood. (2m, 1f) WEATHERS p32-41.
Birds in the Wilderness. DEPEW p280.
*Birds of a feather. (2) EASY-BLACKOUTS p71-75; FRICK-FALL p7-8.
*Birds, trees and flowers. (4b, 5g) IRISH—CHILDREN'S p45-48.
The birth of a nation, by Estelle Martin. ROHRBOUGH p92-98.
*The birth of freedom. (6m) STAHL—LAND. p25-37.

Birth stones. JOLLY p82.

Birthday for all. PARTIES p13.

Birthday greetings. DEPEW p180.

*The birthday party. (4b, 5g) BUGBEE—LIVELY p27-33.

The birthday surprise. TARBELL—SUNDAY p77-81.

Birthdays
   *Double tribute
   *Happy birthday
    Happy birthday stunts
   *Happy birthday to you
   *Let's go to the movies
   *No more murders
    "Personal" readings from the signs of the zodiac
   *Three birthdays
   *Triangle
    Your horror-scope

Birthdays. (2) FRICK—SUMMER p69-70; by Mabel Tuttle
    Craig. JOLLY p89.

A bit of blue ribbon. EASY-BLACKOUTS p83-86.

"Black and white". FERRIS p72.

Black and white minstrels. FERRIS p124.

Black magic. (2) BRINGS—MASTER p383; DRUMMOND—STUNT
    FUN p55.

*The black sheep. (3m) HUBER—TV p5-10.

Blackface. See Dialect—Negro; Minstrels

*Blackmail. (2m, 1f) DRUMMOND—THREE p13-16.

*Blackout in black. (2m, 1f) TAGGART—FIVE p63-67.

Blackouts
   *À la Eugene O'Neill
   *About time (2)
   *Accuracy
   *All one-sided
    Alternate choice
   *"Always bragging"
   *And he never came back
   *An apartment for rent
   *As the Byrd flies
   *Asleep in the deep (2)
   *Aunt Emma brings Dickie (2)
   *Auto suggestion (2)

*Baby's first word
The Barrys
Bashful lover
*Being poor is no disgrace
Big mystery
Bills lost
Birds of a feather (EASY—BLACKOUTS)
A bit of blue ribbon
*Blackmail
*"Bravest of the brave"
*Brotherly revenge
*Browned biscuits
*Buck Private's dream
By the teeth
*The candy shop
*Carrot topped
*"Cashed"
*Cats is cats
*"The census taker" (HUBER—THREE)
*Childish prattle
*Chiseling on chivalry
Chivalry is not dead
*City feller
*"The columnist"
*"The consultation"
*Corn but not forgotten
*Corn cure
Cough syrup
Court scene
*The customer is right (2)
A day in Dog Patch
*Death
*Design for dueling
The dinosaur specialist
Divorce
*A doctor's dilemma (BRINGS—MASTER; STAHL—MORE)
The donkey's tail
Don't brush them on me
*"Don't cry"
*Don't displease your husband

*Don't ever speed
*Don't get excited
*Don't stop us if you've heard these
*Down on the farm
 Dramatized jokes (BRINGS—MASTER; KASER—AMATEUR)
*Eat and like it
 Efficiency expert
*Fifty dollars worth of dog
*Finish the rubber
*The first date
*Fishing
 "Follow the leader" (HUBER—THREE)
*"Football hero"
*The fountain of youth (EISENBERG—HAND.)
*A friend in need
*Front page stuff
*"The game hunters"
*Giving you the jeeters
*The goat
*"Good guy"
*Gratitude
 "A great discovery"
*Guess what
*Guilty
*Happy birthday to you
*Hard to handle
*He's not so dumb
*"Help! Help! (HUBER—THREE)
*"Help the blind" (HUBER—THREE)
*Her souvenirs
 Here, have another rope! The vanishing wife
*Here's a hair
*"High pressure" (2)
*Her sister
*A hit with papa
*Home, sweet home
*Honor man
*Hospitality
 How to live long
*"Hurry, doctor"

I asked her first!
I'll bite
*"The inquiring reporter"
*The insomniac
*Instant dramas
*Insurance
*"Interlude"
*"It's colossal" (HUBER—THREE)
*It's only propaganda
*Ivan Vosco, sanitary inspector, is jailed
*"Juror number twelve"
*Just a love nest (EASY—BLACKOUTS)
*Just ask father
*Just one more
  Just too tired to move
  Kittle for sale
*Last request
*Leave it to mother
*"Let's ask mother"
  Little folks
*Little Sir Echo
*Live a hundred years
*The logical guess
*Lost and found (EASY—BLACKOUTS)
*The lover's errand (EASY—BLACKOUTS)
  Lumbering along
*The lying hunter
*Man of action
*"The Masher"
*"A mathematical wizard"
*Matter of smell
  Meat
  Meat on Friday
*"Medicine man"
*Memories (SNAPPY)
*"Memory course"
*Misinformed
*The monster (PROVENCE—KNOCKOUT)
*Morning
*Mr. and Mrs. Newberry

*Mrs. Clarke wins seat in Congress
*"The muscle dancer"
*Nature cure
*Naughty nudist
*A near tragedy
*"The new invention"
  The New York visitor
*The newlyweds (DRUMMOND—THREE)
  Niagara Falls
*Night
*The night before the morning after Christmas eve
*"Nine"
*No connection
*No sale
*No visitors allowed
*Noon
*Not so crazy (2)
*Oh, doctor (2)
*"The old and the new"
  On with the dance! (LEVIS—TEN)
*One conclusion (2)
*"Opera" (MILLER—BROADWAY)
*Opera opens
*Operations (2)
  Out for a walk
*Parsing a sentence
*The parting tear
*Partners (LEVIS—TEN)
*The passing of Bruno
  Peach pie
*"Physical culture"
*Polite but firm (EASY—BLACKOUTS)
*The poor boob
*Pop goes the heart
*"Power in numbers"
*The pride of the Van Smythes
  The proof
  Pure water
*Razzberry
*"Reader of lips"

*Romance
* A sailor's technique
*Sambo am a dangerous man
*Sandy, defunct
*Scourge of the desert
*"The secretary"
*Seeing father
*"The sharpshooter"
*"Sideshow"
*"Sign up"
 Sixty dollars a week
*"Snakes"
*Sold (EASY—BLACKOUTS)
*Some of them begin young
*"Some story"
*"Something important"
*The speech of acceptance
 Spirit world
 The stamp nut
*The stars and the stripes
*Statistics (2)
*Stop thief (2)
*"Stripes"
*The suicide
*Sure cure (PROVENCE—KNOCKOUT; PROVENCE—LIGHT)
*Taking Maw's advice
 Telephone booth
 That's it!
 That's love
*Their golden wedding anniversary
*There are badges and badges
*There's one born every minute (EASY—BLACKOUTS)
*Thursdays
 Time's up (DRUMMOND—STUNT FUN)
*Time's up (DRUMMOND—SPOT)
*Tit for tat
 Toothbrush
 Tragedy!
*The training camp
*Trouble in Paradise

*The unemployed
*The ventriloquist (EISENBERG—HAND.)
*We want your business
*Wedded bliss
  What a breath!
*What a mess"
  What a night
*What price roommate?
*What's going on
*Who's a hick?
*The winning ticket
*"Won't grandpa be surprised"
  The wrong cup
*"A wronged husband"
*Your change
*Blank check. (3f) HUBER—TV p63-68.
A blank old lady. GEISTER—NEW p68,90.
*The Blankville bus. (5m, 2f) PARSONS p23-25.
Blarney stone. (3) BUGBEE—LIVE WIRE p56; CORMACK p37;
    HUBER—EASY p39-41.
Blind
  *By your hand
Blind alley. ABELL—PEP p88-89.
Blind boxers. JOHNSON—BAKER'S p94.
*Blind date. (2m, 2f) MIKSCH—TEEN p60-65.
Blind dating. GEISTER—NEW p119.
Blind man's journey. YOUNG—GAMES p25-26.
Blind man's meal. YOUNG—GAMES p21.
Blindfold boxing. DEPEW p175.
Blindfold race. DEPEW p323.
Blindfold test. DEPEW p335.
Blindfolded handshakers. GEISTER—NEW p110.
*Blood red roses. (5m, 4f) WEATHERS—MYSTERIES p30-39.
*The blood-stained bread knife. (9m, 2f) MILLER—LANDS
    p40-48.
Blowing race. DEPEW p315.
Blue swells of sportland. LLOYD p63-65.
"The blue waltz". STAHL—AMAT. p103-106.
"Bluebeard". ENTERTAIN—STUNTS p4.
*Bluebeard up-to-date. (1b, 2g) BARBEE p5-9.

"Blushes". HUBER—EASY p55-57.

*The board meeting. (7m, 1f) TAGGART—FIVE p93-106.

*Boarding house tidbits. (6b) IRISH—CATCHY p15-17.

Boarding houses
  *Morning

Boats and Boating
  *The ship-shape show

*Body, body, who's got the body? (11m) PRESTON—FUN p20-37.

"The bogey man". FERRIS p78.

The bold warrior. EISENBERG—HAND p69-70.

The bologne phone. TARBELL—CRAZY p33-35.

The Bon Ton hat shoppe. BUGBEE—GOOFY p83.

The Bon Ton saloon. BAKER'S-GAY p31.

Boners; other boners. EISENBERG—FUN p49-57.

The boob. BUGBEE—GOOFY p42.

*Boobology. (2m) KASER—ACTS p52-58.

Booby. March music. GEISTER—NEW p20.

*The book agent. (2m, 1f) GEORGE—TEN p36-40.

Book competition. YOUNG—GAMES p66-67.

The booking agency. BUGBEE—LIVE WIRE p114.

"Booking for vaudeville". FERRIS p142.

Books and reading
  See also Literary; names of authors, e.g. Shakespeare, William
  A festival of books, or Our trail of books
  *The 4-H quintuplets
  "The hall of fame, or Heroes and heroines from bookland"
  *Our friend—the books
  Quick reading contest
  Which book?
  *Worming around

*Books! Books! Books! (8 students) STARR—RADIO p75-78.

The bookworm. DEPEW p348.

Boomerang, by Robert N. McGregor, BREEZY p67.

Booths. MACDONALD—CARNIVAL p81.

*The boots-and-saddle gang. (7b and glee club) STARR—JR. p92-96.

*The bored king and the bandit. See *Persia presents

Borrowing
  *An even exchange
  *"Fraternity row"
*"Borrowing Bessie", by Charles George (2) (3f) EASY—
  IMPR. p89-96; JOHNSON—EASY p51-54.
*The boss of the king, by Arthur L. Rice. (4m, 1f) ROHRBOUGH
  p40-46.
*"The botany hike". (4m, 3f) DRUMMOND—STUNT FUN p46-
  52.
Bottle and cork. DEPEW p339.
Bottled tea. (2m) TARBELL—COMEDY p90-92.
The bottleneck. HUBER—GIANT p147-148.
Bottles
  The magic bottle
Boulevard ball. YOUNG—GAMES p81.
The bouncing baby. DRUMMOND—STUNT FUN p67-68.
*Bound to please, by Wilmer Baffle. (1m, 2b, 2g) QUICK—
  COM. p104-108.
The bowler's nightmare, by Beatrice M. Casey. CASEY—PEPPY
  p13-15.
*"A box of trouble". (10f) DRUMMOND — FUNNY p24-32.
Boxing
  Blind boxers
  Blindfold boxing
  Championship boxing bout
  Distance boxing
  *Fight to a finish
  Hello, Bill
  Pedigree unknown
  Rattle boxing
  Rope boxing
  Sack boxing
  Smudge boxing
  *"Tom goes sissy"
  *The training camp
  *What was that?
Boxing match. CORMACK p25; by A. W. Buley. ROHRBOUGH
  p105-106; RYAN p114.
*Boy bites dog. (2m, 1f, 1g, 1b) KASER—ACTS p65-71.
Boy in a toy shop. PARTIES p10.

Boy on a train. DEPEW p362.
A boy scout demonstration. FERRIS p167.

Boy scouts
  See also Camps and camping
  *Afternoon at Central station
  "Do a good deed daily"
  A "flivver" party
  *"Lost" (PROVENCE—VAUD.)
  A processional
  A scene at troop headquarters
  Summer camp

Boys
  *Bad boy
  *Dreadful boys
  *A joker in disgrace
  Personal service to boys
  *Tenting tonight

*Boys' glee club fantasy. (1b, boys' glee club, announcer)
    STARR—RADIO p57-59.

Boy's Town
  *Not wanted

Bragging
  *"Always bragging"
The Brahma rooster trot. BUGBEE—LIVE WIRE p57.
"The brain finder". HUBER—EASY p67-69.
Brain food. TARBELL—FUN p65,67.
Brain tester. DRUMMOND—STUNT FUN p85-86.
Brain testers. *See* Mathematics; Puzzlers; Quizzes; Word games
Brain-testing machine. DEPEW p99-100.
"The brand". HUBER—EASY p85-87.
Brandt, Theodore
  The reward
*Braves, arise! By Jean Provence. QUICK—COM. p38-42.
*"Bravest of the brave". (1m, 2f, extras) HUBER—THREE p65-66.
Brazos Pete, by Thomas A. Gere. BAKER'S—GAY p30.
Break the camera. DEPEW p149-150.
*Breakfast for superman. (3m, 3f) STARR—JR. p43-49.
Breaking an egg on your head. EISENBERG—HAND. p52
Breaking into print. DRUMMOND—STUNT FUN p115-116.

Breaking the China. DEPEW p194.

*The Brewer's great white horses or Life with fodder, by Kurtz Gordon. (4m, 2f) BAKER'S GAY p5-6.

*The bride of the dragon—China. (more than 6 char.) MILLER —STUNT p107-111.

*"The bridegroom cometh". (4m, 4f) STAHL—HEARTY p67-69.

Bridegrooms
"A cook's tour"
*She's a beauty

Brides
*Browned biscuits (2)
*The first biscuit
"June echoes"—"Brides of long ago and today"
*Just a love nest (EASY—BLACKOUTS)
Keep the home tires turning
*She's a beauty

Bridge (game)
*"Card party night"
*Finish the rubber
*The flat below
If football players were bridge players
*Partners (EASY—IMPR.)
Trump, trump, trump

*Bridge and poker. (4m, 4f) PARSONS p95-109.

Bridges. GEISTER—NEW p20-22.

The brig. GEISTER—NEW p38-39.

*The bright world. (2m, 1f) HUBER—TV p69-74.

Brine, Mary D.
She was "somebody's mother"

Bringing out a lesson. BUCHANAN p82.

Broadcasting. See Radio; Television

A broadcasting fanstasy. ABELL—STUNTS p15-18.

Broomstick twist. DEPEW p330.

*Brotherly revenge. (2m, 1f) DRUMMOND—THREE p29-32.

Brothers
*Entertaining sister's beaux (2)
Sister's beau

Brought to court, by Harry Githens. GITHENS p17.

*Browned biscuits. (1m, 1f) by Jean Provence. BRINGS—MASTER p202-203; PROVENCE—LIGHT p23-25.

Bruin, the tame bear. BUGBEE—LIVE WIRE p42.

The brutal miner. PARTIES p14-15.

Bubble bath, by Grace Keith Samuelson. "THAT GOOD", p49.

"Bubble-blowers". FERRIS p69.

"Bubble books". FERRIS p77-78.

Bubble dance. EISENBERG—FUN p39.

*Buch private's dream (3m, extras) TAGGART—MEN p104-108.

Bucking the broncho. BUGBEE—GOOFY p79.

Bugbee, Willis N.

  After-dinner speeches

  Around the world quiz

  *Atomic energy

  A Biblical tug-o'-war

  Cross road follies

  *The hobby parade

  Irish symbols, a game

  The kidnapping of Percy Bogelwinkle

  Lub yo' nabors

  Malachi Jimson's farewell sermon

  *Martha Biggers' pumpkin

  The missionary and the cannibals

  Noah's ark charades

  The retro-moviescope

  Shaughnessy's ball

  *Some people are goofy

  Who's who? or The rogue's gallery

Building words. YOUNG—GAMES p50.

Buley, A. W. The boxing match

Bullfights

  A day in Seville

  El Toreador

  Mexican bull fight

Bum's rush. EISENBERG—FUN p114-115.

Bumpity, bum, bump, bump. DEPEW p300-301.

*"Bundles from heaven". (2m, 1f) STAHL—HEARTY p50-52.

*Bungling burglars. (4m, 3f) KASER—ACTS p45-51.

*Bunny bargain bloom is on the air, by Nora Casey. (4f, 1b)
    JOHNSON—EASY p121-128; SHANNON p101-109.

Bunny rabbit. TARBELL—SUNDAY p23-30.

Burdens. (2m) KAUFMAN—HIGHLOWBROW p53-58.

Burglars and burglary
*"And spooking of ghosts"
*The big stunt
*Bungling burglars
*The case of the Gobi pearls
*The customer's right
*The defective detective
*The doctor's dilemma (2) (BRINGS—MASTER; STAHL—
    MORE)
*"Good gracious"
*He always gets his man
*Imagination
*Kid games
*Night school
*"Oh, marry me"
*"Safety first" (PROVENCE—FLASH)
*Sold (EASY—BLACKOUTS)
*Stop thief (2)
*A thief in the house
*Thieves in the night
*The thirteenth trump
*Three strokes too many
*"Tom goes sissy"
*Too late
*Where's Henry?
*Without benefit of license
The burial of the giant. DEPEW p114.
Buried booty. HANLEY—STUNTS p23-25.
Burlesque campaign parade. BUGBEE—LIVE WIRE p30.
Burlesque Greek dance. BUGBEE—LIVE WIRE p30.
Burleque olympics. BUGBEE—NUTTY p80.
Burlesque trial. CANOPY—HIGH p66.
Burlesques
    Always a gentleman
    Hisses and kisses
*"The king's highway"
    Mother Goose grand opera. (FUNNY)
    Old King Cole
    Pyramus and Thisbe
*Red Riding Hood (PRESTON)

*School days at Porcupine Junction
Shipwreck today; or, Robinson Crusoe up to date
The silent house
The simpleton
Telling the world
*"The village band rehearses"
*Burnt crackers. (2m) KASER—SURE p23-34.
Burying Jacksonville. DEPEW p89-91.
Burying the seniors. DEPEW p123-124.
*Bus ride. (5m, 4f) WEATHER—MYSTERIES p4-12.
Bus stop. YOUNG—GAMES p10-11.
*The bus stops at Cactus Junction. (7m, 3f) DEASON—SKIT
   p91-97.

Buses
*The Blankville bus
Chivalry is not dead
*Hurry, hurry
The proof

Business
*"Big business"
Talk on business or profession
Unlucky number
*Business is booming. (2m) BUGBEE—NUTTY p33-44.
The business meeting. EISENBERG—FUN p81.

Business men
*The no man

Business offices
*The best laid plan
*Colossal
*Fame in half an hour
*Forget-me-not!
*Good front
*I'm hungry
*The new secretary
*Polite but firm (EASY—BLACKOUTS; SIX—MORE)
Busted, by gosh. BUGBEE—LIVE WIRE p33.
*Bustin' up the old quartet. (4m) KASER—ACTS p72-76.
*Busy business (1m, 3f) HUBER—FOUR p148-151.
The busy waiter. (1m) TARBELL—CRAZY p72-75.

Butcher Shops
  Kiddlies
Butlers
  *Who's your butler?
  Button up your coat. EISENBERG—FUN p37.
  Buttoning up the vest. TARBELL—CRAZY p16-21.
  *Buying eggs. (1m, 2f) IRISH—CATCHY p104-106.
  Buzz—the oldest known game and always good fun. YOUNG—
      GAMES p53-54.
  *By the teeth. (3m) PROVENCE—KNOCKOUT p42-44.
  *By your hand. (4f) HUBER—CHAR. p29-38.
  *Byron's accident (4m, 3f) IRISH—CATCHY p60-64.

Caesar, Julius
  *"Scrambled dates"
  When Julius Caesar
  A café chantant, "pop" concert, club cabaret. FERRIS p136-
      138.
  Cake-eating contest. DRUMMOND—STUNT FUN p60-61.
  The cake in the hat. TARBELL—COMEDY p59-68.
  The cakewalk. EISENBERG—FUN p95.
  The calabozo. DRUMMOND—STUNT FUN p67.
Calendar
  Resolved—that the calendar . . .
  The calender. JOHNSON—BAKER'S p47-50; PRESTON—FUN
      p144-147.
"Caliph Stork"
  *The magic word—Persia
  A call for the ambulance. BUGBEE—GOOFY p46-48.
  *The call for volunteers. (5b) BUGBEE—LIVELY p65-66.
  *Call me dear. (3m, 3f) HUBER—CHAR. p99-111.
  *Call the next case. (7m, 1f) KASER—MERRY p42-49.
  *Call the police. (4m, 2f) HUBER—SIX p120-126.
  Calling all cars, by Grace Keith Samuelson. CASEY—PEPPY
      p57-58.
  *Calling all cars! By LeRoy Stahl. (3m) EASY—SKITS p91-98.
  Calliope tunes. DRUMMOND—STUNT FUN p88.
  The camel and the owner. CROWLEY, p38, 40-41.
  The camels. DEPEW p340-341.

*Camera study, by Albert G. Miller. (2m, 2f) MILLER—BROAD-
WAY p41-45.

Camp and scamp minstrels. FERRIS p124.

*Camp Crowhill here we come. (4m, 3f) MIKSCH—TEEN
p103-112.

Camp drill. WILLIAMS p19-21.

A camp fire pageant number. FERRIS p160-164.

Camp-song. WILLIAMS p32.

Campaign speeches by presidential candidates. CANOPY—HIGH
p108.

Camper's nightmare, or "A day that never was" by Harry
Githens. GITHENS p59-61.

Cabins
  *The magic cabin
  *Taking Maw's advice

Cablegrams. YOUNG—GAMES p48.

Camps and camping
  See also Boy scouts; Contests; Games, Campfire; Games,
    Outdoor; Girl Scouts; Races; Relays
  Ball game deluxe
  Bat kicking for distance
  Bean bag baseball
  Bean bag boards
  Bean bag gold
  Bean bag grab
  Bean bag shuffleboard
  Bean bag snatch
  Bean-passing relay
  Blindfold test
  Blue swells of sportland
  Broomstick twist
  Camper's nightmare
  The cannibal king
  Changing attire
  Circle pass
  Circle rope jump
  A day in a boy scout camp
  A day in camp
  Discus throw
  Distance boxing

Diving between legs
Diving for duck
Dodge ball
Enroute to camp
Funnel stunt
Greased pole climb
Greased water pole
Hello, Bill
Hog tying
Human tug of war
Hundred-yard dash
In the dining-room
An indoor camping party
Indoor field meet
Jug balance
Jumping the rope
Lifting 150 lbs. with 5 fingers
Lifting seven boys
Logrolling
Major Blows' amateur hour
Memory test
Musical object hunt
Nail driving
Names of states
Object hunt
Old clothes antics
Old MacDonald's farm
Peanut punch
Peanut throw
Pick up
Pill-carbonic orchestra
Plunging
Poison Indian club
Pull fingers apart
Rattle boxing
Rooster fight
Rope boxing
Sack boxing
Shoe hunt
Shot put

Silent conversation
Sink the ship
Skin the snake (2)
Smudge boxing
Spinning on a stick
Stork tag
Summer camp
Swim under water
The table
Ten nails
*Tenting tonight
Tug of war (DEPEW)
Water baseball
Water basketball
Whip tag
Whistling marathon
Wiping up water
Zig zag bean bag
*Can this be love? (2m, 1f) STAHL—MORE p49-51.
Can you name the presidents? DEPEW p345-346.
Can you poke a quarter through a ring? EISENBERG—FUN p42.
Can you read this letter? DEPEW p345.
Can you tell what is missing? YOUNG—GAMES p73-74.
Candidates for congress. YOUNG—GAMES p39-40.
*A candle burns tonight. (6m, 3f, or 4m, 5f) WEATHERS p55-72.
Candle lighting ceremony. PARTIES p60.
*The candy shop, by Robert Lewis Shayon. (1m, 2b, 1g) MIL-LER—BROADWAY p77-81.
Candy under hat. EISENBERG—FUN p41.
*Canned opera. (3m, 2f) HUBER—GIANT p56-60.
The cannibal king, by Harry Githens. GITHENS p61-62.
Cannibals
  The missionary and the cannibals
Cannibals and missionaries. DEPEW p364.
Canoe song (from Sanders of the sea). ABELL—STUNTS p85-86.
*A capable servant. (3m) IRISH—CATCHY p77-84.
Capsule friends. JOLLY p33-40.
Capsule revelation party. DEPEW p294-295.

Captain Jinks. GEISTER—NEW p27-28.
*Captain of the ball nine. (3b, 1g) IRISH—CHILDREN'S p53-55.
*Captain Paul. (3m, 2f) WEATHERS—MYSTERIES p20-29.
Caravan. GEISTER—NEW p16.
Carbolic acid. EISENBERG—HAND. p84.
*"Card party night". (2m, 2f) STAHL—HEARTY p84-86.
A card trick. (2) BRINGS—MASTER p382; DRUMMOND—STUNT
    FUN p54.

Cards, playing
    See also Bridge (game); Poker (game)
    Playing cards introduction
    Playing solitaire
    A trick with cards
*Cards on the table. (4m, 1f) HUBER—No p12-16.
*Carefully yours. (3m, 3f) HUBER—No SCENE p98-108.
Caricatures. BUCHANAN p71.
Carmen. EISENBERG—HAND. p132-133.
Carnival suggestions. DRUMMOND—SPOT p51-52.

Carnivals
    See also Bazaars; Fairs; Side shows
    *Androcles and the lion (CONNOR)
    Astronomical observatory
    The bearded lady
    Bed-time hour (for adults)
    A century of progress
    Championship boxing bout
    The country school
    The country store
    The crystal gazer
    Dance of the nymphs
    The deadly bat
    The fan dancer
    The fat man
    The food and candy booths
    For men only (2)
    The freak horse
    The greatest curiosity in the world
    Hawaiian serenaders
    Hints for the crystal gazer
    Hot dogs (DEPEW)

The human marimba
Japanese tea garden
Kisses for sale
The little flapper, or Follies of 19—
Menagerie
Mexican bull fight
Musical specialties
No man's land
Nursery rhymes (for adults) (CONNOR)
Old curiosity shop
The parade
Parade of the nations
The passenger aeroplane
Read 'em and weep
The rogue's gallery
Siamese twins
"Sideshow"
Side show and freak tent
Sportlight minstrels
Styles of a century
The tatoo shop
*The trial of George Washington
*Vaudeville skit
Walking, talking, singing and dancing dolls
The war in song
The wild man from Borneo (a variation)
*Winter carnival
The wonder cornet
*The carol singers. (5b, 5g) BUGBEE—LIVELY p24-27.
*Caroline bakes a cake. (1g, announcer) STARR—RADIO p47-50.
*Carpet rags. (6f) VAN DERVEER—ANY p20-28.
Carrie from Cantaloupe county. (1f) KASER—BUSHEL p24-28.
Carroll, Lewis
  *"Queen Alice"
*Carrot topped. (3m) EISENBERG—HAND. p99-101.
"Carry me back to Ol' Virginny". FERRIS p106.
Carry on the song. DEPEW p204.
Carry relay. FRICK—FALL p22.
The case of John Imbecile. DEPEW p66-68.
*Case of necessity. (5m) HUBER—NO SCENE p75-84.

*The case of the Gobi pearls. (2m, 2f) SULLIVAN—MORE p52-56.

The case of the lost word. CROWLEY p76-77.

Casey, Arten
  Man to man
  *Matrimony bumps

Casey, Beatrice M.
  Bells
  The bowler's nightmare
  Crr-uel wrr-etch!
  The fiery finger
  The giant and the midget
  Gulliver and the lil'mutts
  Hungry spooks
  In the bag
  Manny-kins
  Murder on the High C
  The sign painter
  A soloist so low
  The spark of love
  The tragic tintype
  Two benches in the park

Casey, Nora
  *Bunny Bargain Bloom is on the air (2)

Casey at the bat. BAKER'S GAY p32-33.

Casey's revenge, by James Wilson. BAKER'S GAY p33-34.

*"Cashed". (3m) HUBER—THREE p72-73.

The cast out. (1m) BRINGS—MASTER p379; DRUMMOND—STUNT FUN p50.

*The casual casualty. (8m) HUBER—GIANT p99-102.

Cat chatter. BRINGS—MASTER p389.

Cat fight, by Grace Keith Samuelson. BUGBEE—NUTTY p100.

Catch a bat. FRICK—FALL p46-47.

Catch questions. GEISTER—NEW p81-82,90.

Catchy verses. CASEY—PEPPY p95.

Cats
  *"Anything to get votes"
  "Mee-ow-ooooo"
  *The reward (QUICK)

Cats and rats. DEPEW p344.

*Cats is cats. (2m, 1f) Drummond—Three p17-20.
*The cat's meow, by Alfred Dykes. (4) Quick Com. p109-115.
Cave man stuff. Eisenberg—Fun p126-129.
Cedric's return, by Arthur L. Kaser. (3m, 2f) Brings—Master p310-315; Kaser—Funny p112-117.
Celebrities. *See* Biography; Historical; names of special groups, e.g. Artists
Celebrities. By Beatrice Plumb. Brings—Master p431; Geister—New p114.
*Celebrity day. (2b, 2g, extras) Starr—Radio p23-26.
Census
   *What are you selling?
*"The census taker". (1m, 2f) Huber—Three p86-87; (1m, 1f) Preston—Fun p80-83.
A century of progress. Connor p59-60.
Chain schemes
   Missing links are morons
Chair circle. Geister—New p40-41.
Chair pass. Geister—New p45.
Chair scramble. March music. Geister—New p13-14.
Chalk talks
   Alphabetic faces
   Animals that didn't win at the fair
   A beautiful view
   Betty's misfortunes
   The bird with the big bill
   The birthday surprise
   Brain food
   Bringing out a lesson
   Bunny rabbit
   The camel and the owner
   Caricatures
   The case of the lost word
   The chemist's jug
   The chicken and the farmer
   Christmas stunts
   The circle, the triangle, and the square
   Closing numbers
   College "bred"
   The college freshman

Color pictures
Coloring a picture
A comedy chalk talk
Comic endings
Comic types and expressions
A commercial relay
The cone and the man
The cow man
The cud-chewing and a basket bawl
The darky and the ghost
David and Goliath
The discontented blacksmith
The dog and the old woman
The donkey and his master
Drawing from photographs
A drink to order
The eagle and the Indian chief
An Easter lesson
Easy human figure drawing
An easy way to make money
The eternal question
Evolution pictures
The fatal bottle
FFA and 4H—a good opening stunt
The FFA emblem
Football stunts
The 4-H club emblem
Fresh fruit
Garden chalk talk
The grateful Samaritan
The gun man
Have a banana
Hip, hip hooray!
The hitch hiker
Holiday suggestions
The honorable Mr. Donkey, esquire
How a General is made
How to make a grouchy man smile
The hunting knife
Joseph and his brethren

The kid and the squid
The lazy man's chalk talk
A lemon while you wait
Let me fish in an Oregon stream
Life's illusions
The light headed gentleman
Lines that count
Love and I.O.U.
A love letter
The loving cup
The medicine bottle and the chemist's jug
Men who have never been president
Military stunts
Modern birds' nests
Money or love
The months of the year
My pet parrot
A novelty telephone stunt
Number men
The old bear
Old bottles
The 105-pound bullfrog
One line stunt
The owl's tale
A pair of spectacles
Paul Revere's ride (SHANNON)
Persuasive pictures
The Pharisees
Phases of the World War
The pirate's chest
The poor man's lamb
The pop bottle
The pumpkin and the witch
The "punch" bottle
The rabbit in the hat
The red rabbit
The rising card
The rising sun
Roman art
The school bell and the professor

The Schotchman's greeting card
The Scotchman's hat
Scrambled states
Seeing things
The shadow of the cross
The shepherd's hut
The shoeman
The soda jerk
Songs of fashion
The state of Idaho
The state of Maine
The state of Nevada
The state of Utah
The story of Ruth and Naomi
Strawberry blonde and mom
A study in transformation
A stylish gentleman
The tea kettle
Thanksgiving stunts
These United States
The three wise men
Tires for defense
Transformation pictures
The treble clef and the musician
Uncle Sam
Upside down stunt
The valentine (CROWLEY)
The vanishing line
The vulture and the tough
The whatzit bird
Your boy—the farm's best product
Zulu Zu
Chalk talks, or Tableaux—The art department. LAMKIN &
    FLORENCE p53.
Chambers of commerce
    Heaven's gate
Chameleon socks. TARBELL—CRAZY p67-71,73.
*Championship. (2m, 2f) HUBER—FOUR p30-34.
Championship boxing bout. CONNOR p15-20.
Changed names. DEPEW p213.

Changing attire. DEPEW p318.
Character sketch. JOHNSON—BAKER'S p104.
Characters in fiction
  See also Dramatizations, Literary
  Book competition
  "The hall of fame, or heroes and heroines from bookland"
Charades
  Accident
  Baltimore
  The eternal charade
  Funny flowers
  Illustrated
  Innocent
  Jiffy plays or charades
  Mendicant
  Minnesota
  Misfortune
  Noah's ark charades
  Romantic
Charades. (2) EISENBERG—HAND. p31-33; PARTIES p16-18.
Charades and stunts. KEMMERER—GAMES p84-87.
Charades, simple. FRICK—SUMMER p60-61.
A chariot race. (2) ABELL—STUNTS p19; DEPEW p334.
Charity luncheon. DEPEW p214.
*Charlie Slasher's mistake. (1b 5g) IRISH—CHILDREN'S p40-42.
*Charlie the wonder horse. (3b) PRESTON p44-46.
The charmer in the dell. LLOYD p34-35.
Chart committee report. DEPEW p245.
The chartreuse murder case. EISENBERG—FUN p129-136.
Chase, Frank E.
  Drink
Chauffeurs
  *Social climbing
Cheap jokes. KASER—BUSHEL p106-108.
Check room. MACDONALD—CARNIVAL p83-84.
Checkers. DEPEW p295.
Checking up, by Robert N. McGregor. JOLLY p76.
"Cheer in Erin". FERRIS p83.
Cheerfulness
  Sunshine in your heart

*The cherrio clinic. (6m, 6f) KASER—FUNNY p95-112.

Cheers and cheer leaders
   Pep—old and new
   Visiting cheerleaders
   Yells, cheers, etc.

Cheese
   The siege of limburger
   The chemist's jug. CROWLEY p57.

Chemistry and chemists
   *All due to chemistry
   What it takes to make a man
Cherry tree stunts. BUGBEE—LIVE WIRE p50.
Chestnuts. WILLIAMS p45-46.
Chewing the rag. CORMACK p35.

Chicago
   Writin' home
Chicago. DEPEW p102.
The chicken and the farmer. CROWLEY p31,33-34.

Chickens
   Cy Perkins' hen
   *Eggs while you wait
   Hand me down a quart of corn
   *The singing hen

Child psychology
   It's all in knowing how
   *Use the book
*Childish prattle. (2m, 2f) DRUMMOND—THREE p50-53.

Children
   See also Babies; Boys; Chorus, Children's; Daughters; Girls
   A baby show (FERRIS)
   "Don't be a goop"
   The gimmes
   "Her first piece"
   The kindergarten kids
   *"The old and the new"
   *Old fogy
   "Our treasures"
   School days (FERRIS)
Children's entertainment. JOHNSON—BAKER'S p74-76.

Children's stunts. *See* Fairy tales; Mother Goose; etc.

The Chinaman and the mouse. (1m) BUGBEE—LIVE WIRE
p115-116.

Chinese

See also Costume, Chinese; Dialect, Chinese

*The bride of the dragon king—China

*The fairy serpent—China

*"The mail-order dragon", A Chinese extravaganza

The moon maiden

*The moon maiden—China

The peculiar Chinese

*Service

Chinese auction. DEPEW p178-179.

The Chinese folder. DEPEW p352-353.

The Chinese paddles. TARBELL—CRAZY p80-85.

Chinese school, by Gladys Lloyd. JOLLY p97.

Chinese wall. FRICK—SUMMER p19.

Chinese writing. DEPEW p303.

*Chip off the old block, by George M. Rideout. (3m) EASY—
IMPR. p123-125.

Chiropodists

*Corns

*Chiseling on chivalry, by Walter F. Kerr. (2m, 1f, announcer)
SNAPPY p70-76.

Chivalry

*Chiseling on chivalry

Chivilary is not dead. EISENBERG—HAND. p87-88.

Choosing partners. BUGBEE—CATCHY p10; JOHNSON—BAKER'S
p98-99.

*"Chop suey". (2m, 1f) GEORGE—TWELVE p39-44.

Choral speaking. KEMMERER—GAMES p126-128.

Chorus

"At the ball"—"Love's dream after the ball"—"Love's
dreamland"

"Bandits bold"

"Black and white"

"Cupid's little dart"—"Cupid never misses a shot"

"Dance and song in far-away lands"—"Brothers all"

"Dances of yesterday and to-day"

"Echoes of the glorious Fourth"

A finale number
"Glowing glow-worms"
Hallowe'en minstrels
"Happiness in every box"
"Help wanted" (FERRIS)
"Little Bo-Peep"
"Maud Muller revue"—"Rebecca of Sunnybrook farm and co."
"My rainbow dream"
"The nation's sweetheart in review"
Newspaper minstrels
"An old-fashioned garden"—"Laces and graces"—"The charmers of long ago and today"
Sportlight minstrels
Summer (girl) minstrels
"Vanquishing vamps"
"When the cows come home"
"Wig-wag"—all's well

Chorus, Baseball
Baseball minstrels

Chorus, Children's
"The bogey man"
"Bubble books"
"Cones! Cones! Cones!"
"Do a good deed daily"
"Little—but oh, my!"
"Santa Claus land"
"School days" (FERRIS)
"Skipping skippers"

Chorus, Christmas
"Christmas holly and red ribbon"

Chorus, Fashion show
"Fifth Avenue fancies"
"June echoes"—"Brides of long ago and to-day"
"Moods of the mode"
"My magazine cover girl"—"My lady's trousseau"—"Off to college"
"Never-mind-the-weather girls"—"My girl—in sunshine or in rain"
"When artists frolic"—"Mind-the-paint girls"

Chorus, Flower
"Daisies won't tell—or will they"?
"Flower girls—all in a row"
"Flowers for sale"
"Say it with flowers"—"The flowers he sends her"
"When it's apple-blossom time in Normandy"
"When you look in the heart of a rose" by Leo Feist;
"Mighty lak' a rose", by E. Nevin
Chorus, Gypsy
"The gypsy trail"
Chorus, Hallowe'en
"A gathering of witches"
"The ghosts are out"
"A jack-o'-lantern frolic"
Chorus, Hard-times
"Rags and tags"
Chorus, Hawaiian
"Aloha-oe"
Chorus, Indian
"In the shadow of the tepee"
Chorus, Italian
"In Venice"
" 'Neath the Italian moon"
"See-a-da-monk"
Chorus, Japanese
"Meet me where the lanterns glow"
Chorus, May day
"The queen of the May"—"Upon a throne sits the queen"
Chorus, Patriotic
"With the colors"
Chorus, Sailor's
Merry middy minstrels
Chorus, St. Patrick's day
"Cheer in Erin"
Chorus, Western
"Across the plains"—"The Texas rangers"
Christian endeavor
We're forever boosting C.E.
Christie, Ray
*Three in one

Christmas
  See also Chorus, Christmas; Santa Claus
  *Bargain present
  *A candle burns tonight
  *The carol singers
  A community Christmas
  Copy cat Christmas story
  "Do your shopping early" or "A shopper's dream"
  The "Favor-ite" box hunt
  The first Christmas
  Fun leaves
  *Gift exchange
  *Holiday homecoming
  *Jingle bells
  *Just another one
  *"Markheim"
  *The night before the morning after Christmas eve
  *Peter's Christmas tree
  *The Purdy's Christmas package
  A quarter to Christmas
  "Santa Claus land"
  "Santa Claus serenade"
  Sleuthing customs
  *To Ellen—from Dad
  Under the hanging mistletoe
  Up on the house-top
  The wail of the Christmas ties
  The week before Christmas
  *What is Christmas Day for?
  The window of Charvel
Christmas Belle minstrels. FERRIS p124.
*Christmas carols. (1g, glee clubs) STARR—RADIO p99-100.
*Christmas conundrums. (6g) IRISH—CHILDREN'S p15-17.
Christmas (decorations). YOUNG—GAMES p110-111.
Christmas (games and stunts). KEMMERER—GAMES p28-32.
*Christmas high jinks. (2b, 3g, glee clubs, band) STARR—RADIO
    p101-109.
*Christmas holly and red ribbon". FERRIS p82-83.
*Christmas presents. (3m, 3f) HOPE p21-22.
Christmas savings. DEPEW p362.

A Christmas story. ELSENBERG—FUN p46-49.

Christmas stunts. BUCHANAN p66,68,70.

*A Christmas surprise. (3f) IRISH—CATCHY p70-73.

Christmas toys. DEPEW p182-183.

Chuckle ads, by Mabel Tuttle Craig. CASEY—PEPPY p114.

Church
  An evening with the American girl
  The house by the side of the road
  If you think your church is best
  The inharmonious choir
  *The ladies' aid church supper
  Now and then program
  *"She's from Hollywood"

The church choir. YOUNG—GAMES p24.

The cigarette smoker. WILLIAMS p15-16.

Cigarettes
  "Don't displease your husband
  *Happy birthday to you
  The spark of love

"Cinderella"
  *After the ball
  Out of the garret
  The romance of little Cinderella

Cinderella. (1f) GODDARD—CHILDREN'S p8-10.

Cinderella Goldlilocks. PRESTON—PANTOM. p51-61.

Cinderella Hassenpfeffer. EISENBERG—FUN p65-66.

Cinderella on the screen, by Harry Githens. GITHENS p74-78.

*Cinderella—quite modern. (1b, 4g) BARBEE p30-33.

Cinderella up-to-date, by Olga E. Gunkle. ROHRBOUGH p33-37.

*Cindy Ella slips, or "Those who wear glass slippers shouldn't skate on ice", (2m, 2f, reader) BREEZY p15-20.

*Cindy swings it. (4m, 7f) LAUFE—EASY p24-44.

Circle and line games. KEMMERER—GAMES p33-46.

Circle pass. DEPEW p311.

Circle race. GEISTER—NEW p46-47.

Circle rope jump. DEPEW p321.

Circle shift. GEISTER—NEW p79-80.

Circle stunt. FRICK—FALL p32.

The circle, the triangle, and the square. TARBELL—CHALK STUNTS p65-69.

Circus
See also Animals; Clowns; Sideshows
*Animals in the circus
*Ballyhoo
Creating a circus
*Mademoiselle Tania
Putting out a fire
*School circus
Circus. BRIDGE (3) p31-34; FERRIS p133-134; PRESTON—FUN p94-98.
Circus parade tumblers. DRUMMOND—STUNT FUN p116.
Circus sideshow, by Harry Githens. GITHENS p11-16.
Citizens of Venus and Mars. BUGBEE—NUTTY p64.

Citizenship
*"I am an American"
*Meeting of the better city campaign committee
*Seven is the perfect number
Students are good citizens, I, II, III
City adventures! Perils to pedestrians. FERRIS p55.
*City feller. (1m, 1f) PROVENCE—KNOCKOUT p17-19.
*City ignorance. (5g) IRISH—CHILDREN'S p62-65.

Civil Betterment. *See* Citizenship

Civil war
*Scenes of the sixties
Clancy to the rescue. EISENBERG—HAND. p66-69.
Clap your hands. FUNNY p53-54.
Clapping stunt. EISENBERG—HAND. p51.
Clara Belle the flea. EISENBERG—HAND. p57-58.
Clash and clatter band. ROHRBOUGH p82-84.

Class banquets. *See* Banquets

Class day
History of class day
The class historian speaks. LAMKIN & FLORENCE p35.

Class histories
The class historian speaks
High flying—class history
*A class in geography. (6b, 6g) IRISH—CHILDREN'S p37-39.

Class orations
Subjects for class orations

Class parties
  Program for a class party
A class poem. LAMKIN & FLORENCE p20-21.
Class poems
  The sky ride—class poem
Class prophecies
  Another prophecy
  A prophecy (ten years hence)
  A prophecy (fifty years hence)
  Seeing things at night—class prophecy
  Your fortunes told
A class song. FUNNY p27.
Class wills
  The sky line—class will
Clawson, Mrs. E. Richey
  What it takes to make a man
*Clean hands. (3m, 1f) HUBER—CHAR. p59-67.
Cleanliness
  *Coming clean
Clemens, Samuel
  *"The glorious whitewasher" ("The adventures of Tom
    Sawyer")
Cleopatra
  When Julius Caesar
*"Cleopatra, the second". DRUMMOND—FUNNY p49-57.
Clergymen. *See* Ministers
Clerks. *See* Salesmen and salesmanship
Clifford, Vance
      Advice to draftees
      Art (three versions)
    *Aunt Emma brings Dickie
    *The gay nineties barber shop, and a quartette
    *High pressure
      Modern transportation
      Vote for me
*"The clock". (2m, 1f) PROVENCE—FLASH p21-22.
Clock strokes. DEPEW p359.
Clocks
  The human clock
*Close deal. (3m, 3f) HUBER p36-44.

Close observer. DEPEW p216-217.

Close order drill. BRINGS—MASTER p389.

Closing numbers
  A finale number
  Good night!
  *Goodbye, students
  Little man in a fix

Closing numbers. CROWLEY p92-93.

Closing pantomime chorus. WILLIAMS p48.

Clothesline relay. DEPEW p321-322.

Clothing and dress. *See* Costume; Fashion

The clown. FRICK—FALL p39.

A clown act. (2) DRUMMOND—STUNT p72-73; FRICK—FALL
  p49-50.

The clown band. FRICK—FALL p40.

Clown minstrels. (2) BUGBEE—LIVE WIRE p102-105; FERRIS
  p125.

The clown wagon. DRUMMOND—STUNT FUN p68.

Clowns
  Circus parade tumblers
  *Mademoiselle Tania
  Tight rope walk
  Tippo's horse

Club memories, by Beatrice Plumb. BREEZY p59.

"Club songs". HUBER—EASY p10-12.

Clubs and lodges
  See also Attendance
  The back yard concert
  The barrel parade
  Blarney stone (BUGBEE—LIVE WIRE)
  *The board meeting
  The Brahma rooster trot
  Come, Fido
  The devil and the deep blue C
  Fresh country butter
  Getting down to business
  The henpecked husband
  Historical opinions
  The hula hula dance
  In Judge Spoofum's court

*"Joining the whole truth club"
*Keep smiling
*The ladies' defense club
 Ladies' initiation stunts
*Local number ten
 The lodge goat
 Lodge stunts for ladies
 The merry-go-round (BUGBEE—LIVE WIRE)
 Names for social clubs or fraternities
 A novel introduction
 On the line
 An organization stunt
 *Organizing a dramatic club at Goose Landing
 The president's dream
 The prehistoric family album
 Rock-a-bye baby
 The surprise camera
 Walking on eggs
 Who's crazy now
 The wind gauge
*Clubs and friends. (1m, 2f) TOPOLKA p69-72.
A clubwoman speaks, by Beatrice Plumb. PRESTON p16.
Coat and vest relay. DEPEW p317.
Coaxing a member to remove his tie. DEPEW p172.
Coffee pot. (2) GEISTER—NEW p63; YOUNG—GAMES p54.
Coin tricks
 Being generous
 The disappearing dime
 The flying quarter
 Money from the air
 Moving coins
 Passing a dime through a table
 A quarter in the yarn ball
 Six on a side
 The slippery penny
 That elusive dime
 'Tis here, 'tis gone
 Traveling coins
 A twenty cent trick
 What coins?

Collection stunt. EISENBERG—HAND. p123.

College and knowledge; Circumstantial evidence; A good joke; An expensive change; Proved. KASER—BUSHEL p102-103.

College "bred". CROWLEY p44,46.

"College days". FERRIS p69.

The college freshman. CROWLEY p48,49,51.

College minstrels. FERRIS p124.

*College never changes, by Jean Provence. QUICK—COM. p101·103.

College revisted. BAKER'S GAY p38.

College rhythm. STAHL—AMAT. p37-41,97-99.

College students
  *All who enter
  *Chip off the old block
  *"Good gracious"
  *Honor man
  I'll bite
  *Kupid's kollege
  *Maybelle confesses
  *So you won't talk!
  *Stars of the gay nineties
  *Vacation
  *What price roommate?

Collegiate scramble. ABELL—STUNTS p8.

Colonial life and customs
  The answer is "yes"
  *"Musical dreams"

Colonial minstrels. FERRIS p124.

Color blindness. HUBER—GIANT p157-158.

Color pictures. BUCHANAN p85-87.

Colored kin. DEPEW p351.

Coloring a picture. TARBELL—CHALK STUNTS p94-99.

*Colossal, by Selden M. Loring. (3m, 2f) EASY—IMPR. p97-104.

Columbus, Christopher
  *"The arrival of Columbus"
  The landing of Columbus
  *Landing of Columbus, in verse
  *This brave new world

Columbus. DRUMMOND—STUNT FUN p68.
Columbus day (decorations). YOUNG—GAMES p110.
Columbus discovers America. (2) BUGBEE—GOOFY p91-93; by John G. Peters. ROHRBOUGH p109-113.
Columbus discovers Minnie who-who. EISENBERG—HAND. p64-66.
*"The columnist". (1m, 3f) HUBER—THREE p75-76.
"The colyumist". FERRIS p20.
The comb orchestra. FRICK—FALL p40.
Combing the air waves. EISENBERG—FUN p144-152.
Come, Fido. BUGBEE—LIVE WIRE p55.
*Come to the basket ball game". BARBEE p43-45.
Come to the game. ABELL—PEP p82-86.
Comedians
  See also Clowns
  *Protection or else
A comedy chalk talk. TARBELL—CRAZY p54-61.
A comedy deviation. TARBELL—CRAZY p96-102.
Comedy song titles. LYONS p121-124.
Comic endings. BUCHANAN p37,41.
Comic orchestra. BUGBEE—CATCHY p11.
Comic quartet. DEPEW p257.
The comic section, by Harry Githens. GITHENS p16-17.
Comic types and expressions. CROWLEY p88,89,91.
Comic valentines. (3) by Sidney Steele. BRINGS—MASTER p292-294; BUGBEE—NUTTY p62; DRUMMOND—STUNT FUN p75-77.
Comics
  A day in Dog Patch
  In the land of Schmozz
  The still in the night
Comin 'round the mountain, by Harry Githens. GITHENS p62.
"Comin' thro' the rye". FERRIS p106.
*Coming clean. (2m, 2f) TOPOLKA p19-23.
Commencement exercises, or schoolroom burlesque. CANOPY —HIGH p65-66.
Commencement week. LAMKIN & FLORENCE p36-50.
Commercial Department
  A shadow graph for the commercial department
A commercial relay. ABELL—STUNTS p5-7.

Commercials, Singing
Singing commercials
*The committee. (2m, 3f) HOPE p10-13.

Committees
Rabbit (DEPEW)
A community Christmas. BUGBEE—CATCHY p36-38.
*Community fund play. (1m, 3f) TOPOLKA p95-99.
Community house minstrels. KENT—ONE p103-112.
*A community leader. (4m, 2f) ROGERS—PLAYS p63-68.
The community news. BRIDGE p17,18.
A community pageant. BUGBEE—CATCHY p18-20.

Community "sings"
"Hello neighbor, let's sing". A "community sing"
A community song-leader. FERRIS p17-18.
Community songs. BRIDGE p13-15.
*"Company, 'tention!" (5m) CASEY p69-77.
Comparisons. BREEZY p48-49.
Compass facing. PARTIES p10-11.
*Competition. (3m, 2f) HUBER—CHAR. p39-48.
Competitive games. BRIDGE p35-51.
*"Con Cregan's legacy". (3m, extras) PROVENCE—EASY
    p18-23.
Concealed goodies. YOUNG—GAMES p12-13.
Concealed jewels. YOUNG—GAMES p64.
Concentrate and do the opposite. DRUMMOND—STUNT FUN
    p22.

Conduct of life
See also Advice; Courage, etc.
*Advice to students
*Life
The cone and the man. CROWLEY p31,34,35.
"Cones! Cones! Cones! FERRIS p79.
Conference chorus. DEPEW p277-278.
*The confession. (3m, 1f) LYONS p131-132.
Confessions. GEISTER—NEW p59-60.
Confusion. JOHNSON—BAKER'S p96.
*Congratulations, my dear. (2f) REACH—QUICK p70-76.
Conk, Audrey Burdell
United by love

Connor, J. Hal
   The trained horse, Battle-Axe.
Consequences. YOUNG—GAMES p44.
Constantinople. DEPEW p306.
*"The consultation". (1m, 2f) HUBER—THREE p32-33.
*Contest. (3m, 2f) HUBER—FOUR p74-77.
A contest tournament. BUGBEE—NUTTY p81-82.
Contests
   See also Prizes; Quizzes; Races; Relays
   Apple-eating contest
   Art contest
   Attendance contest
   Bantam fight
   Biological contests
   Cake-eating contest
   Cracker marathon
   Diving contest
   Eating contests for boys
   Egg race
   An endurance test
   *First prize
   Folding chairs
   A gory battle
   Half and half
   *The jackpot
   Kiddy kar polo
   Kiddy kar race
   Lucky words
   Mile-tug-of-war
   Miscellaneous contests
   "Mystery" contest
   One-eyed threading-the-needle contest
   Oratorical contest
   Other contests
   Peanuts and milk bottles
   A perfect picnic
   Piano stool sparring
   Pie eating contest (2)
   Pillow fight
   Plate race

Punkin pie
Quick reading contest
The siege of limburger
Singing stunt
Slogan contest
*Some people are goofy
Spear 'em alive
Spooning contest
Suckers
Talk-fest
Through a hoop
Two men and a girl
Tying them up
Vanity bags
Watch night stunt
Who's a poet?
Winning that candy bar
Contest. (2) BUGBEE—CATCHY p15-16; BUGBEE—GOOFY p103-107.
Continuous receiving line. FRICK—FALL p7.
Continuous story. DEPEW p306-307.

Conundrums
*Christmas conundrums
Colored kin
Finding partners with conundrums
The king's name
100 conundrums
Parlor conundrums
Relationship
What is it? (DEPEW)
What is it that has?
Who were they?
Conundrums. (2) BUGBEE—CATCHING p17-20; YOUNG—GAMES p84-90.

Conversation
*The French conversation class
Let's talk it over
*The word theory
Conversation. GEISTER—NEW p102.
Converts. EISENBERG—FUN p110-111.

Cook, Edith
  Two marionettes
"A cook's tour". FERRIS p45.
*Cookie bakes a cake. (4f) STARR—JR. p100-109.
The cooking of the prunes. FRICK—SUMMER p57-59.
Cooks and cookery
  *The boss of the king
  *Browned biscuits (2)
  *Caroline bakes a cake
  *Cookie bakes a cake
  "A cook's tour"
  *The first biscuit
  *First prize
  Here's the cook
  Men are the best cooks
  *One a penny, two a penny
  Peach pie
*A coon concert. (3b, 3g) IRISH—CHILDREN's p99-102.
*Coon Creek court cases. (8m) KASER—MERRY p14-22.
*"The Cooper special". (8m, 1f) STAHL—BITS p25-29.
Cooperative artists. DRUMMOND—STUNT FUN p103-104.
Cooperative introductions. GEISTER—NEW p112.
Cootie. GEISTER—NEW p93-94.
Cops and robbers. GODDARD—CHILDREN's p23-25.
Copy cat Christmas story. EISENBERG—FUN p71-72.
Corks
  Fish spearing
Corn baby. FRICK—FALL p61.
*Corn but not forgotten. (2m) EISENBERG—HAND. p163-164.
*Corn cure, by Jean Provence. (3m) BRINGS—MASTER p156-
  157.
Corn song (harvest). PRESTON—PANTOM. p224-227.
Cornfield capers. PRESTON—PANTOM. p120-127.
*Corns. (2m) PROVENCE—LIGHT p44-45.
Corpse. YOUNG—GAMES p30.
Cosmetics
  A goofy debate
Cost of apples. DEPEW p347.
Costume
  Alice in wonderland

Alice-in-wonderland tea dance
"Belle and Bill"
*The blood-stained bread knife
A café chantant, pop concert, club cabaret
Christmas belle minstrels
Columbus discovers America (2)
"Dance of yesterday and today"
The delectable ballad of the Waller lot
An evening with the American girl
Fashion tableaux
The fatal ride
Freak quadrille
*Fun from Norway
*The heroine's husband
Hisses and kisses
How the fire was saved
*A Hungarian tragedy
The laidly worm
The law of the camp fire
*The merchant of Venice
Newspaper minstrels
"An old-fashioned garden"—"Laces and graces"—"The charmers of long ago and today"
The old woman in the wood
*One Arabian night was stunt night
Paul Reveres ride (SHANNON)
Pep—old and new
*Persia presents: the bored king and the bandit
St. George and the dragon
St Patrick minstrels
Sir Ronald the ruthless
*So this is Paris
Summer (girl) minstrels
The wail of the Christmas ties
When ghosts walk
"Wig-wag"—"All's well"
Costume, Artist's
"When artists frolic"—Mind-the-paint girls"
Costume, Baseball
Baseball minstrels

Costume, Bridal
"June echoes"—"Brides of long ago and to-day"
Costume, Chinese
*The bride of the dragon kings—China
*The fairy serpent—China
*The moon maiden—China
Costume, Colonial
The answer is "yes"
Colonial minstrels
*"Musical dreams"
Costume, Fairy tale
The proud princess
The romance of little Cinderella
*The truth about Sleeping Beauty
Costume, Historical
*Scenes of the sixties
Costume, Indian
Indian love call
Costume, Italian
*A little stunt from Italy: the generous fisherman
Costume, Japanese
"Meet me where the lanterns glow"
A night in wonder-wander land, a Japanese party
The pink persimmon tree—Japan
*A thrill from Japan
Costume, Nineties. *See* Gay nineties
Costume, Persian
*The magic word—Persia
Costume, Royal
*"The king's highway"
Costume, Sailor's
Merry middy minstrels
Costume, Spanish
A day in Seville
Costume, Swedish
*The squire's bridge—Sweden
Cough syrup. EISENBERG—HAND. p93-94.
A counselor's council. HANLEY—STUNTS p19-20.
*Count it. (5m) HUBER—FOUR p44-48.
Count to thirty. EISENBERG—FUN p36-37.

Count Twenty's revenge (2) EISENBERG—HAND. p144-148; by
   Ruth Putnam Kimball. JOHNSON—BAKER's p20-25.
"The counter". HUBER—EASY p82-84.
Counter marching. (2) FRICK—FALL p28; GEISTER—NEW
   p123.
*Counting on the Count. (3f) BUGBEE—LIVE WIRE p138-140.
*The country cousin. (4f) HUBER—VAUD. p77-83.

Country life
   See also Dialect, Country; Farmers; Quizzes—Country life
   Are you from the country?
   Community house minstrels
   *Competition
   *The country cousin
   *Down on the farm
   The farm
   Grandmaw and grandpaw at the railroad track
   "Little Bo-Peep"
   "Maria Hayseed visits New York"
   "Maud Muller revue"—"Rebecca of Sunnybrook farm and
      co."
   Rural minstrels
   Rural symphony
   The saga of the farmyard
   "Selina Sue sees the show"
   "When the cows come home"
The country school. CONNOR p66-73.
The country store. CANOPY—HIGH p36,37,39.
Couple Virginia reel. GEISTER—NEW p30-31.

Courage
   "Bravest of the brave"
   "Love's labor"
The court. MACDONALD—CARNIVAL p48-53.
*Court classic. (7m) HUBER—NO SCENE p46-55.
Court scene. EISENBERG—FUN p119-121.
*Courtesy in the halls. (3m, 2f) TOPOLKA p87-90.

Courthouse
   "Not today, madame"
The courtin'. ABELL—STUNTS p47.

Courts
> *See also* Mock trials; Judges
> *A-courting we will go
> *Afternoon of October twentieth
> At King Goofus' court
> Brought to court
> *Call the next case
> *Don't ever speed
> *$500 reward
> Gentlemen prefer blondes
> *Good advice
> I asked her first!
> *I object!
> In Judge Spoofum's court
> Jazzy justice
> *Judge Dubois on the bench
> *Judge Hoptoad's court
> *Judge Knott presiding
> *"Juror number twelve"
> The jury convicts
> *"Justice a la rime"
> *Let the punishment fit the crime
> *Man versus dog
> *Memories (SNAPPY)
> *Monday morning in Maloney's court
> *Monkey business
> *Never kick a man's shin
> *Night court
> "Oh, yeah!"
> *Order in the court
> *The pancake divorce case
> *The penalty
> *"Sure cure" (PROVENCE—FLASH)
> *The trial
> *Trial for the murder of Nellie Gray
> *The trial of George Washington
> *"The trial of the house council"
> *You can't try an insane man

Courtship days. BUGBEE—GOOFY p86.

Courtship through the ages. PRESTON—FUN p137-140.

The cow. DEPEW p169-170.
The cow man. CROWLEY p25-26.
Cowboys
  See also Orchestras, Cowboy
  *The boots and saddle gang
  *The bus stops at Cactus Junction
  The delectable ballad of the Waller lot.
  The drug store cowboy
  *Harold meets the cowboys
Cowboys and Indians. GODDARD—CHILDREN'S p25-27.
*Cowboys from Brooklyn. (4m) DRUMMOND—SPOT p14-16.
Cracker marathon. JOHNSON—BAKER'S p99.
Cracker relay. DEPEW p320.
Cradle to grave in song. PARTIES p12.
Cradle to grave in stunts. PARTIES p12.
*The craftsman. (3m, 2f) MIKSCH—TEEN p66-75.
Craig, Mabel Tuttle
  *Adopting the baby
  Biographies
  Birthdays (JOLLY)
  Chuckle ads
  Crossword puzzle
  Easter parade
  *Gossip is an art
  Intelligence test (CASEY—PEPPY)
  Know your home town (or country)
  Know your neighbor
  *Mary had a little lamb
  MenTALL tests
  A modern romance
  *The orator ("THAT GOOD")
  Quotation quiz for February
  Scripture spelling match
  Slogan contest
  To start the party
  Tools of the trade
  Vegetable soup
  What is your neighbor like?
Craig, Bernice Pell
  Curfew must not ring to-night

The craziest idea. BUGBEE—GOOFY p48-50.
Crazy questions and answers. DEPEW p305.
Crazy relay. DEPEW p333.
Crazy speeches, by Alta Toepp. CASEY—PEPPY p88.
Crazy stunts. FUNNY p32.
*Cream puffs, by Warren Balentine. (3m) ROHRBOUGH p85-88.
Creating a circus. EISENBERG—HAND. p39-43.

Crime and criminals
  After midnight
  *Baby hands
  *The best laid plans
  *Room service
  *Tell no tales
*The crime club. (4m, 1f) SHELDON p70-75.
Crimebusters. EISENBERG—FUN p122.
*Criminal lawyer at home. (1m, 2f) TAGGART—FIVE p12-16.
The crisis. EISENBERG—FUN p103-104.
*Crisscross. (2m) KASER—BUSHEL p97-100.
Crites, Lucile
  When you and I were young
Crocker, Avis
  *Ill-treated Trovatore
  *Sleight-of-hand (ROHRBOUGH)
A crocodile's tale. WILLIAMS p30,31,32.
Cross questions and crooked answers. YOUNG—GAMES p46.
Cross road follies, by Willis N. Bugbee. JOLLY p30-48.
*"Crossed wires". (1m, 2f) STAHL—HEARTY p8-10.
Crossword puzzle, by Mabel Tuttle Craig. CASEY—PEPPY p98.
Crossword puzzles. DEPEW p308.
The crowning of King Booster. BUGBEE—LIVE WIRE p42.
Crrr-uel wrrr-etch! By Beatrice M. Casey. CASEY—PEPPY p31-35.
*The crucial moment, by Arthur Leroy Kaser. (1m, 1f)
    BUGBEE—LIVE WIRE p136-138.
Crusoe, Robinson
  *Friday's Thursday off
The crystal gazer. (2) BUGBEE—LIVE WIRE p65-66; CONNOR
  p23-24.
Crystal-gazing. *See* Fortune-telling
The cud-chewing cow and a basket bawl. BUCHANAN p56,57,61.

Dance of the goups. BRIDGE p20-21.
Dance of the nymphs. CONNOR p39.
Dance of the races. BUGBEE—NUTTY p63.
The dancers. MACDONALD—CARNIVAL p26-27.
"Dances of yesterday and today". FERRIS p71.
Dancing
   See also Ballet; Mixers, Dance; School dances
  *All ashore
   Animal carnival
  *Bewildering popularity
   "The blue waltz"
   Burlesque Greek dance
   Clap your hands
   College rhythm (STAHL—AMAT.)
   "Dance and song in far-away lands"—"Brothers all"
   "Dances of yesterday and today"
   Doll dance
   Down on de old plantation
   Folk dances
   Frolic
   Gnomes
   Goups
   Grand march figures and folk dance
   "The gypsy trail"
   Harem-scarem jitter bugs
   Hiawatha and Mondamin
   The hula hula dance
   "In the garden"
   Indian pep
   Lucky star
  *Mabel's embarassing moment
   *The modernist
  *"Musical dreams"
   " 'Neath the Italian moon"
  *On with the dance
   On with the dance
   Oriental dance
  *Oshkosh land
   Pan pipes a tune
   "Proximity"

*"Rhythmatic" (2)
Romance in the moonlight
Shimmy shakers
Sweethearts on parade
*Turning the fables on Aesop
Welcome
The dancing lady. EASY STUNTS p5; PARTIES p30,31.
*The dancing master. BUGBEE—LIVE WIRE p12-13.
*Danger, fate at work. (4m, 1f) TOPOLKA p33-37.
*Dangerous water. (2m, spectators) PROVENCE—LIGHT p71-72.
*A daring bicycler. (5b) IRISH—CHILDREN'S p43-45.
Dark, isn't it? EISENBERG—HAND. p57.
*"The darktown strutters' quartet". (4m) CASEY p79-85.
The darky and the ghost. TARBELL—FUN p79-80.
Dashing dramatics. FERRIS p27-28.
Dat dog-gone mule. BUGBEE—LIVE WIRE p14.
The date. MACDONALD—CARNIVAL p72.
*A date with Kate. (2m, 3f) HUBER—TV p75-82.

Daughters
*Blank check
*The girls are home
*How Betty put things over Pa.
David and Goliath. TARBELL—SUNDAY p131-138.
*"David Swan", from the story by Nathaniel Hawthorne. (6m, 3f) PROVENCE—EASY p54-60.
*"A day for dogs". (2m, 1f) STAHL—BITS p9-11.
A day in a boy scout camp. FERRIS p168.
A day in camp, by Harry Githens. GITHENS p63,64.
A day in Dog Patch. EISENBERG—HAND. p97-98.
A day in Seville. DEPEW p86-88.
A day in the life of Ma and Pa Settle. EISENBERG—FUN p19-21.
*Day of departure. (4m, 3f) MIKSCH—CURTAIN p5-19.
*Days gone by. (2m, 2f) HUBER—CHAR. p112-119.
A dazzling exhibition of skill, concentration, and rhythm. FERRIS p34-35.
De golden rule (darky sermon) JOLLY p83-85.
Dead finger. EISENBERG—FUN p38.
The deadly bat. CONNOR p38.

Deaf
  *The customer is right (2)
  *Just a love nest (EASY—BLACKOUTS)
  *"A little deaf"

Deaf mutes
  *Charlie Slasher's mistake
  *Excuse it, please! (2)
  *So you won't talk! (BRINGS—MASTER; GEORGE—TWELVE)
  The deaf stunt. GEISTER—NEW p105-106.
*Dear Doctor. (2m, 3f) HUBER—SIX p106-112.
"Dear ole pal of mine". FERRIS p43.
The dearest spot. LLOYD p17-18.
*Death. (2m, 1f) EASY—BLACKOUTS p36-39.
Death-dealing quartette, by Bob Royce. BRINGS—MASTER
    p394-395.
*"The death of Santa Claus". (1m, 1f, 2 children) STAHL—
    HEARTY p73-75.

Debates
  A goofy debate
  Mock debates
  Resolved, that banana oil is . . .
  Resolved, that halitosis is a greater menace . . .
  Resolved, that Sarah Brum . . .
  Resolved, that the calendar . . .
  Resolved, that the oyster is . . .
  Resolved, that there is more nourishment . . .
*A decision must be made. (2m, 3f) WEATHERS p20-31.
Decisions. EISENBERG—HAND. p81-82.

Declaration of Independence
  *America begins
Decorations (by month and holiday). YOUNG—GAMES p102-
    111.
Deep in the heart of Texas, by Mary Jane Woodard. THREE
    —STUNTS p1-2.
Deer hunt. FRICK—SUMMER p20.
*The defective detective. (6m) HUBER—NO p51-56.
Definitions. GEISTER—NEW p56-57.
The delectable ballad of the Waller lot. MILLER—STUNT p167-
    173.

DeMaupassant *See* Maupassant, Guy de

Democracy
　*After the history test
　The dentist. PARTIES p22.

Dentists
　The berth of an upper or howareya
　Heroes are made
　*In the dentist's office
　"It's out"
　"I've got it now"
　The molar's farewell
　*Next!
　*No chances
　*Painless dentistry
　*The pen is mightier than the word
　"That one, Doctor"
　*Too many teeth
　*Turning tail

Department stores
　See also Salesmen and salesmenship
　*Agatha's errands
　*Keep smiling
　*Noonday nightmare
　*Pardon, madame
　*Willoughby's window
Departmental vaudeville. LAMKIN & FLORENCE p51-57.
The departure. BUGBEE—LIVELY p68-69.

Depot agents. *See* Railway stations
Derby, Mary H.
　*Tunetown gossip or Carol entertains the musical club
Descriptions. DEPEW p308.

Desert
　Sand in the desert (or, "The desert symphony")
　*Scourge of the desert
　Water, water! (EISENBERG—FUN)
*Deserted, by William Milligan. (2m, 1f) QUICK—COM. p21-26.
*The deserted wife comes back. (4m, 1f) KASER—HALF p53-59.
*Design for dueling, by Jay Tobias. (3m, 1f) SNAPPY p57-61.
Detective. YOUNG—GAMES p25.

Detectives

See also Mysteries

*Body, body, who's got the body?

*Boy bites dog

*Call the police

*Carefully yours

*The defective detective

Donald Dare, demon detective

*The great thud and blunder murder case

"Stealthy Steve the sleuth"

*There are badges and badges

*The thirteenth trump

When a sleuth sleuths

The devil and the deep blue C. BUGBEE—LIVE WIRE p53.

Diagonal cross. GEISTER—NEW p123.

Diagonal march. FRICK—FALL p29-30.

Dialect, Chinese

The Chinaman and the mouse

*The winning ticket

Dialect, Country

*Balm of life

Carrie from Cantaloupe county

*Dr. Dobb's assistant

"The farmer's daughter"

Fresh roasted peanuts

*A glass in time

"He ain't done right by little Nell"

*The lost pocket-book

*The lover's errand

Oh! To be an actoress

*A practical use for peddlers

Sally in the city

*School days at Porcupine Junction

Something loose

Soup

*Uncle Cy at the talkies

Writin' home

Dialect, Drunken

Prohibition in the home

*Three o'clock in the morning

Dialect, Dutch
  *Almost the last day of school
  *"The baby show" (MacDonald)
  *Dr. Dobb's assistant
  *Oshkosh land
  *Such a nice mix-up

Dialect, English (Cockney)
  *'Arry and 'Arriet

Dialect, German
  *At your service
  Cinderella Hassenpfeffer
  The free clinic
  *Interviewing servant girls
  Keyboard funnies
  *The old village school
  *Professor Sniderschmultze's pupils
  Reddisch Riden Hood
  *Veteran veterinaries
  *"The village band rehearses"

Dialect, Hill-billy. *See* Dialect, Mountaineer

Dialect, Illiterate
  Bill Tell
  *No trading today
  United by love
  Where's gran'paw?

Dialect, Irish
  *Animated freight
  *Around the world in bed
  *"The baby show" (MacDonald)
  *Bustin' up the old quartet
  *"Con Cregan's legacy"
  *Death
  *Interviewing servant girls
  *It happens every day
  *Mrs. Murphy isn't home
  Mulligan's pig
  *Sarah Perkins' hat shop, a parody song sketch
  Shaughnessy's ball
  *Two cops off duty

*Where's Henry?
  Working on the dry squad
Dialect, Italian
  *African aria
  *The merchant of Venice
  *Monkey business
  *The philosopher
  *Sofapillio (2)
  *A thief in the house
Dialect, Jewish
  *"Anuuder lankwich"
  *"The baby show" (MACDONALD)
  *Cream puffs
  *Don't stop us if you've heard these
    Goldberg's beauties
  *Here comes the bride (QUICK—COM.)
  *"In the class room"
  *It's how you say it
    Jake and his family
  *The merchant of Venice
  *Musical eggs
  *Partners (LEVIS—TEN)
    A proved salary
    Signing of the declaration
  *Sleight-of-hand (ROHRBOUGH)
  *Sold (EASY—BLACKOUTS)
  *Some class (KASER—SURE)
  *Some show á la masculine
  *Ye olde junke shoppe
Dialect, Mountaineer
    A day in Dog Patch
    Fatalism
  *Feudin' and fightin'
  *A lucky shot
  *Mountain magic
  *"Out yonder"
  *Taking Maw's advice
Dialect, Negro
    All blowed to pieces
  *Animated scarecrows

*At your service
*"The baby show" (MacDonald)
*Blackout in black
 Blind alley
*Burnt crackers
*A capable servant
*A coon concert
*Coon Creek court cases
*Curing a fresh fish
*The darktown strutters' quartet
 Dat dog-gone mule
 De golden rule
 Dixie pep
*A double date
*"An eye-opener"
*The ghostoscope
*The haunted house ("That Good")
*Hocus-pocus
*In Grandma Perkins' store
 In the bag
 King for a day
 Lather harmony
 Lub yo' nabors
 Malachi Jimson's farewell sermon
 Memories of the dog-show
 Miss Kate Pennoyer
*The newlyweds (Drummond—Three)
*Nothin' but work
*Parsing a sentence
*The prevaricator
*A prospective recruit
 A proved salary
*Pulling Sam's tooth
 Rastus and the ventriloquist
*Sambo am a dangerous man
*Sambo and the mule
*A sudden discovery
 Talking business
*Tethered viciousness
*Tillie's arrival

*Waitin' for de snipes
*"Wait'll you sees Mah man!"
*The wasted tip
*Wedding bells for Hepsidee
*Who stole the world?
 Ye olde medicine show
Dialect, Scotch
 *"The baby show"
 *Sandy, defunct
Dialect, Southern
 *Charlie Slasher's mistake
 *Chiseling on chivalry
 *"Fair enough"
Dialect, Swedish
 *I'll fix it
 *Interviewing servant girls
 *Needle, thread and jabber, a sewing circle entertainment
Dialogs
 *A la Eugene O'Neil
 *About time
 *Absent-minded
 *Accuracy
 *And so it goes
 *Animated freight
 *At the day nursery
 *At the zoo (REACH—QUICK)
 *The backward helper
 *Better not be bettor
 *Boobology
 *Burnt crackers
 *Business is booming
 *City feller
 *Congratulations, my dear
 *Corn cure
 *Crisscross
 *The crucial moment
 *Cupid is speedy
 *The dancing master
 *The doctor's dilemma (EASY—STUNTS)
 *Don't get excited

*Don't spill the salt (2)
*A double date
*Dunk that doughnut!
*Eggs while you wait
*Evidence
*Father's quiet evening
*Fire! Fire!
*The first biscuit
*Fishing
*Front page stuff
*The ghostoscope
*Girl chatter
*The goat
*Golden wedding
*Gratitude
*Guests for dinner
*Hamlet and the ghost
*Hard to handle
*Help waited (EASY—STUNTS)
*Her souvenirs (2)
*Here's a hair
*His sister
*His sweetheart
*Hocus-pocus
*Home sweet home (KASER—SURE)
*A horse of another color
*The hoss race
*How does your garden grow?
*How's your golf?
*I'll fix it, Mom
*In a ballroom
*In the best of families (2)
*Information, please (KENT—ONE)
*Insurance
*It was then as now
*Jake and his family
*Just another one
*Kitty Dawn, stennygrapher
*Live a hundred years
*Logical advice

*A lot of bunk
*The lover's errand (3)
*Marital mishaps
*Matrimony bumps
*Matter of smell
*Maybelle confesses
*Midsummer night's ring
*Miser's last request
*A mono-word play
*Mr. and Mrs. Newberry
*Nature cure
*New maid
*No sale
*Not today, Madame
*Nothin' but work
*Oh, Doctor! (BRINGS—MASTER)
*One conclusion (2)
*One hundred years old
*Out of the bag
*Painless dentistry
*Partners (LEVIS—TEN)
*A prospective recruit
*The rivals
*Romance
*Same old thing
*Say, Dad
*Seeing stars
*Service
*So this is love
*Some like them thin
*Something loose
*The stars and the stripes (EASY BLACKOUTS)
*Statistics (2)
*Success story (JOHNSON—EASY)
*The suicide
*Sure cure (PROVENCE—KNOCKOUT; PROVENCE—LIGHT)
*Telephone tactics
*Ten-minute egg
*Thank you for coming
*That's different

*Tit for tat
*Two cops off duty
*The um-brellah sisters
*The unemployed
*Uraniusm or bust
*Vaudeville skit
*A ventriloquist stunt
*A very good reason
*Was his face red!
*What are you selling?
*What would you do?
*The whole truth
*Wise and otherwise
*Diamond ring. (3m, 3f) WEATHERS—MYSTERIES p66-79.
Diana turns dramatic critic. STARR—JR. p61-63.
Diaries of the distinguished. by Alta Toepp. CASEY—PEPPY
    p102-103.
*Dick and the dictionary. (1m, 1b) STARR—JR. p13-17.
Dickens, Charles
    *"Sam Wellers' valentine
Dictionaries
    *Dick and the dictionary
"Did you ever hear that ——?" FERRIS p42.
Dieting
    Beauty and the clock
    How to reduce
    The joys that once through gullet walls
    *Let's eat
    *"The perfect thirty-six"
    *Thick and thin
Difference between 6 and half a dozen. DEPEW p341.
Digit problem. DEPEW p347.
The dime museum. BRIDGE p34.
Dinner parties
    See also Banquets
    Balloons (GEISTER—NEW)
    Conversation
    The deaf stunt
    Down by tht Old Mill Stream
    *Guests for dinner

Pass it
Place cards
What would you do if
The dinosaur specialist. TARBELL—COMEDY p84-87.

Diogenes
The New York visitor
The search is ended
*Diogenes reincarnated. (4m) DRUMMOND—STUNT p44-45.
*"Direct from the 16th century". (4m, 3f) DRUMMOND—STUNT p55-59.
*Direful doin's. (3m, 1f) RYAN p112-113.
Dirt in a hole. DEPEW p360.
The disappearing dime. DRUMMOND—STUNT p27-28.
The disappearing quartet. (2) EISENBERG—FUN p190; EISENBERG—HAND. p133-134.
The discontented blacksmith. TARBELL—SUNDAY p57-62.
Discordant encore. DEPEW p259.
Discovery of America by the Irish. BUGBEE—LIVE WIRE p67-68.
Discus throw. DEPEW p315.

Disease
The famous Dr. Pillsendoper
*The fight against disease
*Home remedy
Dish the fish, by Beatrice Plumb. BRINGS—MASTER p419.
Dishing out the dirt. YOUNG—GAMES p19-20.

Dishwashing
Song of the dish towel
The disjointed finger. EISENBERG—FUN p27.
A disrobing act. BRINGS—MASTER p379; DRUMMOND—STUNT p51.
Distance boxing. DEPEW p323.
*"The district school at Carrot Corners". (6m, 5f). DRUMMOND—IMPR. p54-61.
*A disturbance in the family. (3m, 3f, 2 children) BUGBEE—LIVELY p110-114.
"The dive of doom". HUBER—EASY p88-89.
Dividing the farm. DEPEW p346.
Diving between legs. DEPEW p325-326.

Diving contest. DEPEW p326.

Diving for the duck. DEPEW p326.

Divorce

  *The pancake divorce case

  *Somewhat divorcified

Divorce. EISENBERG—HAND p91.

Dixie pep. ABELL—PEP p21-23.

The dizzy orchestra. YOUNG—GAMES p35.

"Do a good deed daily". FERRIS p78-79.

*Do I bother you? (2m, 2f) HUBER—NO p70-76.

"Do it yourself"

  *I'll Fix it

Do not open. HUBER—GIANT p126-127.

*Do they? By Pearl Williams. (2m, 4f) ROHRBOUGH p78-79.

*Do you believe in signs, by Charles F. Wells. (6m) JOHNSON
      —EASY p42-43.

"Do your shopping early" or "A shopper's dream". FERRIS
      p145-147.

Do your stuff. FUNNY p33.

*Doctor (1m, 3f) KELLEY p10-13.

*Doctor, come quick! By Anne Martens. (2m, 1f) QUICK—
      COM. p90-96.

Dr. Cutemupsky' free clinic. BUGBEE—LIVE WIRE p88-89.

*Dr. Dobb's assistant. (6m) JOHNSON—BAKER'S p38-46.

*Dr. Killemquick's medicine show, or The friendly quack,
      by A. L. Fisher. (2m, 1b, 1g, extras) BRINGS—MASTER
      p71-80.

Dr. Peppo's medicine show, by Harry Githens. GITHENS
      p17-20.

Dr. Quack and Miss Little Girl. BRIDGE p19.

A doctor's dilemma. HUBER—PRACT. p87-91.

*A doctor's dilemma (3. (2m, 1f) by LeRoy Stahl.
      —MASTER p186-188; 1m, 1f) EASY—STUNTS p27-28.
      (2m, 1f) STAHL—MORE p7-10.

Doctors

  *About time (2)

  *"Angel child"

  *"An apple a day"

  *Asleep in the deep (2)

  *The casual casualty

*Cats is cats
*The cheerio clinic
*"The consultation"
 The crisis
 The curing machine
 Cutting up
*Dear doctor
*Fit as a fiddle
 The fixit clinic
*The fountain of youth (EISENBERG—HAND.)
 The gimmes
*Hospitality
*"Hurry, doctor" (HUBER—THREE)
 I'll call the doctor
*In the doctor's office
*Keep the patient quiet
*"Medicine man" (HUBER—THREE)
 Mental clinic
*The mills that grind
*Mythical medicine
*Nature cure
*Oh, Doctor! (3)
 The operation
*"The operation"
*Quiet, please
*Same old thing
*The sick maid
*"Snakes"
*"Sure cure" (PROVENCE—FLASH)
*The surgery
*Tell no tales
 There's one born every minute (JOHNSON—EASY)
*Thick and thin
*With complications
*You're just the man
Dodge bail. DEPEW p329.
The dog and the old woman. CROWLEY p62, 65.
Dog star, by Arthur L. Kaser. BRINGS—MASTER p345-347;
        KASER—BUSHEL p16-18.
*Dog tricks. (2m, 1f) McCOY—SIXTEEN p21-25.

Dogs
*"Be kind to animals"
*"A day for dogs"
Dog star (2)
*Dog tricks
*Fifty dollars worth of dog
*His first case
Hot dog machine
I got a dog
The magical dog
*Man versus dog
Memories of the dog-show
*A minister's mistakes
The nudist
*The passing of Bruno
*The poor little dear
*Pop goes the heart
*Prefabricated ideas
*The pursuers
*The rivals
Sh! (DRUMMOND—STUNT FUN)
The trained dog
Doing a folk festival. EISENBERG—HAND. p193-201.
Doll dance. RYAN p114.
A dollar in a candle. DRUMMOND—STUNT p38-39.
Dolls
*Keep the patient quiet
The mystery doll
Rag dolls
Walking, talking, singing and dancing dolls
Domestic science
The kitchen symphony—Domestic science department
    (LAMKIN & FLORENCE)
Domestic science. DEPEW p299-300.
Donald Dare, demon detective. HUBER—PRACT. p45-51.
The donkey and his master. CROWLEY p75,76.
*The donkey' tail. (2m, 2f) LEVIS—TEN p19-28.
"Don't be a goop". FERRIS p56-57.
Don't brush them on me! EISENBERG—HAND. p92-93.
*"Don't cry". (2f, 1g) HUBER—THREE p95-96.

*Don't cry baby. (1m, 4f) HUBER—ALL p5-10.
*Don't displease your husband. (2m, 1f) LEVIS—TEN p7-10.
*Don't ever speed. (3m) PROVENCE—KNOCKOUT p38, 39.
*Don't get excited, by Jean Provence. (2f) BRINGS—MASTER p171-173.
*Don't put off being honest. (1m, 2f) McCOY—SIXTEEN p15-20.
*Don't say. (7g) BARBEE p76-77.
*Don't spill the salt, by Arthur L. Kaser. (1m, 1f) BRINGS —MASTER p237; KASER—FUNNY p52-56.
*Don't stop us if you've heard these, by Albert G. Miller. (3m, 1f, 1b) MILLER—BROADWAY p47-53.
Doodles. EISENBERG—HAND. p 53.
Doodles and droodles. EISENBERG—FUN p23.
The door prize. JOLLY p74.
Dots and shapes. YOUNG—GAMES p46-47.
Double circle. GIESTER—NEW p109-110.
*A double date. (2b) KASER—BUTTON p91-94.
*Double or nothing. (4m) HUBER—SIX p54-61.
Double quartet. DEPEW p139.
Double relay. FRICK—FALL p22.
Double scrambled names. DEPEW p298.
Double Tandem. GEISTER—NEW p53.
Double time. FRICK—FALL p28.
*Double tribute. (1m, 3f) McCOY—HOLIDAY p18-23.
Doubtful prizes. GEISTER—NEW p111.
Dous. GEISTER—NEW p67, 90.
Down below where all is owe. FRICK—FALL p44-45.
Down by the Old Mill Stream. GEISTER—NEW p103.
Down on de old plantation. ABELL—STUNTS p62-63.
*Down on the farm. EISENBERG—HAND. p101.
Down the center by two's. FRICK—FALL p29.
Down with all you shrikers. DEPEW p281.
*Drafted. (2b, 1g) BUGBEE—LIVELY p67-68.
Draftee deferred, by Grace Keith Samuelson. "THAT GOOD" p51.
Drama. *See* Acting
Drama at KQZ; or The bat in the belfry. PRESTON—PANTOM. p72-85.
Dramatic medley. BRIDGE p30.

Dramatizations
 Accident
 Charades, simple
 Minnesota
 Nursery rhymes (FRICK—SUMMER)

Dramatizations, Literary
 *"Con Cregan's legacy"
 *"David Swan"
 *An error
 *"The glorious whitewasher"
 *"Handy Andy"
 *"Markheim"
 *"The purloined letter"
 *"Queen Alice"
 *"Sam Weller's valentine"
 *"The tapestried chamber"
 *"Three Sundays in a week"
Dramatized jokes. By Arthur L. Kaser. (2) BRINGS—MASTER p371-377; KASER—AMATEUR's p67-72.
*"Dramatized jokes". (2m, 1f) DRUMMOND—STUNT p62-71
Drawing for the baby. DEPEW p147-148.
Drawing from photographs. BUCHANAN p72-74.
*Dreadful boys. (2b, 5g) IRISH—CHILDREN's p77-80.

Dreams
 The bachelor's dream
 *Dick the dictionary
 *Madeline gets analyzed
 Your dream interpreted
Dreams. FERRIS p147-148.

Dress. *See* Fashion

Dress shops
 Style show (DEPEW)
Dress-up mixer. GEISTER—NEW p111.
Dressing relay. DEPEW p318.
The drill. MACDONALD—CARNIVAL p53-55.
A drill take-off. FERRIS p37-39.

Drills
 Bag and Baggage
 Close order drill

A dazzling exhibition of skill, concentration, and rhythm
The old maid's drill
Drills, setting-up. FRICK—SUMMER p73-81.
Drink, by Frank E. Chase. BAKER'S—GAY p39-42.
Drink to me only with thine eyes. LLOYD p50.
A drink to order. TARBELL—FUN p47-51.

Drinking
  See also Dialect, Drunken
  Drink
  "Ten barrooms in one night"
Drinking five gallons of wine. TARBELL—COMEDY p34.
Driven from home, by Kate Alice White. BUGBEE—LIVE
      WIRE p121.
Driven speechless. EISENBERG—HAND. p122.
*The driver's test. (2m) HUBER—SIX p47.
Driving. *See* Automobiles
The driving lesson. (2) ENTERTAIN—STUNTS p5; PARTIES
      p28.

Drouth
  *Thunder in the East
*The drug store. (4b, 5g) EDGERTON p119-122.
The drug store cowboy. BUGBEE—NUTTY p47-49.

Drug stores
  See also Soda fountains
  *"At the corner drugstore"
  Cough syrup
  *Nerve on display
  *"The perfect thirty-six"
  The remedy
Drummond, Richard
  *Bachelor husbands
  *Curtain time
  Even as you and I
  *No, no, a thousand times, no!
  Ramble on
  "T" is for Texas
  *That's different
  *Tit for tat
  The true story of Capt. John Smith

*Uranium or bust
Very short shorts
The drunkard maker. BAKER'S—GAY p36.

Drunkards. *See* Dialect, Drunken; Drinking
*Duck luck. (1m, 2f) DRUMMOND—STUNT p45-46.
Duck on a rock. FRICK—SUMMER p18-19.
Ducks fly. EISENBERG—FUN p44.

Dude ranches
*By the teeth
The duel. BUGBEE—GOOFY p44.

Duels
*Chiseling on chivalry
*Design for dueling

Dues, collection of
Ima Rotarian
Why Jack was late
The dumb lecturer. BUGBEE—GOOFY p50-52.
The dumb painter, by Arthur L. Kaser. BRINGS—MASTER
   p364-365.
Dumb quartet. FUNNY p11.
The dumb symphony. BUGBEE—GOOFY p42,43.
The dummy. BUGBEE—LIVE WIRE p40.
*Dunk that doughnut! By Grace Keith Samuelson. (1m, 1f)
   CASEY—PEPPY p43-44.
The duplicate stunt. WILLIAMS p41-42.

Dutch
See also Dialect, Dutch
Windmills keep turning around
A Dutch auction. DEPEW p179.
Dykes, Alfred
*The cat's meow
*Let's go to the movies

Each for his own art. BARBEE p72-74.
Each one, grab one, by Beatrice Plumb. BRINGS—MASTER
   p417.
*Each Sunday morn. (2m, 2f) STAHL—MORE p26-28.
The eagle and the Indian chief. CROWLEY p44-45.

Earth, air, water. YOUNG—GAMES p74-75.

*The earth and the sky. (7) STAHL—LAND. p61-74.

Easter

  Girl buys an Easter hat

  *Two hats for Easter

- Easter bonnet. GEISTER—NEW p45-46.

An Easter lesson. TARBELL—SUNDAY p46-50.

Easter parade, by Mabel Tuttle Craig. JOLLY p91.

Easter party (decorations). YOUNG—GAMES p106.

Easy human figure drawing. TARBELL—CHALK STUNTS
  p69-75.

Easy magic numbers. GEISTER—NEW p86.

An easy way to make money. TARBELL—FUN p53-55.

*Eat and like it. (2m, 1f) PROVENCE—KNOCKOUT p14-17.

Eating a package of cigarettes. TARBELL—COMEDY p29-34.

Eating candles. DRUMMOND—STUNT FUN p12.

Eating contests for boys. DRUMMOND—STUNT FUN p60.

Eating goldfish. DEPEW p194.

Eating raw eggs. DEPEW p198.

Eating the goldfish. TARBELL—CRAZY p11-13.

Eaton, Norman Bridge

  *Anxious moments

Echo. PARTIES p28.

Echo answers. EASY—ENTERTAIN. p11-17.

*Echo point. (2m, 2f, extras) PROVENCE—LIGHT p120-124.

"Echoes of the glorious Fourth". FERRIS p83.

The eclipse, by Marjorie G. Stephens. EISENBERG—HAND.
  p140-143; ROHRBOUGH p72-77.

Economy

  *Sandy, defunct

*The editor's busy day. (3m, 4f) BUGBEE—LIVELY p97-101

Editor's mailbag. YOUNG—GAMES p45.

The educated horse. DRUMMOND—STUNT FUN p12-13.

Education

  Higher education

Education don't pay. KASER—ACTS p77-79.

Efficiency

  *Just plain efficiency

  Modern efficiency

  *The word theory

Emergencies
*Meeting an emergency
Emergencies. GEISTER—NEW p55-56.
*Emergency broadcast. (4m, 3f, quartet) KASER—BUTTON
p5-15.

Employment agencies
*A matter of names
*"The sharpshooter"
The employment office. DEPEW p103-104.
Empty chair. DEPEW p304-305.
The empty hatful. DRUMMOND—STUNT p35-36.
Empty pockets. DEPEW p173.

Encores
An Indian massacre
The end of a perfect day. KASER—BUSHEL p101-102.
*End of the line. (4m, 3f) MIKSCH—TEEN p33-43.
Ending words. DEPEW p307.
Endless thread. DEPEW p308.
An endurance test. FERRIS p35-36.

Engaged
*The higher art
*Midsummer night's ring

English
See also Dialect, English (Cockney); Grammar
*Bluebeard up-to-date
*Good English
*"My dear!"
*Off with their heads
*Reverse English (2)
Shakespearean hash—The English department
"English as she is spoke" PRESTON p20-24.
*Enroll in the Red Cross. (3b, 5g) BARBEE p85-87.
Enroute to camp, by Harry Githens. GITHENS p64,65.
*Enter the hero. (2m, 1f) HUBER—NO SCENE p25-31.
*Entertaining sister's beau. (1m, 3g) IRISH—CATCHY p67-70.
*Entertaining sister's beaux, by Charles George (2). (2m,
2f) BRINGS—MASTER p108-112; GEORGE—TEN p24-28.
Entertaining the ambassador. DEPEW p151-152.
*Entertainment committee. (1m, 4f) MIKSCH—TEEN p53-59.

Epigrams. *See* Proverbs
The episode. FERRIS p160.
Epitaphs
Read 'em and weep
Ergro. GEISTER—NEW p67,90.
*"An error." From the story of Guy de Maupassant. (3)
    PROVENCE—EASY p32-35.
Escape. GEISTER—NEW p119.
The escaped prisoner. CASEY—PEPPY p68.
The Eskimo tragedy. EISENBERG—FUN p141-143.
Essay on anatomy. EISENBERG—HAND p44.
The eternal charade. EISENBERG—FUN p22-23.
The eternal question. TARBELL—FUN p56-57.
Etiquette
  *The best people
  *Fourteen points
  Johnny learns about etiquette
The etiquette of the flag. BARBEE p88.
Even as you and I, by Richard Drummond. BRINGS—MAS-
    TER p308-309; DRUMMOND—STUNT FUN p73-74.
*An even exchange. (4m) HUBER—FOUR p139-142.
*Evening bells. (2m, 3f) MIKSCH—TEEN p95-102.
*The evening paper, by Dorothy M. Tilden. (1m, 1f) ROHR-
    BOUGH p69-71.
An evening with the American girl. DEPEW p41-52.
The ever-filled cuspidor, by Robert N. McGregor. BREEZY
    p68,69.
Ever see a lassie. DEPEW p279.
Everybody likes him. DEPEW p278.
Everybody likes it. DEPEW p280.
Evesdropping. EISENBERG—HAND. p86.
*Evidence. (1m, 1f) SIX—MORE p33-36.
Evolution pictures. TARBELL—CHALK STUNTS p21.
*"Examination". (3m) PROVENCE—FLASH p86-88.
Exchange. GEISTER—NEW p113-114.
Exchanging white elephants. DEPEW p210.
Ex-convicts
  *Last chance
*Excuse it, please, by McElbert Moore. (3m, 1f) JOHNSON—
    —EASY p21-23; QUICK (2m, 2f); QUICK p7-12.

Excuses for being late. DEPEW p197-198.

*Executives of the nut factory. (4m) KASER—TOP p19-28.

An exhibition of wax figures. MacDONALD—CARNIVAL p7-9.

Exhibits. DRUMMOND—STUNT FUN p63-64.

Explorers

*The African Explorer

*"Bravest of the brave

Extra! Extra! (2) ABELL—PEP p127; DEPEW p148.

Extravagance

*The letter

Eye

How quick is your eyesight?

Right-eyed or left-eyed?

Sense of sight

*"An eye-opener". (3m) DRUMMOND—IMPR. p79-83.

*"Eye trouble", by Selden M. Loring. (3m) EASY—IMPR.
p105-111.

"The eyes have it". HUBER—EASY p51-54.

*The eyes have it. (1m, 1f) HUBER—NO SCENE p60-66.

The face on the barroom floor, by D'Arcy. BAKER'S GAY
p34-35.

The faculty graveyard. CANOPY—HIGH p43,46,47,49.

Faculty meetings

Mock faculty meeting

Faculty portraits, by Harry W. Githens. GITHENS p108.

*The failure. (5m, 5f, extras) ROGERS—PLAYS p77-80.

*"Faint heart ne'er won fair lady", by Charles George. (1m,
2f) BAKER'S GAY p7-10.

*"Fair enough". (3m, 1f) PROVENCE—VAUD. p45-47.

Fairs

See also Carnivals; etc.

An indoor block party and a county fair

*The lost pocket-book

*The fairy serpent—China. (more than 12 char.) MILLER—
STUNT p27-106.

Fairy tales

See also "Cinderella"; etc.

*After the ball

Alice in wonderland
Alice-in-wonderland tea dance
The bare facts
"Bluebeard"
Cinderella
Cinderella Goldilocks
Cinderella Hassenpfeffer
Cinderella on the screen
*The fairy serpent—China
*The fatal quest
*Fun from Norway
*"Goldilocks and the three tigers"
*The obedient princess
 The old woman in the wood
 Out of the garret
*"The prince and the sleeping beauty"
 Prindella and the since
 The proud princess (2)
*"Queen Alice"
*Red Riding Hood
 Red Riding Hood
 Reddisch Riden Hood
*Robin Hood
 The romance of little Cinderella
 Snow-White and her dwarfs
 The three bears
 The three modern bears
*Tom Tit Tot
*The truth about Sleeping Beauty
Fairy tales and Mother Goose. EISENBERG—HAND. p27-28.
Fake cornet solo. DEPEW p258.
Fake initiation. DEPEW p246.
Fake musical stunt. (2) EASY—STUNTS p7-8; PARTIES p34.
The fake musician. EISENBERG—HAND. p134.
Fake peanut hunt. DEPEW p294.
Fake radio political broadcast. DEPEW p153-154.
A fake seance. BUGBEE—LIVE WIRE p51.
Fakes. *See* Quacks
Fame
 *The heroine's husband

*Fame in half an hour. (2m, 1f) STARR—JR. p80-87.
"Familiar folks in familiar poses". FERRIS p56.

Families
  *Each Sunday morn
  The whole 'fam damily
The family album. (3) DRUMMOND—STUNT FUN p26-30;
    EISENBERG—FUN p117-118; FERRIS p56.
The family car. YOUNG—GAMES p34-35.
Famous advertisements you see every day. CANOPY—HIGH
    p73-74.
The famous Dr. Pillsendoper, by Arthur L. Kaser. BRINGS—
    MASTER p360.
Famous lovers. FRICK—FALL p12.
The famous men quiz. SHELDON—GIANT QUIZ p61-70.
Famous riders of history. BUGBEE—GOOFY p58-63.
The fan dancer. CONNOR p54-55.
*Fan mail. (1m, 4f) HUBER—TV p83-90.
*Fancy football. (3) HUBER—GIANT p80-87.
Fancy pitches. EISENBERG—FUN p81-82.

Fantasy
  *Around the world in bed
  *At the gates
  *Atavism or women are so brave
  The bachelor's dream
  *Buck Private's dream
  Green hat and yellow feather
  *"It might happen"
  *"Not qualified"
  The pink persimmon tree—Japan
  *The sewing club meets
  *"The ultra-modern school"
Farces
  *Reversal in rehearsal
*Farewell to Easter. (3m, 4f) WEATHERS p127-140.
Farewells. *See* Closing numbers
The farm. YOUNG—GAMES p9-10.
*A farm for sale. (2m, 1f) BUGBEE—LIVELY p93-96.
Farm life. *See* Country life
The farmer goes to the city. KERR p63-66.

Farmer quartet. DEPEW p257.

"The farmer's daughter". EISENBERG—HAND. p177-186.

Farmers

  See also Dialect, Country

  *Call me dear

  Crrr-uel wrrr-etch!

  *Stars up above

  *Thunder in the East

  *The traitor

  *"West wind"

  *Who's a hick?

The farmers' quartet. CANOPY—HIGH p63-65.

Fashion

  See also Chorus, fashion show; Dress shops

  Beauty parade

  The dummy

  "Fifth Avenue fancies"

  French mama dolls

  "June echoes"—"Brides of long ago and to-day"

  Lids off!

  *Male model

  Mannykins

  "Moods of the mode"

  "My Magazine cover girl"—"My lady's trousseau"—
    "Off to college"

  "Never-mind-the-weather-girls"—"My girl in sunshine
    or rain"

  Parent's night

  Pre-showing of next season's styles in clothes

  The rising style

  *Style show á la masculine

  Style show for men

  Styles of a century

  The styles of other days

  "When artists frolic"—"Mind-the-paint girls"

Fashion revue, by Harry Githens. GITHENS p20.

Fashion show. GEISTER—NEW p74; PARSONS p45.

Fashion show de luxe. BUGBEE—GOOFY p81,82.

Fashion show from Hollywood, by June Astaire. JOHNSON
  —EASY p73-76.

Fashion tableaux. DRUMMOND—STUNT FUN p73.

The fat man. CONNOR p40.

Fat man and lean man. PARTIES p22.

The fatal bottle. CROWLEY p57,59,61.

*The fatal pickle. (4m) STARR—JR. p64-68.

The fatal plunge. KASER—BUSHEL p103-106.

*The fatal quest. (3m, 3f) ROHRBOUGH p17-22.

The fatal ride. MILLER—LANDS p67-76.

The fatal scream. SHELDON p81-84.

*The fatal wedding. (3m, 1f, 1b) KERR p76-89.

Fatalism. ABELL—PEP p95.

Fate of Mary Ellen Van Twerp, a mock wedding in rhyme, by Jeff Gannett. BRINGS—MASTER p86-89.

*The fateful bargain. (4m, 7f) WEATHERS—MYSTERIES p40-53.

*Father and child doing well, by Mel Tyler and Marriott Wilson. (2m, 2f) EASY SKITS p29-32.

Father Time reviews the accomplishments of the past presidents. DEPEW p158-159.

Father Time's art gallery. CHAPLIN p61-69.

Father Time's visit. BUGBEE—GOOFY p13-15.

Father's Day
  *Instant dramas

*Father's Day. (3b, 5g) GODDARD—CHILDREN'S p88-95.

*Father's quiet evening, by Jean Provence. (1m, 1b) JOHNSON—EASY p12-15.

Fathers
  Balance sheet
  *A date with Kate
  *Doctor
  *The nervous father
  *Seeing father (2)
  *Where's the baby? (BRINGS—MASTER)

The "favor-ite" box hunt, by Beatrice Plumb. CASEY—PEPPY p113-114.

"A feast of fun and frolic". FERRIS p141.

Feats. EISENBERG—FUN p242-252.

Features. BRIDGE p15.

February
  Great loves, by the Griddle Theatre group

Quotation quiz for February
Feed the animals. YOUNG—GAMES p29-30.
Feed the blind man. YOUNG—GAMES p38.
Feel the pain. EISENBERG—FUN p32.
Female impersonations. *See* Impersonations; Ladies' night
*Feminine bravery. (1b, 5g) IRISH—CHILDREN'S p72-75.
Fencing tournament. JOHNSON—BAKER'S p99.
Ferguson, Katherine
  *At the school ball game
  A bag of tricks
*Ferry fare, by Arthur LeRoy Kaser. (4m) QUICK—COM.
    p86-89.
A festival of books or Our trail of books. LAMKIN & FLOR-
    ENCE p77-84.
The festival of No-Ruz, a Persian party. MILLER—LANDS
    p177-187.
Festivals
  Doing a folk festival
  Harvest festival
*Feudin' and fightin'. (6b, 5g) GODDARD—CHILDREN'S p40-
    52.
A few toasts. BREEZY p102-103.
FFA and 4H—a good opening stunt. BUCHANAN p27-29.
The FFA emblem. BUCHANAN p35,40.
Fiction. GEISTER—NEW p96.
Field, Eugene
  The delectable ballad of the Waller lot
Field, Floyd S.
  Lily of the alley (2)
"Field of honor". HUBER—EASY p29-31.
The fiery finger, by Beatrice M. Casey. CASEY—PEPPY p7-9.
"Fifth Avenue fancies". FERRIS p80.
*Fifty dollars worth of dog. (1m, 1f, 1b) DRUMMOND—
    THREE p61-64.
*The fight against disease. (6m, 2f, 2b) STAHL—LAND.
    p91-106.
*Fight to a finish. (3m, 2f) HUBER—CHAR. p5-11.
Figures never lie. JOHNSON—BAKER'S p102.
Fill them up. YOUNG—GAMES p64.
A finale number. FERRIS p112-113.

Finales. *See* Closing numbers
Finding associates with a song. DEPEW p262.
Finding partners with conundrums. DEPEW p297.
Finding the stars, by Alta Toepp. CASEY—PEPPY p97.
Fine chili-sauce. WILLIAMS p22,24.
Fingerprints, by Gladys Lloyd. JOLLY p91,92.
*Finish the rubber! (5m, 1f) LEVIS—TEN p1-5.
Finish-them stunt, by Lettie C. VanDerveer. GITHENS p20-21.
*Finishing school. (3b, 3g) ROGERS—PLAYS p42-49.
*Fire! By Selden M. Loring. (2m, 1f) EASY—IMPR. p56-60.
Fire. EISENBERG—HAND. p83.
The fire bug. ROGERS—PLAYS p94-95.
*Fire! Fire! By Jeff Gannett. (2m) BRINGS—MASTER
    p267-269.
*Fire station number one and a half. (3m, 4f) KASER—
    BUTTON p16-25.
*"Fired". (3) PROVENCE—FLASH p12-14.
*"Fireman, save my house!" (3) PROVENCE—VAUD. p31-32.

Fires and firemen
    Clancy to the rescue
    *A glass in time
    *He remembered
    The midnight fire alarm
    *Our miniature fire brigade
    Putting out a fire
    Save my child
    *What price carelessness?
The firing squad. BUGBEE—NUTTY p37.
*First! (10g) BARBEE p77-79.

First aid in illness and injury
    See also Red Cross
    *The ambulance always
    *An honored tradition
*First and ten. (2m, 2f) HUBER—ARENA p11-18.
*The first biscuit. (1m, 1f) REACH—QUICK p88-91.
The first Christmas. PRESTON—PANTOM. p230-232.
*The first date. (1m, 1f, 1b, 1g) EISENBERG—HAND. p104-105.
*First prize. (3m, 1f) HUBER—FOUR p126-130.
First puppets. PARTIES p23-24.

*The first rehearsal, by Sidney Steele. (5m, 4f) BRINGS—
    MASTER p27-34; DRUMMOND—IMPR. p5-12.
Fiscus, R. Paul (and Ken Kelly)
    The tune the salesman played (JOHNSON—EASY)
Fish and fishing
    *A-fishing I have been
    *"Always bragging"
    *The big bribe
    *Do you believe in signs?
    *The generous fisherman
    *A little stunt from Italy
    Out in the deep
    Piscatorial art (2)
    The usual way
The fish bowl magician, by Arthur L. Kaser. BRINGS—MAS-
    TER p406-407.
*Fish business, by Selden M. Loring. (3m) EASY—IMPR.
    p14-19.
The fish pond. HUBER—GIANT p149; MACDONALD—CARNI-
    VAL p78.
Fish ponds
    Catch a bat
Fish spearing. YOUNG—GAMES p40.
Fisher, A. L.
    Dr. Killemquick's medicine show, or the friendly quack
The fisherman. (2) EISENBERG—FUN p97; PRESTON p11.
*The fisherman's line. (2m) PROVENCE—LIGHT p38-39.
Fisherman's luck. BRINGS—MASTER p398.
*Fishing, by Jean Provence. (2m) BRINGS—MASTER p158-160.
"The fishing fool". HUBER—EASY p17-19.
*A fishing party. (4b) IRISH—CHILDREN'S p20-21.
*Fit as a fiddle. (3m) SULLIVAN—MORE p9-12.
Fitzwater, Don
    *Uncle Tom's nabbin' or The effervescent evaporation of
        Eva
Five fingers. GEISTER—NEW p88-89.
*$500 reward (2m, 1f) KASER—HALE p60-75.
A five-minute minstrel show. PRESTON p17-18.
Five minutes to go. WILLIAMS (#40)
Five on a side. DEPEW p360.

The fixer, by Minnie L. Peterson. ROHRBOUGH p162-164.
The fixit clinic. EISENBERG—FUN p16-18.
The flag. ABELL—STUNTS p94-96.
Flag Day
   The etiquette of the flag
   *Past, present and future
   *The stars and stripes
Flag day (decorations). YOUNG—GAMES p108.
Flag trick, by Beatrice Plumb. BREEZY p57.
Flash! Flash! BUGBEE—NUTTY p63.
Flash light hikes. FRICK—SUMMER p8.
Flashlights
   Wink! Wink!
*The flat below. (3m, 2f) STAHL—MORE p85-88.
Flea hounds and alley rabbits. YOUNG—GAMES p77.
The flimflam television. BUGBEE—NUTTY p51-54.
Flinging filing cards. YOUNG—GAMES p80-81.
Flip the cork. EISENBERG—HAND. p53-54.
A "flivver" party. FERRIS p168-169.
The floating man. EISENBERG—HAND. p26.
The Flora Dora sextet. by Kurtz Gordon. BAKER'S GAY
   p42-43.
Floral fancies. HANLEY—STUNTS p13-16.
Florida
   Burying Jacksonville
Florida, our fair southern state. EISENBERG—HAND. p45.
Florists
   *A tragedy in rhyme
Flow smoothly, sweet sonnet. LLOYD p9-10.
Flower competition. YOUNG—GAMES p46.
"Flower girls—all in a row". FERRIS p69-70.
Flower market minstrels. FERRIS p125.
Flower-pot walk. YOUNG—GAMES p36.
Flowers
   See also Chorus, Flower; Florists; Gardens and gardening
   *Birds, trees and flowers
   Floral fancies
   Funny flowers
   "In the garden"
   My garden is lovely

The state flowers
*The sunflowers' wooing
*"Flowers and weeds". (8m, 8f) DRUMMOND—IMPR. p25-29.
"Flowers for sale". FERRIS p70.
Flowers or fruits. YOUNG—GAMES p49.
The flying quarter. DRUMMOND—STUNTS p28.
*Foiled again. (3m, 2f) HUBER—GIANT p103-109.
*Foiled again, or saved by fate. (2m, 2f) DRUMMOND—
     SPOT p81-84.
Folding chair race. DEPEW p174-175,
Folding chairs. GEISTER—NEW p77.
Folk dances. KEMMERER—GAMES p107-114.
Folk tales. *See* Fairy tales
Follow the arrow. HUBER—GIANT p148.
Follow the leader. BRIDGE p15.
*"Follow the leader". (2m, 1f) HUBER—THREE p80-81.
Follow your impulse. HUBER—GIANT p127-128.
*Fond farewell. (2m, 2f) HUBER—SIX p19-26.
The food and candy booths. CANOPY—HIGH p34-35.
Foolish answers. WILLIAMS p36-37.
Football
   Dixie pep
   *End of the line
   *Fancy football
   *First and ten
   Formation of letters
   "A great discovery"
   High power pep
   A homecoming pep meeting
   *Honor man
   If football players were bridge players
   Indian pep
   The jail bowl game
   *Meet me at three-thirty
   A mock football game
   *The old fight (2) EASY—IMPR.; HUBER—FOUR
   One man's word
   Parade of the stars
   Professor Von Ribbenbropper's football kindergarten
   The race for the bacon

*"Reverse English" (STAHL—AMAT.)
Roman football game
Sailor's pep
*School spirit
The sidelines
*Sissy football
Streamline deluxe model of 1941
*The swing
The town crier
Victory for our team
"What a game! What a game!"
*"What a mess"
A football broadcast. ABELL—PEP p7-10.
The football fool. HUBER—PRACT. p23-27.
*"Football hero" (3m or more) HUBER—THREE p53-55.
Football quiz. ABELL—PEP p111-113.
A football rally. ABELL—PEP p11-17.
*Football rally. (8b, 2g) STARR—RADIO p11-12.
Football stunts. BUCHANAN p52-56.
For men only. (2) CANOPY—HIGH p43-44; CONNOR p12-13.
For the land's sake, by Arthur L. Kaser. BRINGS—MASTER
    p301-306; DRUMMOND—STUNT FUN p78-84.
*For the love of Larry. (4m, 4f) KASER—ACTS p28-36.
For women only. CANOPY—HIGH p43,45.
"A ford feud". FERRIS p43.
Fore and aft beauty shop. WILLIAMS p46-47.
Foreign legion, French
    *Something free
Foreigners
    *To meet the Duke
Forest follies. HANLEY—STUNTS p25-29.
Forfeits. (2) BUGBEE—CATCHY p31; YOUNG—GAMES
    p112-113.
Forfeits and initiation stunts. EISENBERG—FUN p232.
Forgery
    *To whom it may concern
*Forget-me-not, by Mel Tyler and Marriott Wilson. (3m,
    1f) EASY SKITS p22-28.
Formation of letters. (2) ABELL—PEP p125; FRICK—FALL
    p31-32.

*The senator's visit
*The singing hen
Song of the dish towel
*The spirit of 4-H clubs
Sue's lunch
The 4-H quintuplets. ROGERS—PLAYS p22-26.
Four-legged relay. FRICK—FALL p22.
Four nines equals one hundred. TARBELL—COMEDY p21.
Four unfortunates. VAN DERVEER—ANY p54-56.
*Fourteen points. (7b, 6g) BARBEE p68-70.
Fourth of July
Ain't it a shame
America, the beautiful
"Echoes of the glorius Fourth"
The glorious Fourth
Flag trick
*Holiday hush
Patriotic spelling-bee
Red, white and blue chorus
Revolutionary tea
Sparkler drill
Time to retire
Fourth of July celebration—or Fireworks on parade. PRES-
TON p10.
A Fourth of July program. WILLIAMS p4.
The fox, goose and corn. DEPEW p342.
Fox-hunter-gun. EISENBERG—FUN p37-38.
*Foxy grandpa. (3a) IRISH—CHILDREN'S p75-77.
Frasier, Dulcan
The Laidly worn
Fraternities
See also Initiations
The actor
Antique, mystical, Egyptian order of night owls
Banquet toasts
The barber shop
The blarney stone (CORMACK)
Boxing match (CORMACK)
Chewing the rag
Good rich blood

Greek letter fraternities
Greek letter societies
Hazing the obstreperous
His majesty, the king
*The initiation
Initiation, Part I, II, III
The little rose
Low bridge (CORMACK)
Markmanship
Miscellaneous songs
Molten lead test (courage)
Names for social clubs or fraternities
The north pole
The orator (CORMACK)
Oriental dance
Pledge stunts
The pound of flesh
Punkin pie
The royal bumper
The sacred stone
The scrambled egg
The shampoo
Shimmy shakers
Slogans or mottoes
The social order of the union
Songs, parodies, etc.
Strength test
The test of fire
The thirst
The trained dog
Trick mirror
A trip to the moon
Tug of war (CORMACK)
*Two boys meet girl
Yells, cheers, etc.
*"Fraternity row". (3m) STAHL—HEARTY p78-80.
Freak choruses and orchestras. BUGBEE—LIVE WIRE p83-84.
The freak horse. CONNOR p39.
Freak quadrille. CHAPLIN p81-84.
*Fred's mistake. (1b, 2g) IRISH—CHILDREN'S p51-53.

Frustration
   *Thunder in the East
Fuller, Jack
   *Custom built
   Poison Gulch
   *Same old thing
*Fun at the cross roads. (4m, 7f) KASER—AMATEURS' p55-60.
*Fun from Norway: The youth and the North wind. (2m,
      2f, extras) MILLER—LANDS p109-120.
*Fun in the general store. (6m, 6f) KASER—BUTTON p52-63.
Fun leaves, by Beatrice Plumb. CASEY—PEPPY p111-112.
Funeral of opponent. BUGBEE—LIVE WIRE p65.
Funeral of the giant. DRUMMOND—STUNT FUN p11.
Funerals
   *Ferry fare
Funiculi, funicula. EISENBERG—FUN p190.
Funnel stunt. DEPEW p324.
Funny feats, fast and furious. YOUNG—GAMES p9.
Funny flowers. HANLEY—STUNTS p4-13.
Further clues for black magic. GEISTER—NEW p83.
"Futuristic"
   Skyrocket express leaving
   *Twenty-first century

G.G.G. Grapefruit. DEPEW p275.
*The G-men. (6m, 3f) BUGBEE—NUTTY p20-22.
Galileo
   *The earth and the sky
Gallery of famous pictures. CANOPY—HIGH p39-43.
Gambling
   *"A beauty gets the bird"
   *Better not be bettor
   *Double or nothing
   *A sure bettor
   *The whole truth
*"The game hunters". (2m, 2f) HUBER—THREE p81-82.
Game of curtseying. JOHNSON—BAKER'S p99-100.
The game of Ireland. BUGBEE—GOOFY p75-76.
The game room. MACDONALD—CARNIVAL p82.

Games

See also Athletics; Guessing games; Surprise games; Word games; names of individual games and sports

Aeroplane ride
Aim for the basket
All aboard!
All wound round
Alphabet game
Alphabet meal
Ambush
Animals
Apple pass
April Fool party
Arcades
Auto show
Automobile
Baby pictures
Balloon balance
Balloon battle
Bandanna vagabondia
The beater
Bedtime story
Bell pass
Bell ringers
Birthdays (Jolly)
Blind man's meal
Boulevard ball
The brig
Bus stop
Buzz—the oldest known game and always good fun
Celebrities (Brings—Master)
Chair circle
Chair pass
Chinese school
Christmas (games and stunts)
Circle and line games
Circle race
Coffeepot (2)
Competitive games
Concealed goodies

Confessions
Confusion
Cootie
Cracker marathon
Crazy speeches
The cup that cheers
Cy Perkin's hen
Definitions
Dish the fish
Dishing out the dirt
Double tandem
Each one, grab one
Easter bonnet
Eggshell football
Emergencies
The farm
Fencing tournament
Fingerprints
Flee hounds and alley rabbits
Flinging filing cards
Follow the arrow
Freeze
Friends' meeting
Funny feats, fast and furious
Game of curtesying
The game of Ireland
Games for little tots
Games for special occasions
Games old and new
Getting sociable
Ghosts (3)
Giggling Gertie
Going to South America
Grand slashioned
Grandma's ice-box
Grandmother gooseneck
Granny goes to town
Green sleeves
Group mathematics
Guess who? (2)

Music quiz
Musical mystery
Musical neighbors
The musical wand
Mute replying
My favorite object
My garden is lovely
Mysto magic
Names
New Year's (games and stunts)
Non-competitive games
Number race
Number spin
One only
Orchestra
Partnership
Pass the ball
Pass the clothes pins
Pass the orange
Passing the balloon
Pea marathon
Peanuts!
A penny for your thoughts
A perfect picnic
Picture captions
Pockets to purses
Poison
Poor blind bat
Professions
Progressive poetry
Quiz ball
Quiz program (GEISTER—NEW)
Red tape
Regatta
Relay poetics
Repressions
The ridiculous handkerchief
Ring the bell
Rural symphony
The saga of the farmyard

St. Patrick's Day (games and stunts)
Sardines
Schooldays (GEISTER—NEW)
Schooldays no. 2 (GEISTER—NEW)
Screen test game
Scripture spelling match
See-saw
Seven-league boots
Shadow guessing
Shoppers
Shopping
Shrieking bromides
Siamese national anthem
Siege
Silent menagerie
Skid
Slipper hunt
Smoke screens
Snappy answers
Snatch
Softball
Special games and ideas
Speedy seven up
Spell it
Spelling in reverse
The spool game
Spoon pass
A spoonful of fun
Stations
A story about a cat
Supposing
Sweetest story ever told
Synchronized spooners
Take it away
Tandem
Teapot
Tempus fugit
Terminal tag
Thank you
Thanksgiving (games and stunts)

Thieves
This and that
Three little pigs — and the wolf
The three R's
To start the party
Tools of the trade
Transportation
Trekking is tops
Trick and mystery games
Truck lines
Twenty questions
Two cats and a mouse
Unfinished business
Valentine Day (games and stunts)
Wand race
Washington's birthday (games and stunts)
We don't like coffee
The weaver
What is your neighbor like?
What's this
What's wrong with whom?
Where am I
Where's the collar button
Who hit me?
Who is my neighbor?
Who was who?
Wink! Wink!
Word contest
Zig zag bean bag
Zoological garden
Zoo's zoo

Games, Campfire
Animal hunt (FRICK—SUMMER)
Barley Bright
Chinese wall
Deer hunt
Duck on a rock
Ring toss
Toad in a hole

Games, Musical
  Games to music
  Sing song
  Songs for group singing and musical games
Games, Outdoor
  See also Games, Campfire Games, Picnic; Games; Roadside
  Bean bag baseball
  Dodge ball
  Greased pole climb
  Nuts to you
  Peanut punch
  Skill games
  Spinning on a stick
  Sundown-sunup-breakfast
  The table
  Time!
Games, Picnic
  Carry relay
  Double relay
  Four-legged relay
  Kick ball
  Over and under
  Over one
  Over or under two
  Running relay with stunt
  Simple running relay
  Stealing sticks
  Tunnel relay
  Under one
  Wheelbarrow relay (2)
Games, Roadside
  I see something
  Roadside cribbage
  Trail lists
Games, Spectator
  Amnesia
  Art on the installment plan
  Candidates for congress
  The dizzy orchestra
  The family car

Feed the blind man
Fish spearing
Flower-pot walk
Gwendolyn and marmaduke
House furnishing
How's your memory
Mental telepathy
Opposite actions
Picking a movie star
Public orator
Pussy and Dido
Scat!
Taboo
Tight-rope artists
Whistling magic
Games for little tots. KEMMERER—GAMES p88-91.
Games for special occasions. KEMMERER—GAMES p9-32.
Games old and new. BUGBEE—CATCHY p21-30.
Games to music. BRIDGE p79-86.

Gandhi, Mahatma
Mahatma Gandhi
Gannett, Jeff
Fate of Mary Ellen VanTwerp
*Fire! Fire!
The grumbler
I tell jokes
Privation
Sh! (BRINGS—MASTER)
The treasurer's report
*Where's the baby? (BRINGS—MASTER)
Gano, Nina R.
The handicap
Garden chalk talk. BUCHANAN p59,64,67.

Gardens and gardening
*How does your garden grow?
Indoor diversions of a gardner
My garden is lovely
Garrett, Charles E.
The midnight fire alarm

Gasoleen mavourneen. LLOYD p11-12.

"A gathering of witches". FERRIS p82.

"Gay nineties"
  *A backward march of time
  The Bon Ton saloon
  Brazos Pete
  *The Brewer's great white horses
  Casey at the bat
  Casey's revenge
  College revisited
  Curfew must not ring tonight (BAKER'S GAY)
  Drink
  The drunkard-maker
  The face on the barroom floor
  *"Faint heart ne'er won fair lady"
  "The farmer's daughter"
  The Flora Dora sextet
  *"The great bottleneck diamond or The villainous Shah
    of Shush"
  Guilty or not guilty?
  "He ain't done right by little Nell"
  *It was then as now
  *The lady known as Lou
  *Love will win
  The newsboy's debt
  The old stage queen
  Opening and closing numbers
  'Ostler Joe
  *The pen is mightier than the word
  A sample program for a gay nineties revue
  She was "somebody's Mother"
  Songs of the nineties
  *Stars of the gay nineties
  *Ten barrooms in one night
  *The tonsorial quartette
  Two sinners
  *Uncle Tom's Nabbin'
  The watch fob minstrels
The gay nineties. (2) BUGBEE—GOOFY p102-103; MAC-
    DONALD—CARNIVAL p9-11.

*The gay nineties barber shop, and a quartette, by Vance
Clifford. (7m) BRINGS—MASTER p56-59.
*Gay nineties convention, or The sweethearts of the gay
nineties. (2m, 2f, boys) "THAT GOOD" p20-23.
The gay nineties minstrel. BAKER'S GAY p53-56.
Gazook touch, by Alta Toepp. CASEY—PEPPY p84.
General idea. EISENBERG—FUN p88-89.
*The generous fisherman, by Catherine Miller Balm. EISEN-
BERG—HAND. p212-214.
    See also *A little stunt from Italy
The gentleman's gentleman. HUBER—PRACT. p75-78.
Gentlemen prefer blondes, by Grace Keith Samuelson.
CASEY—PEPPY p54-55.

Geography
*A class in geography
*Interdependence
Modes of travel
New deal geography
North America, South America and Europe
Scrambled states
Stars
Where am I?
Geography. (2) DEPEW 307; YOUNG—GAMES p68.

Geology
*History versus geology
Geometry for moderns. ABELL—STUNTS p9-11.
George, Charles
*Absent-minded
*Borrowing Bessie (2)
*Entertaining sister's beaux (BRINGS—MASTER)
*"Faint heart ne'er won fair lady"
*He remembered
*His sweetheart
*It might happen (2)
*Newlyweds (BRINGS—MASTER; GEORGE—TEN)
*Painless dentistry
*The proposal (2)
*The rivals
*So you won't talk (BRINGS—MASTER; GEORGE—TWELVE)
*Ten barrooms in one night

Gere, Thomas A.
  Brazos Pete
The germ convention. PRESTON p87-91.
A German band stirs up pep. ABELL—PEP p58-60.
Germans
  See also Dialect, German
  The fatal ride
  The proud Princess (2)
  The siege of limburger
  A spoonful of fun
The gesticulator. EISENBERG—HAND p120.
"Get-acquainted" stunts
  All participating
  Birds of a feather (FRICK—FALL)
  Bus stop
  Choosing partners (BUGBEE—CATCHY)
  Concealed goodies
  Continuous receiving line
  Cy Perkins's hen
  The farm
  Funny feats, fast and furious
  Getting sociable
  Give an account of yourself
  Goodbye (FRICK—FALL)
  Half-minute speeches
  Hazelnut treasure hunt
  I'm so and so
  In the water, on the shore
  Incidentally
  Let's talk it over
  Locate your maxim
  Maybe you did, but I doubt it
  The musical wand
  Number spin
  Passing the balloon
  Poor blind bat
  Rural symphony
  The school day
  Shake!
  Siamese national anthem

Spell it
What am I?
What's in a name? (FRICK—FALL)
Where's the collar button
Who am I? (FRICK—FALL)
Zoological garden
Zoo's zoo
Get your picture taken. CANOPY—HIGH p53.
*Getting a job. (3m, 2f) TOPOLKA p49-53.
*Getting acquainted. (5g) IRISH—CHILDREN'S p29-31.
Getting acquainted. WILLIAMS p44-45.
Getting Dad up. BUGBEE—GOOFY p34-35.
Getting down to business, by Beatrice Plumb. "THAT
    GOOD" p40-42.
*Getting ready for a visit. (1m, 2f) IRISH—CATCHY p49-52.
Getting ready for her beau. BUGBEE—LIVE WIRE p43.
Getting ready for the party. FERRIS p22.
*Getting rid of an agent. (1m, 3f) IRISH—CATCHY p11-14.
Getting sociable. YOUNG—GAMES p8.
*The ghost goes home. (2m, 3f) HUBER—GIANT p93-98.
Ghost hike. FRICK—SUMMER p8-9.
The ghost of mathematics. STARR—JR. p68-69.
A ghost story. PARTIES p15-16.
*The ghostoscope. (2m) KASER—SURE p42-48.
Ghosts
    *"And spooking of ghosts ——"
    *The crime club
    Down below where all is woe
    *Hamlet and the ghost
    *Let's haunt
    A night in wonder-wander land, a Japanese party
    Special stunt
    *The spirit is willing
    Spirit television
    A terrible ghost story
    The touch of the ghost
    When ghosts walk
Ghosts, by Beatrice Plumb. BRINGS—MASTER p427; JOHN-
    SON—BAKER'S p72-73; JOHNSON—BAKER'S p91,92.
"The ghosts are out". FERRIS p82.

*The ghosts' minuet, by Evelyn Price. (13 or more) ROHR-
BOUGH p12-16.
Ghosts of yesteryear. BUGBEE—GOOFY p12.
*The G.I. minstrels (a first part) (7m) KASER—FUNNY
p36-51.
The giant and the midget, by Beatrice M. Casey. CASEY—
PEPPY p23-24.
Giant caterpillar. EISENBERG—FUN p83.
Giant sneeze. PARTIES p14; TARBELL—COMEDY p56-59.
Giants
The burial of the giant
Giddy-ep! Whoa! Back up! DRUMMOND—STUNT FUN p107.
*Gift exchange. (1m, 1f) HUBER—FOUR p57-60.
Gifts
*Anybodys gift
Breaking the china
Presentation of gifts
Presenting the boloney
Presenting the grand piano
Gigantic sneeze. DEPEW p193.
Giggling Gertie. YOUNG—GAMES p20,21.
Gilbert, Earl J.
*Guilty
*Home, sweet home (SNAPPY)
*Memories (SNAPPY)
The gimmes. FERRIS p51-52.
The Gink family. BUGBEE—CATCHY p13-14.
Gipsies
See also Chorus, gipsy
A golden hours party
"The gypsy trail"
Girl buys an Easter hat. PRESTON p9,10.
*Girl chatter. (2f) KASER—BUTTON p86-90.
*The girl next door. (3m, 2f) WEATHERS p141-170.
A girl scout number. FERRIS p178-179.
Girl Scouts
"Do a good deed daily"
Girls
The bachelor's dream
An evening with the American girl

*Too many types
*The girls are home. (1m, 4f) HUBER—ARENA p63-71.
*Girls' glee club fantasy. (announcer, 1b, girls' glee club)
        STARR—RADIO p41-42.
Girls of America. VAN DERVEER—ANY p83-89.
Githens, Harry
    All's swell that ends swell
    *Animated scarecrows
    As it might have been
    At the union station
    Ball game deluxe
    Brought to court
    Camper's nightmare
    The cannibal king
    Cinderella on the screen
    Circus sideshow
    The comic section
    Comin' round the mountain
    *Daffydill school
    A day in camp
    Dr. Peppo's medicine show
    Enroute to camp
    Faculty portraits
    Fashion revue
    Fountain of youth (GITHENS)
    *Going somewhere
    Great calamity
    Harem-scarem jitter bugs
    Horse race (GITHENS)
    In the dining room
    Jim and Jerry
    Kitchen orchestra
    Little riddle schoolhouse
    Major Blows' amateur hour
    Manager's chamber of horrors
    Modern tales from Shakespeare
    Mother Goose's family
    Old MacDonald's farm
    The old woman who lived in a shoe
    Operatic movie

A pantomimed melodrama
Pill-carbonic orchestra
Professor Cuckoo—crystal gazer (GITHENS)
*Say, Dad
Singing school at Cyclone Junction
*Sleepy Hollow school
Snow-white and her dwarfs
Telling the world
*Under the spreading chestnut tree (GITHENS)
Whiteface minstrels
Give an account of yourself. FRICK—FALL p9.
"Give me". HUBER—EASY p26-28.
"Giving. EISENBERG—HAND. p121-122.
*Giving Aunt Jane a shock. (4g) IRISH—CHILDREN'S p56-68.
Giving away an automobile. DEPEW p213-214.
Giving out dimes. DEPEW p179.
*Giving you the jeeters. (3m, 3f) LEVIS—TEN p47-56.
*"The glacier". (2m, 2f) PROVENCE—FLASH p17-18.
Glamour
*A student's complaint
Class forfeit. EISENBERG—FUN p40.
*A glass in time. (3m) STAHL—MORE p22-25.
*Glass of poison. (4m, 2f) WEATHERS—MYSTERIES p91-102.
Glass or bottle players. EISENBERG—FUN p39.
Gleanings from the hayfever weekly. KASER—BUSHEL p108-
110.
Glee clubs
*The boots-and-saddle gang
*Boys' glee club fantasy
*Girls' glee club fantasy
*Madeline gets analyzed
*The magic cabin
A glimpse into the future. BUGBEE—NUTTY p12.
The glorious Fourth. JOHNSON—BAKER'S p58-59.
*"The glorious whitewasher, from "The Adventures of Tom
Sawyer, by Samuel Clemens. (5b, 1f) PROVENCE—
EASY p61-69.
Gloves de luxe. TARBELL—COMEDY p9.
The glow worm. ABELL—STUNTS p75.
"Glowing glow-worms". FERRIS p84.

Glowworm. (2) GEISTER—NEW p25; PRESTON—FUN
  p100-101.
Glynn, Patricia and Peleg
  The song of the shoes
Gnomes. FRICK—FALL p53,54.
*The goat. (1m, 1f) LEVIS—TEN p29-32.
The goat quartet. DEPEW p254.
Gob chatter. ABELL—PEP p114-115.
*God's country. (10m) KAUFMAN—HIGHLOWBROW p37-52.
Godiva, by Karin Sundelof-Asbrand. BUGBEE—NUTTY
  p93-94.
Going native, by Gail White. JOHNSON—EASY p46-57.
*Going somewhere, by Harry Githens. (3m) GITHENS
  p21-23.
Going to court. BREEZY p74.
"Going to Jerusalem"
  Booby. March music
  The modern Jerusalem. March music
Going to South America. YOUNG—GAMES p15.
Gold or feathers? DEPEW p348.
*"Goldbaum at Waterloo". (3m) STAHL—BITS p12-14.
Goldberg's beauties. BUGBEE—LIVE WIRE p25-26.
Golden chair. FRICK—SUMMER p83.
A golden hours party. MILLER—LANDS p149-161.
*Golden wedding. (2m) KAUFMAN—HIGHLOWBROW p99-103.
*"Goldilocks and the three tigers". (3m, 2f) STAHL—AMAT.
  p80-84.
Golf
  "A hole in one" (2)
  *How's your golf?
  Putt! Putt!
  *Three strokes too many
The golfer dreams. (2) BRINGS—MASTER p384-385; DRUM-
  MOND—STUNT FUN p56-57.
*Good advice. (4m) PROVENCE—LIGHT p64-66.
"The good club member". FERRIS p177-178.
*Good English. (announcer, student) STARR—RADIO p19-21.
*Good front. (3m, 1f) HUBER—FOUR p122-125.
*"Good gracious". (4f) PROVENCE—VAUD. p17-19.
*"Good guy". (3m) HUBER—THREE p23-24.

Good morning! FRICK—SUMMER p82.

*Goodbye. DRUMMOND—STUNT FUN p109; FRICK—FALL p10.

*Goodbye, Mother. (2m, 2f) HUBER—ARENA p110-116.

*Goodbye, students. (5 students, glee clubs, band, faculty) STARR—RADIO p121-124.

Goodnight. (2) DRUMMOND—STUNT FUN p116-117; RYAN p111.

Goodnight, Elaine. KERR p45-47.

Goodnight, Mollie. LLOYD p76,77.

Good old class. FUNNY p27-28.

Good rich blood. CORMACK p26.

A goofy debate. BUGBEE—GOOFY p29-32.

Gopher girls. EISENBERG—HAND. p119.

Gordon, Kurtz
  *'Arry and 'Arriet
  *A backward march of time
  *The Brewer's great white horses
   The Flora Dora sextet
  *The lady known as Lou
  *Your order, please

A gory battle. DRUMMOND—STUNT FUN p61.

Gossip
  *A back-yard build-up
  *Byron's accident
  *Carpet rags
   Dishing out the dirt
  *It might happen (2)
   Mrs. Buzzy, news dispenser
  *The scandal
  *The Shantytown scandal
  *Slightly exaggerated

Gossip. EISENBERG—FUN p96.

The Gossip Hollow ladies' minstrels. MALCOLM p96-106.

*Gossip is an art, by Mabel Tuttle Craig. (4f) "THAT GOOD" p34-36.

Got the grip. EISENBERG—FUN p189.

Goups. FRICK—FALL p54-55.

The graduates' home coming party (decorations) YOUNG—GAMES p108-109.

Graduation
  Commencement exercises, or schoolroom burlesque
Grammar
  *Don't say
  *Parsing a sentence
  Grand march figures and folk dance. BRIDGE p75-78.
  Grand march medley. March music. GEISTER—NEW p24.
  Grand march mixers. March music. GEISTER—NEW p23-24.
  Grand march stunt, by Beatrice Plumb. PRESTON p11-13.
Grand marches
  Circle race
  Counter marching (2)
  Diagonal cross
  Interlacing
  Partnership
  Regatta
  Serpentine
  Trios
  Grand-opera contest. WILLIAMS p39-40.
  Grand prize, by Robert N. McGregor. BREEZY p75.
  Grand slashioned, by Beatrice Plumb. BRINGS—MASTER p428.
Grandfathers
  *Foxy grandpa
  Where's Gran'paw (2)
  Grandma's ice-box, by Beatrice Plumb. BRINGS—MASTER
      p415.
  *Grandma's sick. (4f) HUBER—GIANT p110-117.
  Grandmaw and grandpaw at the railroad track. DEPEW
      p122.
  Grandmother gooseneck. YOUNG—GAMES p21-22.
  Grandmother remembers. PRESTON—PANTOM. p95-104.
  Grandmother's great grievance, or Who purloined the bustle?
      by Arthur L. Kaser. BAKER'S GAY p46-50.
  Grandmother's problem. DEPEW p349.
  *Grandpa Dean's talking machine. (3b, 3g) BUGBEE—LIVELY
      p12-14.
  Grandpa gets a bomb. BUGBEE—GOOFY p32-34.
  *Granger helps Kate. (2f) TOPOLKA p61-63.
  Granny goes to town. YOUNG—GAMES p20.
  The grapevine. GEISTER—NEW p29-30.

*Fresh fish
*In Grandma Perkins' store
Little shot
*"Memory course"
*Small sale
*Where's the baby? (KASER—FUNNY)
Gross, H. H.
   The rising king
Ground hog day (decorations). YOUNG—GAMES p103-104.
Group acting. EISENBERG—HAND p52-53.
Group dramatization of life situations. PARTIES p19-20.
Group mathematics. YOUNG—GAMES p77.
The grumbler, a poem by Jeff Gannett. BRINGS—MASTER
   p335-336.
"Guaranteed; sixty thrills a minute". FERRIS p45-48.
*Guess what. (3m) DRUMMOND—STUNT FUN p35-37.
Guess who, by Mable Tuttle. CASEY—PEPPY p95; YOUNG—
   GAMES p77-78.

Guessing games
   Observations
   Packages
   Shadow guessing
Guessing musical numbers. DEPEW p257.
Guessing numbers. BRIDGE p15.
*Guests for dinner. (1m, 1f) SULLIVAN—MORE p5-8.
*Guilty, by Earl J. Gilbert. (2m, 1f) SNAPPY p106-109.
Guilty or not guilty? BAKER'S GAY p31-32.
Gulliver and the Lil' Mutts, by Beatrice C. Casey. CASEY
   —PEPPY p9-10.
The gun man. CROWLEY p41-42.
Gunkle, Olga E.
   Cinderella up-to-date
   *Robin Hood
Gustafson, Oscar L.
   A mellerdrammer
Gwendolyn and marmaduke. YOUNG—GAMES p34.

Gypsies. *See* Gipsies
"The gypsy trail". FERRIS p77.

Hail! Hail! the meat's all gone. DEPEW p280.
Hail, Horatius! By Karin Sundelof-Asbrand. BUGBEE—
  NUTTY p91-93.
Half and half. GEISTER—NEW p76.
Half-minute speeches. JOHNSON—BAKER's p102-103.
Half through the night. LLOYD p48-49.
"The Hall of fame, or Heroes and heroines from Bookland".
  FERRIS p57-58.
The hall of terror. MACDONALD—CARNIVAL p61-62.

Hallowe'en
  See also Chorus, Hallowe'en; Fortune-telling; Ghosts;
    Witches
  Bazaar, Hallowe'en
  Catch a bat
  A clown act (FRICK—FALL)
  Down below where all is woe
  Fortunes
  "A gathering of witches"
  Ghosts (JOHNSON—BAKER's)
  "The ghosts are out"
  *The ghosts' minuet
  Hit the cat
  "A Jack-o'-lantern frolic"
  *Look before you screech
  The murder of Jabel Jenkins
  Professor See-all and know-all
  *Public hero number one
  Ring the cat's tail
  Ring the witch's hat
  The R.O.S. initiation
  Special stunt
  A "striking" stunt
  Talloween fortunes (for Hallowe'en)
  Use of the old Halloween stunts
  What is your neighbor like?
  The witches' cauldron
  Witches' den
  Your hooror-scope

*Hallowe'en. (2) (5b, 10g) GODDARD—CHILDREN's p96-108;
  (2b) STARR—RADIO p37-40.
Hallowe'en (decorations) YOUNG—GAMES p110.
*A Hallowe'en frolic. (4b, 4g) BUGBEE—CATCHY p44-48.
Hallowe'en (games and stunts) KEMMERER—GAMES p23-25.
Hallowe'en minstrels. FERRIS p123-124.
Hallowe'en social or party. BUGBEE—CATCHY p32-34.
A Hallowe'en stunt, by Ruth Putnam Kimball. JOHNSON—
  EASY p96-97.

Hallucinations
  *The girl next door
*The ham what am, or Do you want to be an actor? (4m, 2f)
  SHELDON p62-69.
The hamagician. DRUMMOND—STUNT FUN p9.
*Hamlet and the ghost. (2m) BUGBEE—LIVE WIRE p78.
Hamlet's soliloquy. ABELL—STUNTS p31-32.
Hand clues. GEISTER—NEW p81.
Hand me down a quart of corn, by Cressy M. Weaver. CASEY
  PEPPY p65-66.
The handicap, by Nina R. Gano. ROHRBOUGH p146-149.

Handicapped
  *Around the world in bed
  Four unfortunates
Handkerchief and toothpick. DEPEW p362.
Hands up. JOHNSON—BAKER's p101.
*"Handy Andy". (3m) PROVENCE—EASY p70-76.
A handy mustache. TARBELL—COMEDY p9-10.
Hanging in effigy. BUGBEE—LIVE WIRE p65.

Happiness
  *A candle burns tonight
"Happiness in every box". FERRIS p84.
*Happy birthday. (1m, 3f) HUBER—TV p17-22.
Happy birthday stunts, by Beatrice Plumb. "THAT GOOD"
  p58-61.
*Happy birthday to you. (3m) TAGGART—MEN p68-72.
Happy Hooligan trio. WILLIAMS p18-19.
Happy landings. March music. GEISTER—NEW 18-19.
*The happy medium. (2m, 4f) HUBER—GIANT p73-79.
*Hard sledding. (4m, 2f) HUBER—GIANT p70-72.

Hard-times
   "Rags and tags"
   Hard times minstrels. FERRIS p125.
*Hard to handle. (2f) PROVENCE—KNOCKOUT p49-50.
Hard wheeling. JOLLY p85.

Hardware
   *Colossal
Hare, Walter Ben
   The old maid's drill
Hare and hounds picnic. FRICK—FALL p14-16.
Harem-scarem jitter bugs, by Harry W. Githens. GITHENS
   p108-109.

Harems
   Harem-scarem jitter bugs
*"Harmony á la hobo". (4m) DRUMMOND—IMPR. p50-53.
*The harmony laundry. (4f, chorus) KENT—ONE p62-69.
*Harold meets the cowboys. (4m) PRESTON p30-33.
Hartenhome problems. KASER—BUSHEL p110-113.

Harvest
   Corn baby
   Corn song
   Indian corn ceremonial
   Indian harvest customs
   Red ear
Harvest festival. BUGBEE—CATCHY p35-36.
Harvest home celebration. FRICK—FALL p61-62.
Hasty Harry, by R. M. Eliot. (3) EASY STUNTS p11-14;
   EISENBERG—FUN p180-184; ROHRBOUGH p119-124.
Hat arguments, by Alta Toepp. CASEY—PEPPY p88-89.
*A hat for madame. (3f) SIX—MORE p27-32.
Hat rhythm. EISENBERG—HAND. p53-54.
Hat sale. EISENBERG—FUN p82-83.
Hat stunt. EISENBERG—HAND. p123.
Hats, a monologue for a giggling woman, by Sidney Steele.
   BBINGS—MASTER p323-324.

Hats and hat shops
   The Bon Ton hat shoppe
   Girl buys an Easter hat
   Lids off!

*Miss Jones' millinery opening
The new Easter bonnet
*Sarah Perkins' hat shop, a parody song sketch
Whose hat is that?
Hats off, men! By Beatrice Plumb. BRINGS—MASTER p413.
*Hats to you. (2) (1m, 3f) HUBER—FOUR p108-112; (2m, 3f)
HUBER—SIX p5-11.
*Hattie's singing lesson. (2b, 3g) IRISH—CHILDREN'S p55-57.
The haunted house, by Grace Keith Samuelson. BUGBEE—
NUTTY p69-70.
*The haunted house. (2m, 2b) "THAT GOOD" p73-75.
Haunts the jungle, by Jocelyn W. Tyler. BUGBEE—LIVE WIRE
p20-22.
Have a banana. TARBELL—FUN p24-27.
*Have a good time, by Sidney Steele. (any number) BRINGS
—MASTER p19-22.

Hawaiian
"Aloha-oe"
Hawaiian serenaders. CONNOR p41.
Hayford, Harlan
*Success story
Hayes, Agnes Dubbs
*And the villain still pursued her
A pep operation
Hazelnut treasure hunt. YOUNG—GAMES p9.
Hazing the obstreperous. CORMACK p83-85.
"He ain't done right by little Nell". EISENBERG—HAND p153-
155.
*He always gets his man. (3m) DRUMMOND—SPOT p11-13.
(3m)
He can do little. (2) DEPEW p301; YOUNG—GAMES p18.
*He knew all the answers. (5m) TAGGART—MEN p73-86.
*He knew his strength. (3) PROVENCE—LIGHT p101-103.
*He remembered, by Charles George. (3m) QUICK p83-89.
"He works his way". FERRIS p44.
He's crazy. EISENBERG—FUN p96-97.
*He's not so dumb. (1m, 1f, 1b) DRUMMOND—THREE p86-88.
Head and feet. DEPEW p344.
Heads or tails. GEISTER—NEW p91-92.

Heald, J. P.
*At your service
Health
The alphabet is queen
*Breakfast for Superman
*Cinderella—quite modern
The germ convention
*Keep your engine oiled
Skidoo, germs
Health performances. FERRIS p173-174.
*A health stunt.(10f) ROGERS—PLAYS p27-30.
Hear the Southland calling. PRESTON—PANTOM. p243-246.
Hearing
See also Deaf
Sense of hearing
The sound detectors
Hearts and spades. GEISTER—NEW p120.
Heaven
*The lax judgment
Heaven protects the working girl; or, The old homestead gets
its face lifted. PRESTON—PANTOM. p22-31.
Heaven's gate. DEPEW p127-138.
Heel and toe relay. DEPEW p332.
Helen of Troy
*So this is Paris
Hello, Bill. DEPEW p323.
"Hello, neighbor, let's sing". FERRIS p99-101.
Help! Help! BUGBEE—NUTTY p75.
*"Help! Help!" (1m, 2f) HUBER—THREE p62-63.
*"Help the blind". (2) (2m, 2f) HUBER—THREE p35-36; (3m)
REACH—QUICK p32-38.
*Help wanted. (1m, 1f) EASY—STUNTS p22-23.
"Help wanted". FERRIS p84.
*Help wanted—badly. (3m, 2f) MIKSCH—CURTAIN p21-29.
Hen club. DEPEW p191-192.
The henpecked husband. BUGBEE—LIVE WIRE p54.
*Henry, the model husband. By Franklin Phelps. (1m, 2f)
BRINGS—MASTER p23-26; (1m, 2f) DRUMMOND—
IMPR. p84-88.

Hens and eggs. DEPEW p344.
"Her first piece". FERRIS p16-17.
Her first voice lesson. FUNNY p23-24.
Her reverie. FERRIS p109-110.
*Her souvenirs. (2) (2f) EASY—BLACKOUTS p78-82; By
    Charles F. Wells. (2f) SIX—NEW p12-14.
*Herbert's hurt. (3f) HUBER—ARENA p35-39.
Hercules, the strong man. MACDONALD—CARNIVAL p18-21.
Here come three little pigs. YOUNG—GAMES p59.
*Here comes the bride. (2) By William Milligan. (2m, 1f)
    QUICK—COM. p33-37; (2m, 2f) SULLIVAN—MORE
    p21-25.
Here comes the groom; Flag of the free. LLOYD p70-72.
Here comes the weatherman. BUGBEE—GOOFY p55-58.
Here, have another rope! The vanishing wife. TARBELL—
    COMEDY p87-90.
*Here lies a lie. (4m, 2f) HUBER—SIX p33-40.
*Here's a hair. (1m, 1f) PROVENCE—KNOCKOUT p26-27.
Here's the cook. BUGBEE—GOOFY p43.
Here's to the banquet. DEPEW p282.
*Here's to the track team! (cheer leader, six voices) BARBEE
    p66-68.
"Hermione". FERRIS p19.
*Heroes. (4m) PROVENCE—LIGHT p83-85.
Heroes are made. WILLIAMS p43-44.
*The heroine's husband. (7m, 1f) MILLER—LANDS p49-52.
Heyday. GEISTER—NEW p116-117.
Hiawatha
    The picture writing from Hiawatha
Hiawatha and Mondamin. PRESTON—PANTOM. p104-113.
Hickville comes to conference. DEPEW p101.
Hidden animal crackers. DEPEW p171.
Hidden letters. GEISTER—NEW p114.
Hidden personalities. GEISTER—NEW p113.
Hidden prizes. GEISTER—NEW p120.
Hidden words. GEISTER—NEW p68-69.
Higbee, Marjorie
    Sir Ronald the ruthless
Higdon, Raymond
    *A lucky shot

*"High finance". (3m) DRUMMOND—STUNT p3-5.
High flying—class history. LAMKIN & FLORENCE p40-42.
High power pep. ABELL—PEP p24-28.
*High pressure. (2) By Vance Clifford. (2m, 1f) BRINGS—
    MASTER p197-200. (2m, 1f) DRUMMOND—IMPR. p89-92.
High school
  *Advice to students
  *The ambulance always
  *Books! Books! Books!
   Boys' glee club fantasy
  *Caroline bakes a cake
  *Celebrity day
  *Christmas Carols
  *Christmas high jinks
  *Clubs and friends
  *Coming clean
  *Community fund play
  *Courtesy in the halls
  *Danger, fate at work
  *Football rally
  *Getting a job
  *Girls' glee club fantasy
  *Good English
  *Goodbye, students
  *Granger hels Kate
  *Hallowe'en (STARR—RADIO)
  *History versus geology
  *How can I be popular?
  *Industrial progress
  *The interview
  *Interview with Santa
  *Invitation to a wiener roast
  *Is it worth the sacrifice?
  *The jackpot
  *Join the hiking club
  *Keep your engine oiled
  *Mabel's embarrassing moment
  *Not wanted
  *Personality does count
   The play's the thing (ABELL—STUNTS)

A radio interview
*School bazaar
*The school bell
*School circus
*School spirit
*Silly Sally fails again
*Spring revels
*A student's complaint
  Students are good citizens, I, II, III
*Thanksgiving day
*Unwarranted speed
*Wanted: young office assistant
*Welcome, students
*What price carelessness?
*Who wrote it? (TOPOLKA)
High school students
*Arrival in person
*Backfire
*Brotherly revenge
*Cupid on a rampage
*Double tribute
  "A great discovery"
*"High finance"
*"The inquiring reporter"
*It's a silly game
*My kingdom for an aspirin
*No visitors allowed
*Resolution for two
*Through with girls
*"Tom goes sissy"
*"Won't grandpa be surprised"?
*"High speed". (5m, 1f) STAHL—HEARTY p17-19.
  High time minstrels. KASER—ACTS p84-96.
*The higher art. (1m, 2f) STAHL—MORE p62-63.
  Higher education. KASER—ACTS p80-82.
*Highlowbrow. (7m, 2f) KAUFMAN—HIGHLOWBROW p1-15.
  Hi-Fi, the wonder horse. TARBELL—CRAZY p37-39.
Hiking
  Bag and baggage
  *"The botany hike"

Flash light hikes
Ghost hike
*Join the hiking club
I see something
Nature hikes
Roadside cribbage
Trail lists
Treasure hunts
Hilarity. PARTIES p11.
Hill, Conny
Statuesque de silly
"Hill-billies"
See also Dialect, Mountaineer
A day in the life of Ma and Pa Settle
*Feudin' and fightin'
*Lend me five
The mirror
*"Out yonder
The still in the night
*Taking Maw's advice
A hill-billy orchestra. BUGBEE—NUTTY p78.
Hinky dinky parlez vous. GEISTER—NEW p28.
Hints for the crystal gazer. CONNOR p24-26.
Hip, hip, horray! TARBELL—FUN p61,66.
*Hiram and Mirandy. (2m, 1f) ROHRBOUGH p89-90.
*His daughter's hand. (2m, 2f) HUBER—ARENA p103-110.
*His first case. (1m, 2f) KELLEY p53-56.
His line. WILLIAMS p16.
His majesty, the king. CORMACK p32.
His reverie. FERRIS p110.
*His sister, by Jean Provence. (1f, 1g) BRINGS—MASTER
    p175-176.
*His sweetheart, by Charles George. (2m) BRINGS—MASTER
    p247-249.
Hisses and kisses, by Bernice Vandersall. EASY—SKITS
    p99-105.
Historical
See also Biography; Civil War; Costume, Historical;
    "Gay Nineties"; Medieval; Patriotic; Sixteenth Cen-
    tury; U.S. History; etc.

*America begins
America, the beautiful
As it might have been
*The beginning of knowledge
*Big moments in history
The birth of a nation
*The birth of freedom
Columbus discovers America (2)
Famous riders of history
The gay nineties (BUGBEE—GOOFY)
*God's country
*Great men
*Historical hystericals
*History versus geology
How's your history
*Just suppose
Landing of the Pilgrims (2)
*Mabel takes up history
Marching through Georgia
Moments in history
Muddled up history
Paul Revide's rear
The saving of Capt. John Smith
*"Scrambled dates"
Statuesque de silly
*This brave new world
Truthful Betsy
Washington crosses the Delaware
Historical 4-D television. EISENBERG—FUN p110.
*Historical hystericals, or Pocahontas comes to the rescue, by Arthur L. Kaser. (2) (6m, 6f) BRINGS—MASTER p125-132; (7m, 6f) KASER—FUNNY p27-35.
Historical opinions. BUGBEE—GOOFY p77-78.
History of Class day. LAMKIN & FLORENCE p9-11.
A history song (patriotic). PRESTON—PANTOM. p222-224.
*History versus geology. (4 students) STARR—RADIO p61-64.
Hit the cat. FRICK—FALL p46.
Hit the nail. HUBER—GIANT p142-143.
*A hit with Papa, by Edwin Scribner. (4m, 1f) SNAPPY p88-94.

The hitch hiker. CROWLEY p41-43.
Hi-Y
*Coming clean
Hoag, Victor
Scene at the art gallery
Hobbies
A style show (LAMKIN & FLORENCE)
Talk on hobbies
*The hobby parade, by Willis N. Bugbee (MC and several
others) BREEZY p5-10.
The hobby show. MACDONALD—CARNIVAL p74-75.
Hobo day. FRICK—SUMMER p67.
A hobo fight. BRIDGE p20.
*Hobo minstrels. (5m, chorus) BUGBEE—GOOFY p63-67.
Hoboes. *See* Tramps
"Hoboes en routte for Hoboken". FERRIS p42-43.
*Hocus-pocus. (2m) KASER—SURE p115-127.
Hodgkins, Helen C.
*Stop—look—listen
Hog tying. DEPEW p330.
Hokey-pokey, the trained horse. DRUMMOND—STUNT FUN
p68.
Holbrook, Marion
The lover's errand (JOHNSON—EASY)
*A major operation
Polite but firm (JOHNSON—EAST)
*With complications
*The hold-up man. (4m) HUBER—FOUR p49-52.
A hole in one, by LeRoy Stahl. (2) (3m) BRINGS—MASTER
p283-285; STAHL—HEARTY p57-59.
*Holiday homecoming. (4m, 4f) MIKSCH—CURTAIN p73-87.
*Holiday hush. (2m, 3f) McCOY—HOLIDAY p53-61.
Holiday suggestions. TARBELL—CHALK STUNTS p61-65.
Holidays
See also names of Holidays; Parties
Games for special occasions
Shadow review of the holidays
Holidays. FRICK—SUMMER p70-71.
Hollister, Len D.
*Morning

Niagara Falls
*Honor man. (3m, others) PROVENCE—KNOCKOUT p40-41.
Honor-society
  *Who wears the laurel crown?
*Honorable mention, by Mel Tyler and Marriott Wilson.
   (3m, 1f) EASY SKITS p79-84.
The honorable Mr. Donkey, Esq. TARBELL—FUN p34-39.
*An honored tradition. (3m, students) PROVENCE—LIGHT
   p42-43.
Horace. EISENBERG—HAND. p58-60.
Horoscopes. *See* Astrology
Horror song titles. EISENBERG—FUN p23.
A horse of another color. SULLIVAN—MORE p17-20.
Horse race. (3) CANOPY—HIGH p98-99; DEPEW p183;
   By Harry Githens. GITHENS p27.
*The horse race shall not ring today. (5m, 1f) KENT—ONE
   p19-26.
Horse-racing
  See also Kentucky Derby
  The handicap
Horseback. FRICK—SUMMER p84.
Horses
  *"Be kind to animals"
  Clancy to the rescue
  The educated horse
  Hi-Ki, the wonder horse
  The love of beauty
  The old gray mare (2)
  The race
  Tippo's horse
  The trained horse, battle-axe
*Hospital blues. (3m, 2f) DEASON—SKIT p84-91.
*Hospitality, by Robert L. Sherman. (2m, 1f, announcer)
   SNAPPY p143-146.
Hospitals
  *His sister
  *Hospitality
  *No visitors allowed
  *One conclusion (2)
  *Operations (2)

*The reward (QUICK)
*Trouble in Paradise
*What would you do?
*The hoss race. (2m) "THAT GOOD" p85-86.
The hostess spoke French. STARR—JR. p17-20.
Hot and cold. DEPEW p299.
*A hot day. (3m, 1f, 1b) BUGBEE—LIVELY p81-84.
Hot dog machine. (2b) CANOPY—HIGH p77-80.
Hot dogs. (2) DEPEW p292; DRUMMOND—STUNT FUN p106.
Hot news. EISENBERG—HAND. p84.
"Hotel hash". FERRIS p42.
*Hotel Hokum. (2) (12m, 1f) BERLE p63-74; (14m) KASER
    —BUSHEL p58-76.
Hotels
    See also Porters
    *Á la carte
    *The defective detective
    *Excuse it, please! (2)
    *A glass in time
    *The heroine's husband
    Insomnia
    *No, they're married
    *Noon
    *Oh, waitress!
    *Room service
    *Room 213
The house by the side of the road. DEPEW p253-354.
House cleaning. YOUNG—GAMES p57.
House furnishing. YOUNG—GAMES p40-41.
*House guest. (2m, 3f) MIKSCH—TEEN p5-14.
The house of horrors, by Grace Keith Samuelson. BUGBEE—
    NUTTY p65-67.
The house of terrors. CANOPY—HIGH p54-55.
*"The house painter". (2m, 1f) STAHL—BITS p20-22.
The house that Jack built. JOHNSON—BAKER'S p63-69.
Household hints
    Aunt Sophie's household hints
"Household hints by Aunt Matilda". FERRIS p20.
Housework
    *Bachelor Hall medley

How to produce a shadow play. ABELL—STUNTS p79.

How to pronounce it. EISENBERG—FUN p42-43.

How to reduce. BUGBEE—GOOFY p24-27.

*How we started. (7m, 3f, extras) DEASON—SKIT p10-16.

Howdy do, everybody. DEPEW p283.

"Howdy neighbor" social, by Beatrice Plumb. CASEY—
PEPPY p78-79.

How's this for romance? By Lettie V Van Derveer.
GITHENS p24-26.

*How's your golf? By Charles F. Wells. (2m) JOHNSON—
EASY—p67-68.

How's your history? YOUNG—GAMES p61.

How's your memory? YOUNG—GAMES p33-34.

How's your smeller? YOUNG—GAMES p43.

Hudson, H. R.
The newsboy's debt

The hula hula dance. BUGBEE—LIVE WIRE p57.

*Hull House. (12m, 6f, 2 children) STAHL—LAND p137-151.

Human calliope and xylophone. EISENBERG—HAND. p134.

Human checkers. DEPEW p339.

The human clock. HUBER—GIANT p139-140.

Human, cross-word puzzle. WILLIAMS p29-30.

The human fire department. TARBELL—CRAZY p21.

Human jig-saw. DEPEW p291.

The human marimba. CONNOR p30-32.

Human marionettes. PARTIES p24.

Human organ. (2) ENTERTAIN—STUNTS p2; FUNNY p11.

The human renovator. BUGBEE—LIVE WIRE p47.

Human tug of war. DEPEW p328.

Human xylophone. (4) CANOPY—HIGH p77; no. 1. DEPEW
p258; no. 2 DEPEW p258-259; EASY—ENTERTAIN p19-
21.

Humorous tableaux. FERRIS p192-195.

Hundred with 6 nines. DEPEW p341.

Hundred-yard dash. DEPEW p314-315.

*A Hungarian tragedy: The kidnapped bride. (3m, 1f)
MILLER—LANDS. p91-95,

Hungry spooks, by Beatrice M. Casey. CASEY—PEPPY
p36-37.

Hunt the whistle. JOHNSON—BAKER'S p89.

Hunter and squirrel. DEPEW p343.
Hunters and hunting
  *Bang!
  *"The game hunters"
  *Man of courage
  *Tit for tat
The hunting knife. CROWLEY p48-50.
Hunts
  Fake peanut hunt
  Funny feats, fast and furious
  Hazelnut treasure hunt
  Hidden animal crackers
  Hunt the whistle
  Musical object hunt
  Noisy-peanut hunt
  Object hunt
  Slipper hunt
  The treasure box
  The treasure hunt
  Treasure hunt picnic
The hurdy gurdy man. BUGBEE—LIVE WIRE p42.
Hurly-burly. DEPEW p216.
*Hurry, doctor. (2) (3m, 2f) HUBER—ALL p53-58; (2m, 1f)
      HUBER—THREE p24-25.
*Hurry, hurry. (2m, 2f) HUBER—FOUR p87-90.
Husbands
  *All one-sided
  *Bachelor husbands
  *The best people
  Blackmail
  *Can this be love?
  The crisis
  *Fond farewell
  *Henry, the model husband (2)
  *The heroine's husband
  *It's a small world
  *Let's trade places
  *No fight tonight
  *Noon
  *A wronged husband

*You said it Doc
The Hyde Park hecklers. BUGBEE—GOOFY p38.
The hypnotic rug. BUGBEE—LIVE WIRE p31-33.
A hypnotic vanshing. TARBELL—CRAZY p90,91-93,95.

Hypnotism
   The mighty Merlin
   *Sleep softly
*"The hypnotists's assistant, or youth will rise". (4m)
      STAHL—BITS p5-8.
*"Hypnotized". (3m) PROVENCE—FLASH p46-48.

*I always say. (2f) HUBER—NO SCENE p19-25.
*"I am an American". (7b, 6g) BARBEE p35-37.
I arrived at the church. DEPEW p269.
I asked her first! EISENBERG—HAND. p90.
I did it with my little hatchet. EISENBERG—HAND p74-77.
I do bequeath. GEISTER—NEW p58-59.
"I don't have a pain no more". DRUMMOND—STUNT p87-88.
I got a dog. BRINGS—MASTER p386.
I gotta cold. EISENBERG—HAND. p86.
I have written a play, which is explained by the writer, by
      Franklin Phelps. BRINGS—MASTER p333-335.
I just love paintings. STARR—JR. p69-73.
I lost my mummy. GODDARD—CHILDREN'S p20-21.
*I object! By LeRoy Stahl. (4m, 1f) EASY SKITS p12-18.
I resolve! By Bearice Plumb. BREEZY p59.
I see a ghost. GEISTER—NEW p72-73.
I see something. FRICK—SUMMER p9.
I spy. GEISTER—NEW p62-63.
I tell jokes, by Jeff Gannett. BRINGS—MASTER p362-363.
I want to be happy. GEISTER—NEW p27.
Ice-breakers. WILLIAMS p11.
Ice cream race. DRUMMOND—STUART FUN p87-88.

Icemen
   *The logical guess
I'd rather have fingers than toes. DEPEW p285.
The idea of Thanksgiving through the ages. FRICK—FALL
   p65.

Ideas
   The craziest idea
   The identical words. WILLIAMS p24-27.
Identification by a nose. DEPEW p196.
Identifying articles blindfold. DEPEW p93.
Identity. CASEY—PEPPY p87.
*The idol worshippers. (2m, 2f) MIKSCH—TENN p44-52.
If footbal players were bridge players. ABELL—PEP p118-
      120.
If I should return, by Robert N. McGregor. BREEZY p68.
If-I-weren't-myself stunt, by Lettie C. Van Derveer. GITHENS
      p26-27.
If you think your church is best. DEPEW p283-284.
Il Advertiso. EASY—ENTERTAIN p71-81.
"Il Trovatore"
   *Ill-treated Trovatore
*I'll be home Thanksgiving. (5m, 3f) WEATHERS p73-82.
I'll bite. EISENBERG—HAND. p88.
I'll call the doctor, by Sidney Steele. BRINGS—MASTER
      p351-352.
*I'll fix it. (2m,3f) KASER—FUNNY p5-15.
*I'll fix it, Mom, by Sidney Steele. (1m, 1f) BRINGS—MAS-
      TER p269-270.
"I'll tell the world". FERRIS p42.
Ill treated. PRESTON—PANTOM. p254-255.
*Ill-treated Trovatore, by Avis Crocker. (5m, 2f) SHANNON
      p30-35.
Illustrated proverbs, by Beatrice Plumb. BRINGS—MASTER
      p426-427.
Illustrations of famous literary titles. BUGBEE—LIVE WIRE
      p81-82.
I'm a screamer. WILLIAMS p47-48.
I'm as happy as a donkey. DEPEW p280.
I'm forever blowing bubbles. ABELL—STUNTS p33-34.
I'm going to be an actress. GODDARD—CHILDREN'S p12-14.
*I'm hungry. (2m, 2f) HUBER—FOUR p17-20.
*I'm not here. (1m, 5f) HUBER—CHAR. p68-78.
I'm so and so. YOUNG—GAMES p8-9.
I'm thinking. YOUNG—GAMES p55-56.
Ima Rotarian. DEPEW p190-191.

*Imagination. (1m, 3f) HUBER—VAUD. p101-107.
   See Impersonations; Take-offs
Immigrants
   Ellis Island
An imperfect day. FUNNY p28.
Impersonations
   See also Ladies' night; Men's night
   Beautiful, but dumb
   Comic valentines (DRUMMOND—STUNT FUN)
   Easter parade
   The Flora Dora sextet
   "Lightning-change imitations"
   Mahatma Gandhi
Impersonations. ABELL—PEP p125-126.
Impromptu party. GEISTER—NEW p95-96.
Impromptu stunts. DEPEW p203-204.
Impromptu wedding. DEPEW p150.
*In a ballroom. (1m, 1f) KAUFMAN—HIGHLOWBROW p141-
   144.
*In a cinema. (1m, 2f) HOPE p65-66.
In a radio studio. PARSONS p63-68.
In Flanders field. ABELL—STUNTS p93-94.
*In giving thanks. (1m, 3f) HUBER—ARENA p54-63.
*In Grandma Perkins' store. (11f) MALCOLM p46-58.
*In Judge Hashover's court. (5m, 5f) KENT—ONE p5-18.
In Judge Spoofum's court. BUGBEE—LIVE WIRE p57-59.
*In line of duty. (2m, 2f) HUBER—SIX p12-19.
*In Paris. (2m, 2f) KAUFMAN—HIGHLOWBROW p67-73.
In proper order. HUBER—GIANT p128-129.
In the bag, by Beatrice M. Casey. CASEY—PEPPY p15-17.
*In the best of families. (1m, 1f) EASY—STUNTS p18-19;
   (1m, 1f) PARTIES p18.
*"In the class room". (6m) DRUMMOND—FOOT p78-90.
*In the dentist's office. (2m, 2f) DRUMMOND—SPOT p75-77.
In the dining-room, by Harry Githens. GITHENS p65.
*In the doctor's office. (4m, 1f) PRESTON—FUN p73-76.
"In the garden". MACDONALD p67-71.
In the good old wintertime. LLOYD p21-22.
In the king's garden. YOUNG—GAMES p67-68.
In the land of Schmozz. SHELDON p30-34.

In the limelight. BUGBEE—NUTTY p8-9.

*In the music shop. (2m, 6f) KASER—AMATEUR'S p22-27.

*In the nick of time. (2m) (3m, 1f) DRUMMOND—STUNT
     p77-80; (4m, 2f) KASER—MERRY p78-83.

In the park. HUBER—PRACT. p79-82.

In the photograph studio. RYAN p61-62.

*"In the radio store". (2m, 3f) DRUMMOND—STUNT p44-47.

*In the secret drawer. (5b) BARBEE p23-26.

"In the shadow of the tepee". FERRIS p76-77.

In the usual way. EASY—ENTERTAIN p31-35.

In the water, on the shore. YOUNG—GAMES p11.

*In union. (5f) HUBER—CHAR. p120-128.

"In Venice". FERRIS p73.

Incidentally. YOUNG—GAMES p12.

Income tax
   From income tax report last year
   *"The mental marvel" (2)
   *The outcome of income
   *To the ends of the earth

Income tax advice, by Arthur L. Kaser. BRINGS—MASTER
     p356-357.

Inconsequential journeys. SHELDON p35-42.

Independence day (decorations). YOUNG—GAMES p109.

Indian corn ceremonial. FRICK—FALL p63-64.

Indian harvest customs. FRICK—FALL p62-65.

Indian love call. ABELL—STUNTS p64-65.

Indian love songs. HUBER—PRACT. p32-34.

An Indian massacre. MILLER—STUNT p179-181.

Indian medicine. DEPEW p106.

Indian pep. ABELL—PEP p29-34.

Indians
   See also Hiawatha
   *"The arrival of Columbus"
   *Big moments in history
   *Braves, arise!
   Columbus discovers America (ROHRBOUGH)
   Columbus discovers Minnie who-who
   The delectable ballad of the Waller lot
   Discovery of America by the Irish
   *"Examination"

Punkin pie
Rolling the wheelbarrow
"Round and round"
The royal bumper
The sacred stone
The scrambled egg
The secret cavern
The shampoo
Shimmy shakers
"Shocked beyond words"
"Sock savers"
"Soup to nuts"
Staging a fight
Strength test
The submarine club
"Tearing time"
The test of fire
The thirst
Thumbs down
"To the swift"
"Too smart"
The trained dog
Trick mirror
A trip to the moon
Tug of war (CORMACK)
Vaulting the horse
"Walk of death"
"The walking lesson"
"The worm"
Innocent. PRESTON—PANTOM. p252-254.
*The innocent bystander. (4m, 1f) HUBER—ALL p17-23.
*"The inquiring reporter". (6m) HUBER—THREE p29-30.
Inquiry. GEISTER—NEW p65.
Insane
Alternate choice
Are you nutty?
*Assorted nuts
"Big business"
*Birds and blood
*"Cashed"

*The girl next door
*"Goldbaum at Waterloo"
He's crazy
The mental clinic
*"Method in madness"
*Not so crazy (2)
The racing bug
*"War is ——!"
Who's crazy now?
*Woman of Hilltop House
*You can't try an insane man
*An insect stunt. (12 characters) ROGERS—PLAYS p31-36.
Insects
The ant and the grasshopper
Be kind to insects
Clara Belle the flea
Dance of death
The elusive fly
Insomnia. PRESTON p25-27.
*The insomniac, by Charles Sherman. (1m & others) MILLER
—BROADWAY p1-6.
Installation banquet. DEPEW p143-147.
Installations
Father Time reviews the accomplishments of the past
presidents
Menu for installation banquet
*Instant dramas. (6m) TAGGART—MEN p39-42.
Insurance
*We agree
*Insurance, by Jean Provence. (1m, 1f) BRINGS—MASTER
p169-170.
Intelligence test. (3) By Mabel Tuttle Craig. CASEY—PEPPY
p97-98; DEPEW p186-187; "THAT GOOD" p42-43.
Intelligence tests. GEISTER—NEW p71-72.
*Interdependence. (3b, 4g) BARBEE p49-51.
Interlacing. GEISTER—NEW p123.
*"Interlude". (3m, 1f) HUBER—THREE p48-49.
Intermissions
Klaud's klimbing kit
International catastrophe. DEPEW p342.

An international recitation. JOHNSON—BAKER'S p70-71.
The interstellar league. BUGBEE—NUTTY p28-33.
*The interview. (announcer, 1b) STARR—RADIO p15-16.
*Interview with Santa. (2b, 1g) STARR—RADIO p93-98.
Interviewing celebrities. YOUNG—GAMES p48-49.
*Interviewing servant girls. (7f) IRISH—CATCHY p26-32.
Introduce speaker. DEPEW p152-153.
Introducing members at other tables. DEPEW p180.
Introducing motions. DEPEW p196.
Introduction by tables. DEPEW p180.
Introduction ceremony. HUBER—EASY p5-12.

Introductions
    See also Get-acquainted stunts; Mixers
    Asleep with the sheets
    "Do your shopping early" or "A shopper's dream"
    Line introductions
    Playing cards introduction
    *Thank you for coming
    To start the party
    Welcome
    *The welcome
*The intruder. (2m, 1f) LYONS p127.

Invalids
    See also Handicapped
    *Aunty Cheerful's visit

Inventors
    *The robot rebels
Invisible pins. EISENBERG—FUN p81.
*Invitation to a wiener roast. (announcer, 4 students)
        STARR—RADIO p35-36.
The irate dad. BUGBEE—LIVE WIRE p65.
Irish, Marie
    Nellie Gray

Irish
    See also Dialect, Irish; St. Patrick's day
    *Bustin' up the old quartet
    Discovery of America by the Irish
    "Mother Machree"
Irish symbols, by Willis N. Bugbee. BREEZY p78-79.

Is it true or false. "THAT GOOD" p5-8.
*Is it worth the sacrifice? (4m) TOPOLKA p65-68.
Is that right? HUBER—GIANT p138-139.
Islands
   Always a gentleman
It, by Beatrice Plumb. BRINGS—MASTER p419.
*It happens every day. (1m, 2f) KELLEY p33-37.
It makes a difference, by Arthur LeRoy Kaser. JOLLY
      p 75-76.
*It might happen, by Charles George. (2) (4m) BRINGS—
      MASTER p102-107; GEORGE—TWELVE p28-33.
*It was then as now. (1m, 1f) KASER—GAY p4-8.
It's a good time. DEPEW p272-273.
It's a short, short life. DEPEW p272.
*It's a silly game. (1m, 3f) HUBER—No p44-50.
*It's a small world. (1m, 2f) REACH—QUICK p9-13.
*It's against the law. (2m) PROVENCE—LIGHT p16-17.
*It's all in knowing how. (3f) PROVENCE—LIGHT p10-13.
*"It's colossal". (2) (3m, 1f) HUBER—THREE p27-28;
      (1m, 2f) TAGGART—FIVE p25-30.
It's good to be a joy-er. DEPEW p274.
It's happening in Daytona. DEPEW p273.
*It's her or the car, by Sidney Steele. (3m, 1f) BRINGS—
      MASTER p65-66.
*It's how you say it. (3m, 1f) DRUMMOND—SPOT p88-90.
It's impossible. HUBER—GIANT p150-151.
It's in the bag. HUBER—GIANT p125-126.
It's my brother. EISENBERG—HAND p86.
It's never been known to happen. LYONS p128-130.
*It's no picnic. (4m, 3f) MIKSCH—CURTAIN p124—135.
*It's only propaganda. (4m) TAGGART—MEN p93-97.
"It's out". JOHNSON—BAKER's p57.
It's the clock. EISENBERG—FUN p98.
*"It's the law". (2m, 3f) GEORGE—TWELVE p11-16.
Italians
   See also Dialect, Italian
   The employment office
   *The generous fisherman
   "In Venice"
   *A little stunt from Italy

'Neath the Italian moon"
"See-a-da-monk"
"Tony"
*Ivan Vosco, sanitary inspector is jailed, by Norman L. Zeno,
    Jr. (5m, 2f) MILLER—BROADWAY p7-14.
I've got a cold. FUNNY p34-35.
"I've got it now". JOHNSON—BAKER'S p57.
Iwan, Louise
    On a busy street corner

Jack Horner. LLOYD p29.
"A Jack-o'-lantern frolic". FERRIS p82.
*The jackpot. (announcer, 1b) STARR—RADIO p31-34.
The jail bowl game. EISENBERG—HAND. p156-159.
*Jake and his family. (2m) KASER—SURE p49-55.
Jam session, by Beatrice Plumb. BRINGS—MASTER p416.
Janitors
    *Just a love nest (EASY BLACKOUTS)
    *Not for credit (2)
January
    A golden hours party
Japanese
    See also Costume, Japanese
    *The awful fate of a fibber
    "Meet me where the lanterns glow"
    The ogre of Rashamon
    The pink persimmon tree—Japan
    Sixty jokes for stunts
    *A thrill from Japan
Japanese tea garden. CONNOR p38.
Jazzy justice. BUGBEE—NUTTY p41-46.
The jewelry shop. CANOPY—HIGH p48-49.
Jewelry stores
    *You've got to be tough!
Jewels
    Concealed jewels
Jews
    See also Dialect, Jewish
    *At the gates

Modern jokes—sidewalk conversation
Parlor stories
Smile a second—after dinner stories
Under the spreading chestnut tree
The joking singers. BUGBEE—LIVE WIRE p33.
Jolly jugglers. FERRIS p34.
The Jones store buys a radio, by Grace Keith Samuelson.
 BUGBEE—NUTTY p67-69.
Joseph and his brethren. TARBELL—SUNDAY p138-152.
The joy of winter sports, by Ruth Elder. JOHNSON—EASY
 p111-114.
Joy riding. JOHNSON—BAKER'S p84-85.
The joys that once through gullet walls. LLOYD p61-62.
Judd, Richard
 Moments in history
 "Oh, yeah!"
 The Schiltz murder case
 The scissors grinder
 "Suez you"
*Judge Dubois on the bench. (9m, 8f) KASER—BUTTON p64-
 79.
*Judge Hoptoad's court. (9m) KASER—HALF p22-33.
*Judge Knott presiding. (10m, 6f, chorus) KASER—AMATEUR'S
 p5-14.

Judges. *See* Courts
Jug balance. DEPEW p324.
The juggler. (2) BRINGS—MASTER p384; DRUMMOND—STUNT
 FUN p54-55.

Juggling
 Jolly jugglers
Jumbled words. (2) HUBER—GIANT p140; YOUNG—GAMES
 p72.
Jump, then. EISENBERG—FUN p99.
Jumping the rope. DEPEW p321.
"June echoes"—"Brides of long ago and to-day". FERRIS
 p81.

Jungle
 Haunts of the jungle
Jungle adventure. EISENBERG—FUN p69-70.

Junk shops
  *Ye olde junke shoppe
*"Juror number twelve". (4m) HUBER—THREE p39-40.
The jury convicts. ABELL—PEP p91-94.
Just a balloon. HUBER—GIANT p143-144.
Just a kiss at twilight. LLOYD p36-37.
"Just a love nest. (1m, 1f, child) EASY—BLACKOUTS p45-48.
"Just a love nest". JOHNSON—BAKER'S p62.
Just a voice on the radio, by Cressy M. Weaver. CASEY—PEPPY p64.
*Just another one, by Gail White. (1m, 1f) JOHNSON—EASY p18-20.
*Just ask father. (1m, 1f, 1b) DRUMMOND—THREE p92-94.
*Just basketball. (4m) HUBER—GIANT p88-92.
Just before the battle, Maggie. LLOYD p78-79.
*Just like John. (2m, 1f) HUBER—NO SCENE p56-60.
Just married. DRUMMOND—STUNT FUN p68.
*Just one more. (2m, 1f) PROVENCE—KNOCKOUT p36-37.
*Just plain efficiency. (1m, 2f) HUBER—TV p31-38.
*Just suppose. (7b) BARBEE p79-80.
Just too tired to move. EISENBERG—HAND. p94.
*"Just who is crazy"? (5f) DRUMMOND—FUNNY p58-65.
*"Justice a la rime". (7m, 1f) DRUMMOND—FOOT p62-70.
Juvenile delinquents
  *Not wanted

Kangaroo relay. DEPEW p333.
Kansas
  *Thunder in the East
Kaser, Arthur L.
  *A-fishing I have been
  *A bad luck sign
  Cedric's return (2)
  *Counting on the Count
  *The crucial moment
  *Cupid is speedy
  Dog star (2)
  *Don't spill the salt (2)

Dramatized jokes (2)
The dumb painter
The famous Dr. Pillsendoper
*Ferry fare
The fish bowl magician
For the land's sake (BRINGS—MASTER)
*Grandmother's great prievance or Who purloined the
    bustle?
*The great bottleneck diamond or The villainous Shah
    of Shush
*Historical hystericals (2)
How to build a dog house
Income tax advice
It makes a difference
*Landing of Columbus
*The liar's club
Live puppets
*Man versus dog
*Marital mishaps
*The merchant of Venice
*Mr. and Mrs. Newberry
Mrs. Buzzy, news dispenser
On the Isle of Bombalay
*One hundred years old
The optimistic road knight
*The pen is mightier than the word
Pure gold
*Saved by the hero
*Saved, or love's dilemma
*Schooldays (BRINGS—MASTER)
Science of today
A star is born
*Stars of the gay nineties
The tense moment
Thar's gold in them hills
*Their first play
*There's a sandbur in gran'pa's stocking
*There going to be a wedding
*Time for something
*Ventriloquist and his boy

Vote for me (2)
*What a classroom
*When is the train due?
Where's Gran-paw? (2)
*Without benefit of license
Women drivers (BRINGS—MASTER)
*Ye olde time vaudeville
Yeah
Kate. YOUNG—GAMES p51-52.
Katie goes to the zoo. GODDARD—CHILDREN's p10-12.
Keep back the squirrel. TARBELL—CRAZY p52-53.
*Keep smiling. (2m, 4f) MIKSCH—CURTAIN p137-147.
Keep the home tires burning. LLOYD p73-74.
*Keep the patient quiet. (2b, 5g) EGERTON p101-104.
Keep the song going. EISENBERG—HAND. p132.
*Keep warm. (1m, 3f) HUBER—FOUR p104-107.
*Keep your dignity. (2m) PROVENCE—LIGHT p96-97.
*Keep your engine oiled. (11 students) STARR—RADIO p51-53.
*Keeping store. (2b, 7g) IRISH—CHILDREN's p7-10.
Keeping the wolf away. FUNNY p24-25.
Kelly, Ken and R. Paul Fiscus
   The tune the salesman played (JOHNSON—EASY)
Kentucky
   *Taking Ma's advice
"Kentucky babe". JOHNSON—BAKER's p60-61.
Kentucky Derby
   *A horse of another color
Kerr, Walter F.
   *Chiseling on chivalry
   *The night before the morning after Christmas eve
   *The winning ticket
Keyboard funnies. FUNNY p5-6.
Keys
   The treasure box
Kick ball. FRICK—FALL p19-21.
The kid and the squid. CROWLEY p26-27.
Kid day. FRICK—SUMMER p67-69.
*Kid games. (2m, 1f) HUBER—SIX p98-105.
Kiddie car race. DEPEW p177-178.
Kiddlies. EISENBERG—FUN p87-88.

Kiddy Kar polo. GEISTER—NEW p75.

Kiddy Kar race. GEISTER—NEW p75.

The kidnapping of Percy Bogelwinkle, by Willis N. Bugbee.
BREEZY p31-38.

*The kidnapped bride, in A Hungarian tragedy

Kidnapping
*Music hath charms

*Kill the Ump. (3m, 1f) HUBER—ALL p93-99.

Kimball, Ruth Putnam
A backward party for April Fool's day
County Twenty's revenge. (JOHNSON—BAKER'S)
A Hallowe'en stunt
Rob 'em good

Kimono. DEPEW p255.

*"Kind-hearted people". (2m, 1f) DRUMMOND—STUNT p14-
15.

The kindergarten kids. FERRIS p53.

King for a day. DEPEW p69-77.

*"The king's highway". (3m, 2f) DRUMMOND—FOOT p41-45.

The king's name. DEPEW p351.

*The kings toemain, an entertainment of royal nonsense, by
Franklin Phelps. (4m, 1f) BRINGS—MASTER p67-70.

Kings
*Persia presents
The rising king

*Kisses. (2m, 4f) KAUFMAN—HIGHLOWBROW p17-35.

Kisses for sale. EISENBERG—FUN p106.

Kissing the blarney stone. JOHNSON—BAKER'S p100.

Kitchen band. (2) FRICK—FALL p40; FUNNY p10-11.

Kitchen band, or toy orchestra. CANOPY—HIGH p67-71.

Kitchen bands. *See* Orchestras, kitchen

Kitchen cabinet orchestra. DEPEW p111-112.

Kitchen orchestra. (3) BRIDGE p30-31; DRUMMOND—STUNT
FUN p10; By Harry Githens. GITHENS p111-112.

Kitchen orchestra, and semi-minstrel show. CHAPLAIN p28-30.

Kitchen symphony. (2) DRUMMOND—STUNT p72; JOHNSON
—BAKER'S p86.

The kitchen symphony—Domestic science department.
LAMKIN & FLORENCE p53.

Kitchens
 *Twenty-first century
Kittle for sale. EISENBERG—HAND. p93.
*Kitty Dawn, stennygrapher. (1m, 1f) KENT—ONE p98-102.
Kiwanis
 Heaven's gate
 How a person gets into Kiwanis
 Installation banquet
 Since my hubby has joined the Kiwanis
Kiwanis baseball game. DEPEW p217-220.
The Kiwanis court. DEPEW p224-230.
Kiwanis finishing school. DEPEW p159-165.
Kiwanis ladies' night. DEPEW p145-146.
K.K.K. DEPEW p211-212.
Kladd's klimbing kit. EISENBERG—HAND. p126-129.
Kneeling to Buddha. DRUMMOND—STUNT FUN p22-23.
Knight, Stuart W.
 *A grave problem
*The knot is tied. (4m, 6f) DRUMMOND—SPOT p32-40.
Know your home town, by Mabel Tuttle Craig. JOLLY p90.
Know your neighbor, by Mabel Tuttle Craig. CASEY—PEPPY
 p99.
Knowledge
 *The beginning of knowledge
Knowledge bump reader. DRUMMOND—STUNT FUN p89.
The kops and kitchenmaids. BUGBEE—LIVE WIRE p49.
Krazy kritters. EISENBERG—HAND p30-31.
*Kupid's kollege. (9b, 9g) DEASON—SKIT p26-31.

Labor laws
 *It's the law
Laboratories
 *Atomic energy
"Ladder to success". HUBER—EASY p45-47.
Laddergraph. YOUNG—GAMES p62-63.
Laddle rat rotten hut. EISENBERG—FUN p66-68.
*The Ladies' Aid church supper. (6f) SULLIVAN—MORE
 p57-64.
Ladies before gents. WILLAMS p40.

*The ladies' defense club. (5f) "THAT GOOD" p78-80.

Ladies in charge. DEPEW p149.

Ladies' initiation stunts. BUGBEE—LIVE WIRE p63-64.

Ladies' night
The beauty specialist
The Bon Ton hat shoppe
Choosing partners (JOHNSON—BAKER'S)
Fashion show deluxe
Lids off!
The rose vs. the lemon
The sewing bee
What culture has done for man

"Lady Clare". EISENBERG—HAND. p150-151.

*The lady known as Lou. (A crude sketch of the yester-years). By Kurtz Gordon. (4m, 2f) BAKER'S GAY p43-46.

Lady, won't you dance. FUNNY p30-31.

The laidly worm. MILLER—STUNT p155-163.

The lambeth walk. GEISTER—NEW p26-27,116.

The land for me. PRESTON—PANTOM. p240-243.

The landing of Columbus. DRUMMOND—SPOT p27-31.

*Landing of Columbus, in verse that couldn't be worse, by Arthur L. Kaser. (6m) BRINGS—MASTER p135-137.

Landing of the Pilgrims. (2) BUGBEE—GOOFY p96-98; BUGBEE—LIVE WIRE p70-73.

Landlords
*The noble landlord

Lantern slide numbers. FERRIS p171-173.

Larnin' the trombone. FUNNY p20-22.

Laryngitis
*Help wanted—badly

*Last chance. (2m, 1f) HUBER—TV p91-98.

Last line contest. DEPEW p199-202.

*Last request. (3m) PROVENCE—KNOCKOUT p30-31.

"Last rose of summer". JOHNSON—BAKER'S p62.

The last woes of summer. LLOYD p30-31.

Late again. By Sidney Steele. BRINGS—MASTER p342-344; KASER—FUNNY p89-91.

Lather harmony. RYAN p11-16.

Latin
*What about the root?
Laufe, A. L.
*Midsummer night's ring
Laughing relay. FRICK—SUMMER p85.
Laughing song. DRUMMOND—STUNT FUN p10.

Laundry and laundrymen
*The harmony laundry
Lavender, lace and old clothes, by H. Grady Moore.
    GITHENS p34-36.
Law, Arthur
    Two marionettes

Law
    See also Courts; Lawyers
    *"It's the law"
The law of the camp fire. FRICK—SUMMER p46-51.
Lawrance, Lois M.
    Nosey old Lady O'Grady

Lawyers
    *A-courting we will go
    *Criminal lawyer at home
    *His first case
    *No connection
*The lax judgment. (3m, 1f) KERR p68-71.

Laziness
    *"High speed"
The lazy man's chalk talk. TARBELL—CHALK STUNTS p17-
    19.
The League of Nations. BUGBEE—GOOFY p39-41.

Leap frog
    Partner leap frog
    Tunnel leap frog
Leap frog race. DEPEW p328.
Leap frog relay. FRICK—SUMMER p83.
*Learning to say yes. (2b, 2g, extras) IRISH—CHILDREN'S
    26-29.
*Leave it to mother. By Sidney Steele. (1m, 2f) BRINGS—
    MASTER p173-175; DRUMMOND—THREE p68-70.

Lee, Jeanne
  *Too busy
The leg of nations. BUGBEE—LIVE WIRE p39-40.
Legends
  *Captain Paul
  *The moon maiden—China
A lemon while you wait. TARBELL—FUN p27-30.
"Lend a hand". HUBER—EASY p73-75.
*Lend me five. (2m, 2f) HUBER—ARENA p71-76.
Let George do it, by M. Lee Shinkle. BUGBEE—LIVE WIRE
  p129-131.
Let me call you Lizzy. DEPEW p284.
Let me fish in an Oregon stream. BUCHANAN p87.
*Let me off at Sapulpa. (2m) PROVENCE—LIGHT p40-41.
*Let the punishment fit the crime. (3m, 1f) PROVENCE—
  LIGHT p104-109.
*"Let's ask Mother". (2m, 2f) HUBER—THREE p93-94.
  Let's be merry. FUNNY p31.
*Let's deny it. (5m, 3f, extra) HUBER—NO SCENE p66-75.
*Lets eat. (1m, 3f) HUBER—NO SCENE p85-91.
*Let's end it all. (3m, 4f) KENT—ONE p70-83.
  Let's give a cheer. FUNNY p31-32.
  Let's get married. BUGBEE—LIVE WIRE p48.
*Let's go to the movies, by Alfred Dykes. (1m, 2f) QUICK
  —COM. p43-48.
*Let's haunt. (1m, 5f) HUBER—ARENA p95-103.
  Let's join the parade. BUGBEE—NUTTY p84-86.
*Let's modernize. (5f) HUBER—NO p84-90.
*Let's pretend. (2m, 2f) HUBER—ALL p67-73.
*Let's stick together. (3m, 1f) HUBER—FOUR p118-121.
  Let's talk it over. FRICK—FALL p5-7.
*Let's trade places. (4m, 3f) HUBER p73-83.
*The letter, by Tom Taggart. (1m, 2f) QUICK—COM. p27-
  32.
  Letter carrier. EISENBERG—FUN p115.
  Letter game. YOUNG—GAMES p51.
  Letter stunt. FRICK—FALL p32.
  Letterfly. DEPEW p198-199.
Letters
  The purple pen

Letters, Formation of
  Formation of letters (2)
  Letter stunt
Lever, Charles
  *"Con Cregan's legacy" (The confession of Con Cregan)
Liars. *See* Untruth
*Liars and dynamite. (2m, 1f) KENT—ONE p27-36.
*The liars' club, by LeRoy Stahl. (2) (6m) BRINGS—MASTER
    p121-124; STAHL—MORE p81-84.
Liars' convention. RYAN p114.
Librarians
  *Madeline gets analyzed
  Silence, please!
Libraries
  *Granger helps Kate
Lick the stick. CASEY—PEPPY p88.
Lids off! By Beatrice Plumb. PRESTON p51-53.
The lie detector. (2) EISENBERG—HAND. p124; TARBELL—
    CRAZY p47-51.
Lie detectors
  *Here lies a lie
Life
  Such is life
*Life. (6m, 9f) LYONS p143-148.
*Life as it ain't. (char. vary) PARSONS p17-31.
*Life is so dull. (3m, 2f) MIKSCH—TEEN p85-94.
The life of a basketball player. ABELL—PEP p107-110.
Life's illusions. TARBELL—SUNDAY p70-77.
Lifeguards
  Help! Help!
  *There are life guards and life guards
  *Well qualified
Lifelike likenesses: satisfaction guaranteed. FERRIS p55.
Lifting 150 lbs. with 5 fingers. DEPEW p330.
Lifting seven boys. DEPEW p335-336.
The light headed gentleman. CROWLEY p65-66,68.
Light relay. YOUNG—GAMES p79.
Lighthouses
  United by love

Lighting effects
Athletic tableaux
"Lightning-change imitations". FERRIS p28.
Lily of the alley, by Floyd S. Field. (2) EISENBERG—
HAND. p143-144; ROHRBOUGH p66-86.
*The limb of the law. (2m, 1f) LYONS p133-135.
Limburger cheese. RYAN p93.
Limelight limericks. FERRIS p95-99.
Limericking 'round the world, by Willis N. Bugbee. BREEZY
p79-81.
Limericks
Limelight limericks
Limericks á la carte. BUGBEE—LIVE WIRE p29.
Lincoln, Abraham
*Washington or Lincoln
*Lincoln speaks. (7b, teacher) BARBEE p11-12.
Lincoln's birthday. YOUNG—GAMES p104.
Line introduction. DEPEW p296.
Lines that count. TARBELL—FUN p82-87.
Lint on the lung. DRUMMOND—STUNT FUN p15-16.
Lion act. JOHNSON—BAKER'S p87.
The lion hunt. EISENBERG—HAND. p70-72.
Lions
*Androcles and the lion (CONNOR)
Horace
Lisping
Horace
"Listen at the wall". EISENBERG—HAND. p96.
*Listening in on Joe's new radio. (4m, 4f) HOXIE p15-23.
Literary
See also American literature; names of authors, e.g.
Shakespeare, William
Godiva
Hail, Horatius!
Illustrations of famous literary titles
Pippa's song
"Little BoPeep". FERRIS p73.
Little Boy Blue. PRESTON p11.
"Little—but Oh, my!" (3f) FERRIS p79-80.
*"A little deaf". (3f) PROVENCE—VAUD. p13-15.

The little flapper, or Follies of 19——. CONNOR p32-35.

Little folks. LEVIS—TEN p43-45.

The little hills—with gestures. PRESTON p27-29.

Little man in a fix. GEISTER—NEW p35-37.

*A little matter of a motor car. (2m, 1f) SULLIVAN—
MORE p37-43.

Little riddle schoolhouse, by Harry W. Githens. PRESTON
p69-73.

Little Ride Hooding Red. EISENBERG—HAND. p50-51.

The little rose. CORMACK p25.

Little Sally. HUBER—PRACT. p39-44.

Little shot. EISENBERG—FUN p111-112.

*Little Sir Echo. (2m, 2f) DRUMMOND—SPOT p85-87.

*A little stunt from Italy: the generous fisherman. (4m,
extras) MILLER—LANDS p99-102.

*Live a hundred years. (3) PROVENCE—KNOCKOUT p20-21.

Live and learn, by Beatrice Plumb. BRINGS—MASTER p420.

Live puppets, by Arthur L. Kaser. BRINGS—MASTER p408.

Living basketball statuary. ABELL—PEP p78-81.

Living pictures. (6) BRIDGE p24; DEPEW p97-98; EISEN-
BERG—FUN p95; ENTERTAIN—STUNTS p3; PARTIES
30; RYAN p114.

Living songs. FUNNY p58-59.

Living statues *See* Statues, Living

Lloyd, Gladys
   An alarming time
   Auto show
   Bandanna vagabondia
   Chinese school
   The cup that cheers
   Fingerprints
   How many words will a quarter cover?
   How quick is your eyesight?
   A middling-good party
   A penny for your thoughts
   Quiz ball
   Red tape
   Relay poetics
   See-saw

Seven-league boots
Tell down
Tempus fugit
Trekking is tops
Truck lines
What's in a name? (CASEY—PEPPY)
Where am I?

Loans
*Lend me five
*"The pawn shop"
Local art gallery. BUGBEE—LIVE WIRE p44.
Local broadcast, by Grace Keith Samuelson. CASEY—PEPPY
p53-55.
*Local number ten. (9b, 4g) GODDARD—CHILDREN'S p61-72.
Locate your maxim. YOUNG—GAMES p12.
Lochinvar, by Sir Walter Scott. EISENBERG—FUN p137-
140.
Lochinvar Leadbetter. PRESTON—FUN p149-155.
The lodge goat. BUGBEE—LIVE WIRE p61.
Lodge stunts. *See* Club and lodge stunts
Lodge stunts for ladies. BUGBEE—LIVE WIRE p61-63.
*Logical advice, by Franklin Phelps. (2m) BRINGS—MAS-
TER p276-277.
*The logical guess, by Paul S. McCoy. (1m, 2f, announcer)
SNAPPY p127-133.
Logrolling. DEPEW p327.
London bridge. March music. GEISTER—NEW p14.
Long distance. DEPEW p57-59.
*Long live the King. (2m, 3f) HUBER—FOUR p96-99.
Long, long ago. PRESTON—FUN p155-160.
Longevity. *See* Old age

Longfellow, Henry Wadsworth
Quotation quiz for February
*The tables turned
Longman, Lucile
From Eve on down
Looie, by Robert N. McGregor. BREEZY p71.
*Look before you screech. (2m, 3f) McCLOY—HOLIDAY
p62-69.

Look! His trousers! (2) Brings—Master p380; Drummond
—Stunt Fun p53.
The loose that gaid the olden geggs. Eisenberg—Fun p58.
Loring, Selden M.
  *"And they got paid"
  *Ballyhoo
  *"Big business"
  *Colossal
  *"Eye trouble"
  *Fire!
  *Fish business
  *Next!
  *News
  *Number, please!
  *The old fight (Easy—Impr.)
  *Partners (Easy—Impr.)
  *The pay off
  *The third degree
  *You've got to be tough
Lost. Eisenberg—Fun p84-85.
*"Lost". (2m, boys) Provence—Vaud. p71-73.
Lost and found. (2) By Beatrice Plumb. Breezy p58-59;
      Huber—Giant p137-138.
*Lost and found. (2m, 2f) Easy—Blackouts p55-59.
Lost collar button. Funny p45-46.
*The lost pocket-book. (9 or more b, 5g) Bugbee—Lively
      p18-23.
The lost sheep. Eisenberg—Hand. p125-126.
*A lot of bunk. (2m) Kaser—Button p105-109.
  Love
    And the lamp went out
    The answer is "Yes"
    Bashful lover
    *The book agent
    *Cupid is speedy
    A cupid's tour of the world
    Great loves, by the Griddle Theatre group
    *A hit with papa
    How's this for romance?
    Love through the ages

Loyalty
  *Not for sale
  Loyalty test. HUBER—GIANT p125.
  Lub yo' nabors, by Willis N. Bugbee. BREEZY p85-87.
  Lucky circle. DEPEW p304.
*A lucky shot, by Raymond Higdon. (6m, 1f) "THAT
      GOOD" p23-27.
  Lucky spots. GEISTER—NEW p121.
  Lucky star. STAHL—AMAT. p100-103.
  Lucky words (spelling contest), #1,2. By Lettie C. Van
      Derveer. GITHENS p37-39.
*Lucy goes A.W.O.L. (14m) KASER—MERRY p58-68.
  Lullaby: Then and now. ABELL—STUNTS p66-68.
  Lumbering along. EISENBERG—HAND. p83.
Lunatics. *See* Insane
Luncheons
  Advertising favors
  Animal hunt (DEPEW)
  Are you from the country?
  Armistice, 1918
  Art contest
  Athletic meeting
  Attendance chart committee
  Attendance committee
  Attendance contest
  Attendance letters
  Attendance prize
  The babies
  The baby bottle
  Backward luncheon
  Backward program
  Badge place cards
  The bag relay
  Balancing egg on pencil
  Birthday greetings
  Blindfold boxing
  Breaking the China
  Carry on the song
  Changed names
  Charity luncheon

Chart committee report
Chinese auction
Christmas toys
Coaxing a member to remove his tie
The cow
A Dutch auction
Eating goldfish
Eating raw eggs
Empty pockets
Exchanging white elephants
Excuses for being late
Fake initiation
Folding chair race
From income tax report last year
Gigantic sneeze
Giving away an automobile
Giving out dimes
Greased pig
Hen club
Hidden animal crackers
How a person gets into Kiwanis
Hurly-burly
Identification by a nose
Ima Rotarian
Impromptu stunts
Information desired
Initiation for new members
The intelligence test (DEPEW)
Introducing members at other tables
Introducing motions
Introduction by tables
Jig-saw sentences
Kiddie car race
Kiwanis baseball game
Kiwanis court
Kiwanis ladies' night
K.K.K.
Last line contest
Letterfly
Mahatma Gandhi (DEPEW)

Matching them off
Meeting the train
*Musical eggs
Names in the bulletin
New book on psychology
Numbers
Oratorical contest
The ordeal
Over the slide
Passing the buck
Peanuts and milk bottles
Pie-eating contest (DEPEW)
Playing cards introduction
Presenting the boloney
Presidents' meeting
Prohibition in the home
Questionnaire
Removing a shirt
The report of the stunt committee
A resolution
Right and wrong reception
Rolling the wheelbarrow
A rooster race
Rotary friend X
Round table luncheon
Sees all—knows all
Self-introduction
Sense of hearing
Sense of sight
Sense of smell
Singing stunt
Slang (DEPEW)
Speaking from notes
A speaking marathon
Special recognition
Spelling bee
Spelling test
Staging a fight
The submarine club
Suckers

Suit case race
A talk on athletics
Talk on business or profession
Talk on hobbies
Talks on attendance
Talks on travel
Tall story club
Telegram from the district governor
Telegrams
Ten beans
Three men on chairs
A trick with cards
A trick with nuts
Tying them up
The ventriloquist (DEPEW)
Waiter fight
Waiter stunt
A walkout
Why Jack was late
Yardstick balance
The Yowell club
*The lying hunter. (1m, 1f) EISENBERG—HAND. p98-99.
Lyrics, Song
Song lyrics

*Mabel takes up history. (1b, 2g) STARR—JR. p26-33.
*Mabel's embarrassing moment. (3m, 4f) TOPOLKA p101-104.
McCoy, Paul S.
  *An apartment for rent
  *The logical guess
  *A sailor's technique
  *That's love
McGregor, Robert N.
  The battered cyclist
  Boomerang
  Checking up
  The door prize
  The ever-filled cuspidor
  Fresh fish (BREEZY)

Going to court
Grand prize
The great Higginson
How to eat goldfish
If I should return
Looie
Oh—Missus Smith!
Palmistry
The racing bug
Saint Richard
Silent speeches
Spring, beautiful spring
Watch our smoke!
X-Ray eyes
McMullen, J. C.
  *How horrible
  *The sick maid
  Was his face red!
McNeil, Beatrice H. and Edna C. Ammons
  The home town minstrel show
The maddening mandolin mystery. FERRIS p32-33.
*Madeline gets analyzed. (1m, 1f, glee club) STARR—JR.
  p88-92.
*Mademoiselle Tania. (2m, 1f) KELLEY p27-32.
Magazines
  *99 and 44/100% pure
Magic and magicians
  See also Tricks
  "The amateur magician"
  Another egg trick
  Asleep with the sheets
  Being generous
  A big mouth
  Black magic (BRINGS—MASTER)
  Bottled tea
  Brain-testing machine
  The cake in the hat
  The Chinese folder
  Cut the deck
  The dinosaur specialist

The disappearing dime
A dollar in a candle
Drinking five gallons of wine
Eating a package of cigarettes
Egg in a bag
The empty hatful
The fish bowl magician
The flying quarter
The giant sneeze (TARBELL—COMEDY)
Gloves de luxe
The hamagician
A handy mustache
Here, have another rope! The vanishing wife
*Hocus-pocus
Identifying articles blindfolded
Meat on Friday
Money from the air
A mysterious bird cage
The mystery bag
The mystery doll
Out for a walk
Passing a dime through a table
The peculiar Chinese
Plumes from a handkerchief
Presto, the Great
*The professor's magic
The quarter in the yarn ball
The rambling ring
Sawing a man in half
Seeing the winkle bird
Sevens always
*The shirt's off
Sleight of hand (FRICK—FALL)
The slippery penny
The spirit cabinet
Spirit reading
That elusive dime
'Tis here, 'tis gone
Trick and mystery games
A twenty cent trick

A useless clean-up
The vanishing spinach
The vanishing table
Want a hand?
*The watch on the Rhine
A watch trick
The weed in the eye
What shirt?
Magic animals. YOUNG—GAMES p29.
The magic bottle. DEPEW p354-355.
*The magic cabin. (4m, 2f, singers) STARR—JR. p20-24.
The magic mirror. WILLIAMS p14-15.
Magic numbers. GEISTER—NEW p85-86.
The magic pill. MACDONALD—CARNIVAL p21-26.
*The magic wand. (9b, 1g) BUGBEE—LIVELY p42-47.
*The magic word—Persia. (more than 8 char.) MILLER—
    STUNT p118-132.
Magicwriting. EISENBERG—HAND. p117-118.
The magical dog. TARBELL—COMEDY p26.
The magician. MACDONALD—CARNIVAL p41-47.
Magician act. BRINGS—MASTER p388.
A magician—hysterious—marvelous. FERRIS p30-32.
Mahatma Gandhi. (2) DEPEW p212; YOUNG—GAMES p26.
*The maid o' the mandolin. (2m, 2f) MILLER—STUNT
    p185-200.
*A maiden in distress. (2m, 1f, 2 voices) KELLEY p38-42.
*"The mail-order dragon". A Chinese extravaganza. (3m,
    1f) STAHL—IMPRO. p37-44.
Maisie goes to school. GODDARD—CHILDREN'S p6-8.
Major Blows' amateur hour, by Harry Githens. GITHENS
    p66.
*A major operation, by Marion Holbrook. (3m, 2f) SIX—
    NEW p5-11.
Majoress Bow-Wow's amateur hour, by Marion Ogden
    Snyder. CASEY—PEPPY p45-53.
"Make a note of it. (12m) HUBER—GIANT p42-48.
*"Make him talk". (4m) PROVENCE—FLASH p23-24.
Make them equal 17. DEPEW p365.
Make them equal 20. DEPEW p365.
Make-up. MALCOLM p5-7.

*Making the best better. (4m, 2f) ROGERS—PLAY p69-76.
Making three squares. EISENBERG—FUN p34.
Malachi Jimson's farewell sermon, by Willis N. Bugbee.
    BREEZY p82-85.
Male impersonations. *See* Impersonations; Men's night
*Male model. (1m, 3f) HUBER—ALL p39-43.
Mamma and baby relay. DEPEW p335.
Man. *See* Men
*A man arrives, by Anne Martens. (1m, 2f) QUICK—COM.
    p54-62.
*"Man of action". (1m, 3f) HUBER—THREE p51-52.
*A man of authority. (2m, 2b) PROVENCE—LIGHT p69-70.
*Man of courage. (2m, 2f) HUBER—FOUR p78-82.
*Man of many miens. (2m, 1f) HUBER—NO p17-23.
Man to man, by Arten Casey. BRINGS—MASTER p330-332.
*Man versus dog, by Arthur L. Kaser. (3m) BRINGS—MAS-
    TER p133-134.
The man who shops for his wife. FERRIS p15.
Man, wolf, gun. GEISTER—NEW p39-40.
Man's eternal quest for the good life. EISENBERG—HAND.
    p201-207.
Manager's chamber of horrors, by Harry Githens. GITHENS
    p40-43.
Manny-kins, by Beatrice M. Casey. CASEY—PEPPY p11-13.
Many a slip. HUBER—GIANT p131-132.
Marathons. *See* Contests
The march of the light brigade. HANLEY—STUNTS p35-36.
Marchant, Mrs. Lucy C.
    Ellis Island
    The President's dream
Marching
    See also Grand marches; Letters, formation of
    Circle stunt
    Counter marching
    Diagonal march
    Down the center by two's
    Double time
    Formation of letters (2)
    Grand march figures and folk dance
    Grand march stunt

Letter stunt
One right and one left
Opening and closing numbers
Pep squad stunts
Reception marches
Score stunt
Single file marching
Spiral marching
The straw vote
Wheel marching
Wooden soldiers
Marching through Georgia. BUGBEE—GOOFY p101-102.
"Maria Hayseed visits New York". FERRIS p17.
Marionettes. *See* Puppets
"Marital mishaps, by Arthur L. Kaser. (1m, 1f) BRINGS—
MASTER p241-246.
Marked men and women. HUBER—GIANT p124.
Markets and marketing. *See* Grocers and grocery stores
*"Markheim" (from the story by Robert Louis Stevenson).
(2m, 1f, voices) PROVENCE—EASY p7-17.
Marksmanship. CORMACK p36.
Marriage
See also Honeymoon; Husbands; Wives
*Advice aplenty
*Deserted
*Don't spill the salt (2)
*Love is blind
*Marital mishaps
*Matrimony bumps
*Mona's fit of temper
*Newlyweds (2) (BRINGS—MASTER, GEORGE—TEN)
*The penalty
*"The tie that binds"
*Too busy
*The treasurer's report
*A very good reason
*When David woke up
The marriage (?) license. BUGBEE—LIVE WIRE p45.
Mars
Citizens of Venus and Mars

The interstellar league
Mars views the earth. DEPEW p20-23.
Marshmallow race. DEPEW p334.
Martens, Anne
    *Doctor, come quick
    *A man arrives
    *She's a beauty
*Martha Biggers' pumpkin, by Willis N. Bugbee. (6m, 2f)
        JOLLY p62-68.
Martin, Estelle
    The birth of a nation
Marx brothers
    *"Marx time"
*"Marx time". (3m, 1f) STAHL—HEARTY p87-91.
Mary and the lam. RYAN p97.
*Mary Anne's mortgage. (2m, 2f) DEASON—SKIT p73-83.
*Mary had a little lamb, by Mabel Tuttle Craig. (2m, 3f)
        "THAT GOOD" p31-34.
*"The masher". (2m, 1f) HUBER—THREE p20-21.
*The master touch. (2m, 1f) STAHL—MORE p37-39.
Matchbox. GEISTER—NEW p92.
Matches
    Tricks and puzzles with matches
    Matching fingers. EISENBERG—FUN p37.
    Matching them off. DEPEW p242.
Mathematical
    Age and telephone number
    The apples
    Arranging and adding
    At what intervals?
    A billion
    Bottle and cork
    Boy on the train
    The camels
    Cannibals and missionaries
    Cats and rats
    Christmas savings
    Clock strokes
    Cost of apples
    Difference between 6 and half a dozen

Digit problem
Dirt in a hole
Figures never lie
Five on a side
Four nines equal one hundred
Frog in the well
The ghost of mathematics
Grandmother's problem
Group mathematics
Head and feet
How deep was the river?
How far could the bee fly?
How long is the fish?
How many cows?
How much change have you?
How much did he have?
How much greater?
How much is eight digits?
How old?
How to predict the answer
Hundred with 6 nines
Make them equal 17
Make them equal 20
New Year's resolution
Nursery rhyme riddle
Odd mathematics
100 head $100
Pigs in pens
A proved salary
Seven thirteens
Six on a side
Squirrel on a log
The strong man (DEPEW)
Subtraction
They total 80
Thought transmission cards—fake mind-reading stunt
Three times 7 equals 20
*Through with girls
Total 20
Ticks with figures

MORE p68-70.

The medicine show. EISENBERG—FUN p80-81.

Medicine shows

Dr. Killemquick's medicine show, or The friendly quack

Dr. Peppo's medicine show

Ye olde medicine show

Medieval

Count Twenty's revenge (2)

Medley. DEPEW p288.

Medley mixer. GEISTER—NEW p121.

"Mee-ow-ooooo". DRUMMOND—STUNT FUN p69-72.

Meet George and Martha Washington. JOHNSON—BAKER'S p97.

*Meet me at three-thirty. (2m, 2b) BARBEE p26-28.

"Meet me where the lanterns glow". FERRIS p73.

*Meet Mrs. Stuckopf. (3f) TAGGART—FIVE p31-35.

Meet the team. ABELL—PEP p61-63.

*Meeting an emergency. (4b, 4g) ROGERS—PLAYS p37-41.

*Meeting of the Better city campaign committee. (6f) KASER—TEN p23-31.

Meeting the train. DEPEW p199.

Melancholy twilight. KERR p71-75.

A meller dramatic evening at home, by M.Lue Perry. JOLLY p50-54.

A mellerdrammer, by Oscar L. Gustafson. THREE—STUNTS p3-4.

A melodrama sing. FERRIS p104-106.

Melodramas

*And the villain still pursued her

*And the willin still persueder

At home with the range

Bessie of Bar X ranch

Drama at KQZ

*The elopement (DRUMMOND—STUNT FUN)

*Enter the hero

"The farmer's daughter"

The fatal plunge

The fatal scream

*The fatal wedding

*Foiled again

*Foiled again or Saved by fate
For the land's sake (2)
*For the love of Larry
*The great bottleneck diamond or The villainous Shah of
    Shush
"Guaranteed: sixty thrills a minute"
Heaven protects the working girl
Hisses and kisses
*The horse race shall not ring today
*"In the nick of time" (DRUMMOND—STUNT)
It's her or the car
Let George do it
Lily of the alley (2)
Love knoweth no bounds, or Where is Joe?
*Love will win
*The maid o' the mandolin
*Mary Anne's mortgage
A mellerdrammer
*No, no, a thousand times, no! (2)
*"Now we'll play 'East Lynn'!"
Out of the storm, or Love will triumph
A pantomimed melodrama
*The persecuted maiden, or Curses! Foiled again, a syn-
    copated surge of dastardly doings
*Reverse English (TAGGART—MEN)
Rob 'em good
*Saved by the hero
*Saved in the nick of time
*Saved, or love's dilemma
Shakespearean hash (ROHRBOUGH)
*Ten barrooms in one night
*There's a sandburr in Gran'pa's stocking
*A thief in the house
*Tick tock
*Tragedy of the sea
*Uncle Tom's nabbin' or The effervescent evaporation
    of Eva
United by love
*Up from the depths or The rise of Tillie Tureen
*The villain still pursued her

Virtue triumphant
Melody mixer. PARTIES p13.
Memorial Day
  *The stars and stripes
Memorial Day (decorations). YOUNG—GAMES p108.
Memories. DEPEW p17-23.
*Memories. (2) (2m) HUBER—FOUR p69-73; By Earl
      J. Gilbert. (2m, 1f, announcer) SNAPPY p101-103.
Memories of the dog-show. WILLIAMS p37-39.
Memory
  *Absent-minded
  Can you tell me what is missing?
  *Forget-me-not!
  How's your memory
  Something has been disturbed
  *Stringing along
  *The thinkers
  What's this
*"Memory course". (3m) HUBER—THREE p60-62.
Memory test. DEFEW p336.
Men
  *All men are stupid
  *The master touch
  *The sewing club meets
  What it takes to make a man
Men are the best cooks. BRINGS—MASTER p366-367.
Men who have never been president. TARBELL—FUN p89-97.
Menagerie. CONNOR p9-10.
Mendicant. PRESTON—PANTOM. p256.
Men's night
  Courtship days
  Snap shots of busy men
Mental
  The bookworm
  Can you name the Presidents?
  Can you read this letter?
  Dividing the farm
  The fox, goose, and corn
  Gold or feathers?
  Hens and eggs

How old was Bill?
Human checkers
Hunter and squirrel
International catastrophe
The magic bottle
Magical terms
Orange trees in rows
Possibility
Strange animal
Too wise
Unlucky 1930
Water uphill
Which travels fastest?
Word mathematics
The mental clinic. BUGBEE—NUTTY p15-18.

Mental hospitals
*Not so crazy (2)
*The mental marvel, by LeRoy Stahl. (2) (3m) BRINGS—
    MASTER p119-120; STAHL—HEARTY p48-49.

Mental telepathy
Cy the psychiatrist
*Strained interlude
Thought waves
Mental telepathy. YOUNG—GAMES p36-37.
Mentality tests. BUGBEE—GOOFY p37-38.
MentTALL tests, by Mabel Tuttle Craig. BREEZY p41-45.
Menu for installation banquet. DEPEW p144-145.

Menus
"A feast of fun and frolic"
Kiwanis Ladies' night
Mephisto, the educated horse. CANOPY—HIGH p59-63.
*The merchant of Venice, by Arthur L. Kaser. (4m, 2f)
    SHANNON p43-55.
The mermaid. DRUMMOND—STUNT FUN p110.
The merry-go-round. (2) BUGBEE—GOOFY p78; LIVE WIRE
    p55.
Merry middy minstrels. FERRIS p122-123.
The merry wives of Windsor. BUGBEE—LIVE WIRE p73-74.
A message for you. HUBER—GIANT p152-153.

Messengers
 *"Fired"
*"Method in madness". (1m, 2f) PROVENCE—VAUD. p75-77.
Methusaleh. GEISTER—NEW p108.
Mexican bull fight. CONNOR p13-15.
Mexican prisoner. YOUNG—GAMES p26-27.
Mexicans
 *Shoot!
Miami, Florida
   The case of John Imbecile
Mice
 *Love's labor
A middling good party, by Gladys Lloyd. CASEY—PEPPY
   p 92-94.
The midnight fire alarm, by Charles E. Garrett. ROHRBOUGH
   p114-116.
The midnight ride. HUBER—PRACT p13-17.
*Midsummer night's ring, by A. L. Laufe. (1m, 1f) GITHENS
   p90-93.
The mighty hunter. BRINGS—MASTER p395.
The mighty Merlin. PRESTON—FUN p112-116.
Mile-tug-of-war. DRUMMOND—SPOT p73.
Military drills. *See* Drills
Military stunts. BUCHANAN p47,49-51.
Milk language. EISENBERG—FUN p76-78.
Milkmen
 *The lowly milkman
The milky way. (2) By Beatrice Plumb. BRINGS—MASTER
   p416; WILLIAMS p13-14.
Miller, Albert G.
 *Camera study
 *Don't stop us if you've heard these
 *Trouble in Paradise
Milligan, William
 *Deserted
 *Here comes the bride. (QUICK—COM.)
   There's one born every minute. (JOHNSON—EASY)
Millinery. *See* Hats and hat shops
Mills Sisters' quartette. BUGBEE—NUTTY p61.
*The mills that grind. (2m, 2f) HUBER p77-83.

Mind over matter. BUGBEE—NUTTY p11.

Mind-reading. *See* Mental telepathy.

Mind reading. (2) EISENBERG—FUN p35; YOUNG—GAMES p17-18.

Mind reading deluxe. TARBELL—CRAZY p41-47.

The mind reading machine. BUGBEE—LIVE WIRE p15-16.

Minding the house. GODDARD—CHILDREN'S p21-23.

The miniature golf course. MACDONALD—CARNIVAL p77.

*A minister's mistake. (1m, 2f) IRISH—CATCHY p7-10.

Ministers
  *And so the new minister arrives
  Converts
  *A man arrives
  *"Such a hot day"

Minnesota. FRICK—SUMMER p60-61.

Minnis, Jack
  King for a day

Minstrel. LYONS p149-157.

*Minstrel maids. (14g) PRESTON p91-94.

The minstrel show. MACDONALD—CARNIVAL p28-32.

Minstrels
  Advertising minstrels
  Alabama attaboy minstrels
  Athletic minstrels
  Baseball minstrels
  Black and white minstrels
  Buttoning up the vest
  Camp and scamp minstrels
  Christmas belle minstrels
  The clown minstrels (2)
  College minstrels
  Colonial minstrels
  Community house minstrels
  Eating the goldfish
  A five-minute minstrel show
  Flower market minstrels
  The gay nineties minstrels
  *The G.I. minstrels
  The Gossip Hollow ladies' minstrels
  Hallowe'en minstrels

Hard times minstrels
High time minstrels
*Hobo minstrels
The human fire department
Kitchen orchestra, and semi-minstrel show
Merry middy minstrels
The missing finger
Newspaper minstrels
*The old maid minstrelettes
One among the many
"The pocket-size minstrel"
Popular garden pets
Popularity minstrels
A powerful blow
River boat minstrels
Rural minstrels
St. Patrick minstrels
School day minstrels
*School daze minstrels
Sportlight minstrels
Summer (girl) minstrels
The tea room minstrelettes
*A ten-minute whiteface minstrel show
Uncle Sam's singing army
An up-to-date shell game
*"Valley View minstrelettes"
The watch fob minstrels
What shirt?
Whiteface minstrels
Ye olde medicine show
The mirror. EISENBERG—FUN p116.
Miscellaneous contests. KEMMERER—GAMES p55-66.
Miscellaneous songs. CORMACK p91-92.
*Miser's last request. (2m) PARTIES p52.
Misers
Old man Blake
Misfortune. PRESTON—PANTOM. p247-249.
*Misinformed. (1, 2f) DRUMMOND—THREE p83-85.
*Miss Information, please. (4m, 3f) HUBER—GIANT p49-55.

*Miss Jones' millinery opening. (2m, 5f) BUGBEE—LIVELY
   p88-93.
Miss Kate Pennoyer. ROHRBOUGH p91.
Miss Mehitable. BUGBEE—LIVE WIRE p29.
Miss Popular. BRIDGE p19-20.
"Miss Swatt-the-fly; an ardent reformer". FERRIS p18.
The missing false teeth. SHELDON p87-89.
The missing finger. TARBELL—CRAZY p21-23.
Missing letters. YOUNG—GAMES p63.
Missing link are morons. YOUNG—GAMES p16.
Missing syllables. YOUNG—GAMES p49-50.
Missing the hazards. DRUMMOND—STUNT FUN p105.
The missionary and the cannibals, a miniature operetta,
   by Willis N. Bugbee. (4) BREEZY p20-24.
Missions
  *Dangerous water
   The missionary and the cannibals
  *We want your business
Mixed props. EISENBERG—HAND. p120-121.
"Mixed voices". DRUMMOND—STUNT p85.
Mixers
   Advertisers
   Badge place cards
   Blindfolded handshakers
   Celebrities (GEISTER—NEW)
   Cooperative introductions
   Double circle
   Double scrambled names
   Doubtful prizes
   Dress-up mixer
   Exchange
   Finding associates with a song
   Giving out dimes
   Hidden letters
   Hidden personalities
   Initial words
   Introduction by tables
   Methuselah
   Numbers
   Peanut hunt

Receiving line
Scrambled names
Self-introduction (3)
Sign language
Ten beans
Who is my neighbor?
Mixers, Dance
Assembly
Balloon dances
Blind dating
Escape
Hearts and spades
Heyday
Hidden prizes
Lucky spots
Medley mixer
Mixers for extras
Number dance
Old favorites
Skaters
Suffragettes
Mixers, Musical
As you were! March music
Assembly
Booby. March music
Bridges
Captain Jinks
Caravan
Chair scramble. March music
Couple Virginia Reel
Daisy
Glowworm
Grand march medley. March music
Grand march mixers. March music
The grapevine
Green sleeves
Happy landings. March music
Hinky dinky parlez vouse
I want to be happy
The lambeth walk

Little man in a fix
London bridge. March music
Low bridge. March music
The modern Jerusalem. March music
Mountain march
Number mixer. March music
The Paul Jones
Please porridge hot
Popularity
Snail. March music
Tally circles
Tipperary
Touch and go. March music
We won't go home until morning
Mixers for extras. GEISTER—NEW p122.
Mock assembly. FRICK—SUMMER p65-66.
Mock debates. *See* Debates
Mock debates. BUGBEE—LIVE WIRE p27-28.
Mock election. BUGBEE—LIVE WIRE p28.
Mock faculty meeting. ABELL—PEP p126.
A mock football game. ABELL—PEP p124-125.
A mock indoor field meet. BRIDGE p18-19.
Mock marriage in rhyme, by Esther Phelps-Jones.
    JOHNSON—EASY p68-72.
A mock trial. (3) BRIDGE p28-29; CHAPLIN p85-88;
    FRICK—SUMMER p65.
Mock trials
  Burlesque trial
  The case of John Imbecile
  *Coon Creek court cases
  *The deserted wife comes back
  *$500 award
  *In Judge Hashover's court
  *Judge Hoptoad's court
  *"Justice á la rime"
  The Kiwanis court
  *Lucy goes A.W.O.L.
  *Martha Biggers' pumpkin
  *Monday morning in Maloney's court
  *Monkey business

Mulligan's pig
*Never kick a man's shin
*Oswald Oozelpopper, hoss thief
*Somewhat divorcified
Sued for non-support
*Trial for the murder of Nellie Gray
*A welcome entrance
*Who stole the world?
Mock trials. ENTERTAIN—STUNTS p3-4.
Mock weddings
*The elopement (SHANNON)
Here comes the groom
Impromptu wedding
*In the nick of time (KASER—MERRY)
*The knot is tied
*Love, honor and obey
Mock marriage in rhyme
Quaker wedding
*"The substitute bride"
*There's going to be a wedding
*Wedding bells and belles
*Wedding bells for Hepsidee
Wedding of Augustus Peabean and Perlina Eggplant
Womanless wedding (2)
Models (mannequins). *See* Fashion
Models, Artists'
The artists's model
Modern birds' nests
Modern black magic. GEISTER—NEW p82-83.
Modern efficiency. EISENBERG—FUN p29-32.
The modern Jerusalem. March music. GEISTER—NEW
p19-20.
Modern jokes—sidewalk conversation. LYONS p7-19.
A modern romance, or Red Riding Hood in three parts,
by Mable Tuttle Craig. "THAT GOOD" p27-30.
Modern tales from Shakespeare, by Harry Githens.
GITHENS p43-45.
Modern transportation, by Vance Clifford. BRINGS—MAS-
ter p407.
A modern wedding. EASY—ENTERTAIN p23-30.

Hats
Her first voice lesson
Higher education
The hostess spoke French
How to build a dog house
I have written a play, which is explained by the writer
I just love paintings
I lost my mummy
I tell jokes
I'll call the doctor
I'm going to be an actress
Income tax advice
Jiminy Crickets!
Johnny learns about etiquette
The joy of winter sports
Katie goes to the zoo
Keeping the wolf away
Larnin' the trombone
Late again (2)
Maisie goes to school
Malachi Jimson's farewell sermon
Me and Smitty
Meat
Men are the best cooks
Minding the house
Mrs. Buzzy, news dispenser
The murder of Jabel Jenkins
Nobody wants me
Oh! To be an actoress!
The optimistic road knight (2)
Parson Highbrow on wickedness
Pete, the postman
Poor me is married
Portrait of a man thinking aloud
Prince Arthur
The princess
The purple pen
Ramble on
Sally in the city
Science of today

Sister's beau
Soup
Stringing them
Summer camp
The tantalizing tune
The treasurer's report
The tune the salesman played (JOHNSON—EASY)
Uncle George
The vacuum virtuoso
Vote for me (3)
Wandering Willie Willie
When a sleuth sleuths
When Johnny practices
Where's Gran-paw?
Working on the dry squad
Writin' home
Yeah!
Your future is at stake

Monroe, Elbert Henry
   *Three birthdays
*The monster. (2) (1m, 2f) GEORGE—TWELVE p8-10; (2m,
   2f) PROVENCE—KNOCKOUT p6-8.
Monster. PARTIES p52.

Months (of the year)
   See also names of months, names of holidays
   The calendar (JOHNSON—BAKER'S)
   Father Time's art gallery
   Who am I? New Year's entertainment (JOHNSON—
      BAKER'S)
The months of the year. CROWLEY p80-88.
"Moods of the mode". FERRIS p81.
The moon maiden. EISENBERG—HAND. p222-225.
*The moon maiden—China. (more than 6 char.) MILLER—
   STUNT p112-117.
*Moonrise Island. (4m, 5g, extras) PRESTON—FUN p62-68.
Moore, H. Grady
   Lavender, lace, and old clothes
Moore, Judge John L.
   King for a day

Mothers
*Bad boy
*Herbert's hurt
*His sweetheart
Our Father
*Triangle (EASY—IMPR.)
* Vacation
*What was that?
Whistler's farewell to his mother
Mothers-in-law
*Goodbye, Mother
*That's different
Moths and the flame, by Grace Keith Samuelson.
    CASEY—PEPPY p56-57.
The motion picture. BRIDGE p34.
Motion pictures. *See* Moving pictures
Motor trouble. (2) DRUMMOND—STUNT FUN p53-54;
    BRINGS—MASTER p381.
*Mountain magic, by Mel Tyler and Marriott Wilson. (2m,
    1f) EASY—SKITS p42-47.
Mountain march. GEISTER—NEW p33-34.
Mountaineers. *See* Dialect, Mountaineer; Hillbillies
Mouthophonic phonograph. CANOPY—HIGH p75.
*Movie camera pageant. (6m, 5f) ROGERS—PLAYS p10-21.
A movie fade-out. WILLIAMS p21-22.
The movie mystery, by Charles F. Wells. JOHNSON—EASY
    p65.
Movie stars. YOUNG—GAMES p63-64.
Movies. (2) FERRIS p49; FRICK—SUMMER p61-63.
Moving coins. DEPEW p363.
Moving pictures
    See also Actors and actresses; Quizzes—Moving pictures
    As we see the movies (2)
    At the movies (3)
    Bessie of Bar X ranch
    *Braves, arise!
    *"The Cooper special"
    *Don't stop us if you've heard these
    *"Goldbaum at Waterloo"
    Hasty Harry (3)

*Here comes the bride (QUICK—COM.)
*"A Hollywood romance"
*In a cinema
*Let's go to the movies
*The pay off
Screen stars
Screen test game
*Success story (QUICK)
This is a movie
*Uncle Cy at the talkies
Your screen test
Moving pictures. MACDONALD—CARNIVAL p60-61.
Mr. and Mrs. ("Reuben and Rachel") LLOYD p40-42.
*Mr. and Mrs. Newberry, by Arthur L. Kaser. (1m, 1f)
    BRINGS—MASTER p212-224.
*Mr. Chubb's housekeeping trials. (3b, 3g) BUGBEE—
    LIVELY p7-11.
Mr. Totten takes a rest. PRESTON—FUN p134-137.
Mrs. Buzzy, news dispenser, by Arthur L. Kaser. BRINGS—
    MASTER p353-354.
*Mrs. Clarke wins beat in Congress, by Norman L. Zeno,
    Jr. (2m, 2f) MILLER—BROADWAY p83-87.
*Mrs. Murphy isn't home, by Wilmer Baffle. (3f) QUICK—
    COM. p70-74.
Mrs. Santa Claus' reception. MILLER—LANDS p189-198.
Muddled up history. YOUNG—GAMES p65-66.
The mule he is a funny sight. DEPEW p284-285.
A mule named Joe and the circus show. VAN DERVEER—
    ANY p57-59.
Mulligan's pig (mock trial). BUGBEE—LIVE WIRE p90-94.
Mumbo jumbo. HUBER—GIANT p132-133.
Murder
    *Carefully yours
Murder. DEPEW p302.
The murder of Jabel Jenkins. BUGBEE—CATCHY p49-51.
Murder on the High C., by Beatrice M. Casey. CASEY—
    PEPPY p26-27.
Murder will outsky. EASY—ENTERTAIN p51-54.
*"The muscle dancer". (1m, 1f) HUBER—THREE p15-16.
The museum. CANOPY—HIGH p51-53.

Museum of World War II relics. MACDONALD—CARNIVAL
    p75-76.
The music box revue. CANOPY—HIGH p57.
Music department
    We always stress harmony—The Music department
*Music hath charms. (6m) HUBER p62-72.
Music quiz. GEISTER—NEW p95.
Musical
    See also Ballads; Games, Musical; Mixers, Musical;
        Orchestras; Parodies; Piano; Quartets; Quizzes—
        Musical; Singing; Song titles; Songs; Tableaux, Singing;
        Trios; etc.
    Bell backs
    *A-courting we will go
    *Aladdin and the vamp
    All's well that ends swell
    America first
    *Around in the world in bed
    "At the country club
    *At the music counter
    *Audition
    Baby Lon
    "Balloons! Balloons! Who said Balloons?"
    "Bubble-blowers"
    A café chantant, "Pop" concert, club cabaret
    Canoe song
    *Christmas carols
    *Christmas high jinks
    *Cindy swings it
    Clap your hands
    Clash and clatter band
    The clown band
    "College days"
    The comb orchestra
    Community house minstrels
    Culinary symphony
    Dance of death
    Doing a folk festival
    Double quartet
    Echo answers

The kitchen band (2)
Kitchen cabinet orchestra
Kitchen orchestra (3)
Kitchen orchestra, and semi-minstrel show
The kitchen symphony (2)
Larnin' the trombone
Living pictures (DEPEW)
Lochinvar Leadbetter
Lost collar button
Lullaby: Then and now
*Mabel's embarrassing moment
The maddening mandolin mystery
Major Blows' amateur hour
Man's eternal quest for a good life
Melancholy twilight
Memories
Miss Kate Pennoyer
A modern wedding
Mother Goose grand opera (2)
Mother Goose tableaux
A mule named Joe and the circus show
Murder on the High C
Murder will outsky
Musical Jack-in-the-box
Nellie Gray
Oh, Hamlet, Hamlet
Oh, my darling Clementine
The old gray mare (PARTIES)
Old man river
Old time records
*The old village school
*On the good ship Moonbeam
One finger keeps moving
Opening chorus
The opera
*"Opera"
*Opera opens
Operatic advertisements (EISENBERG—FUN)
Operatic movie
Orchestra

An orchestra without note
Organ grinder man
*Oshkosh land
"Over the hills and far away"
Parade of the stars
Passing the balloon
Past presidents' chorus
Piano duet
Pickaninny chorus
The Pied Piper of Hamelin
Pigmy orchestra
Pippa's song
Playing a one-string instrument
*Powah of music
*The professor's magic
Put it to music
*Pygmalion and Galatea
Queer quartets
Report to the Board
"The rhythm band travesty"
Romantic notes
*School days (CHAPLIN)
"See-saw"
Sharps and flats
Skaters of skill and fame
Solo
A soloist so low
Some musical settings
Speeding up the housework
*Spring revels
*Stars of the gay nineties
The stars, the night, the moon
Start early to do this
Styles
"Summer resort specialties"—"Those alluring girls"—
    "On the board walk"
Sweethearts of mine
"Swing high—swing low"
*Swing low, sweet Juliet
"Take me out to the ball game"

The tantalizing tune
*"Television'"
"Tennis teasers—love all"!
*Thankgiving Day
That last rose of summer
There were three maids of Lee
Tony and his monk
Topsy turvy concerts (2)
A tribute to music
The tune the salesman played (2)
*Tunetown gossip or Carol entertains the musical club
Tuning in on the past
Up and down the scale
U.R. next
Victrola musical
*"The village band rehearses"
The vintage of 1880
*Welcome, students
*What price carelessness?
When Johnny practices (2)
When you're right, you're wrong
While the organ peeled
*Who wrote it? (Topolka)
Womanless wedding (DEPEW)
The wonder cornet
Wynken, Blynken and Nod
You can't go to heaven
You can't stay away from me
You-uns and we-uns got religion
Musical answers. SHELDON p49-54.
A musical date. ABELL—PEP p96-97.
*"Musical dreams". (any no. of f.) DRUMMOND—FUNNY
    p66-69.
*Musical eggs. (6m) KASER—TOP p29-42.
Musical hungarian goulash. FERRIS p24-25.
Musical jack-in-the-box. PARTIES p11.
The musical kitchen. EISENBERG—FUN p191.
Musical mystery, by Beatrice Plumb. BRINGS—MASTER
    p423.
Musical neighbors. JOHNSON—BAKER's p93.

Musical object hunt. DEPEW p317.
A musical quiz. SHELDON—GIANT QUIZ p46-51
Musical specialties. CONNOR p40.
Musical terms. DEPEW p359.
A musical voyage. FERRIS p103-104.
The musical wand. YOUNG—GAMES p10.
Mute replying. YOUNG—GAMES p55.
Mutes. See Deaf mutes
My Bennie. LLOYD p26-27.
My Bennie is out on the gold links. DEPEW p271.
*"My book". (4f) MALCOLM p40-45.
*"My dear!" (3g) BARBEE p16-18.
My favorite object. GEISTER—NEW p64-65.
My gal Sal. EISENBERG—FUN p68-69.
My garden is lovely. YOUNG—GAMES p59.
My hat. EISENBERG—FUN p96.
*"My kingdom for an aspirin. (5m, 5f) KASER—ACTS p7-19.
"My little grey home in the West". FERRIS p106.
"My magazine cover girl"—"My lady's
    trousseau"—"Off to college". FERRIS p81.
"My old Kentucky Home". RYAN p94.
My pet parrot. CROWLEY p22-23.
"My rainbow dream". FERRIS p71-72.
My wandering boy. HUBER—GIANT p146-147.
My wife is into my pockets. LLOYD p54-57.
Mysteries
    See also Murder; Quizzes—Mystery
    *Blood red roses
    *The blood-stained bread knife
    *Body, body, who's got the body?
    *Bus ride
    *Captain Paul
    The chartreuse murder case
    *Diamond ring
    *The fateful bargain
    *Glass of poison
    *The great thud and blunder murder case
    *Green hat and yellow feather
    *No more murders
    The Schlitz murder case

*The spirit of Montague Manor
*Twelve skulls mean death
A mysterious bird cage. TARBELL—COMEDY p73-81.
Mysterious signs. HUBER—GIANT p152.
The mystery bag. DRUMMOND—STUNT p37.
"Mystery" contest, by Beatrice Plumb. "THAT GOOD" p44-45.
The mystery doll. DRUMMOND—STUNT p32-34.
*The mystery of the bath-tub. (2m, 1f, 1b, 1g) BARBEE—
GOOFY p52-55.
*Mystery of the green room. (3m, 1f) KAUFMAN—HIGHLOW-
BROW p75-86.
Mystic circle. DEPEW p302-303.
Mysto magic. JOHNSON—BAKER'S p95-96.
*Mythical medicine. (1m, 3f) HUBER—VAUD. p93-100.

Nail driving. DEPEW p316.
The name of your future wife. EISENBERG—FUN p42.
Name relay. FRICK—SUMMER p82.

Names
*A Christmas surprise
Greek letter societies
*A matter of names
Synthetic celebrities
What am I?
What's in a name? (2)
*What's in a name? (2)
Who am I? (FRICK—FALL)
Names. YOUNG—GAMES p57-58.
Names for social clubs or fraternities. CORMACK p7.
Names in the bulletin. DEPEW p243.
Names of states. DEPEW p336.
Napkin bite. EISENBERG—FUN p40.

Napoleon Bonaparte
*"Scrambled dates"
Napoleon's farewell to his grandmother. DEPEW p126.
"The nation's sweetheart in review". FERRIS p84.
National parks. *See* Parks, National

Nature
   See also Animals; Flowers; Gardens and gardening; etc.
   "A student of nature"
   *What we'd like to be
*Nature cure, by LeRoy Stahl. (2m) BRINGS—MASTER p182-183.
   Nature hikes. FRICK—SUMMER p9.
*Naughty nudist, by Robert L. Sherman. (1m, 1f, announcer) SNAPPY p147-150.
   Navy. *See* Sailors; U.S.—Armed Forces
*Navy Day. (3b, 3g) BARBEE p28-29.
*A near tragedy. (2m, 1f) DRUMMOND—THREE p71-73.
   " 'Neath the Italian Moon". FERRIS p74.
*Needle, thread and jabber, a sewing circle entertainment. (10f) KASER—TEN p55.
Negroes
   See also Dialect, Negro; Revivals, Negro
   Colored kin
   *"Crossed wires"
   Down on de old plantation
   "Kentucky babe"
   "Old Black Joe"
   Wha' dat wattahmilyun gone?
   You-uns and we-uns got religion
Neighborly songs, by Beatrice Plumb. CASEY—PEPPY p79-80.
Neighbors
   *A back-yard build-up
   *Busy business
   *An even exchange
   "Howdy neighbor" social
   Know your neighbor
   More neighborly songs
   *Mrs. Murphy isn't home
   Neighborly songs
   *New neighbors
   What is your neighbor like?
Nellie Gray, by Marie Irish. BUGBEE—LIVE WIRE p79-80.
Neptune's court. BUGBEE—NUTTY p72-74.
*Nerve on display. (3m, 1f) McCOY—SIXTEEN p26-33.

*The nervous father. (3m, 1f) EISENBERG—HAND. p167-168.
Never fail breath tester. BUGBEE—LIVE WIRE p11-12.
*Never kick a man's shin. (7m) KASER—HALF p41-52.
"Never-mind-the-weather-girls"—"My girl-in-sunshine
   or in rain". FERRIS. p82.
New book on psychology. DEPEW p176-177.
New deal geography. YOUNG—GAMES p67.
The new Easter bonnet. by Grace Keith Samuelson.
   "THAT GOOD" p52-53.
*"The new invention". (1m, 2f) HUBER—THREE p30-31.
*The new maid. (2f) KASER—SURE p66-69.
*New neighbors. (5f) HUBER—NO SCENE p31-40.
*The new secretary. (4m) HUBER—ARENA p83-88.

New Year's Day
   Even as you and I
   Father Time reviews the accomplishments of the past
      presidents
   Father Time's visit
   Fun leaves
   Now and then program
   *Resolutions for two
   Sleuthing customs
   Who am I? New Year's entertainment
New Year's eve (decorations). YOUNG—GAMES p102-103.
New Year's (games and stunts). KEMMERER—GAMES p9-11.
New Year's resolution. DEPEW p354.

New York City
   *What's going on?
The New York visitor. EISENBERG—HAND. p92.
Newell, Prof. H. A.
   Mars views the earth

Newlyweds. *See* Bridegrooms; Brides; Moneymoon; etc.
*Newlyweds. (3) By Charles George. (2m, 1f) BRINGS—
      MASTER p249-253; (2m, 1f) DRUMMOND—THREE
      p33-36; (1m, 2f) GEORGE—TEN p19-23.
*"News, by Selden M. Loring. (5m, 1f) QUICK p112-122.

News commentators
   The telenews machine
News of the war. BUGBEE—LIVELY p72-73.

Newsboys
*Some of them begin young
The newsboy's debt, by H. R. Hudson. BAKER'S—GAY
    p30-31.
Newspaper advertisement relay. DEPEW p315-316.
Newspaper columnists
*"The columnist"
"The colyumist"
"Household hints by Aunt Matilda"
Newspaper editors
*The editor's busy day
*News
The newspaper idea. FERRIS p138-141.
A newspaper medley. BUGBEE—LIVE WIRE p33-34.
Newspaper minstrels. FERRIS p120.
*Newspaper nightmare. (4m, 3f) HUBER—No p63-69.
Newspaper office. EISENBERG—FUN p83-84.
Newspaper relay. DEPEW p316.
Newspapers
    See also Newsboys; Reporters; School papers; etc.
    The animated newspaper
    Big mystery
    *The evening paper
    *The mystery of the bath-tub
    *News
    Scooping the scoop
*Next! By Selden M. Loring. (3m, 2f) EASY—IMPR. p84-88.
Niagara Falls. EISENBERG—HAND. p91-92.
The nickel and the penny. GEISTER—NEW p86-87,90.
*Nice cream. (2m, 2f) HUBER—FOUR p100-103.
*Night, by Len D. Hollister. (2m, announcer) SNAPPY p30-33.
*The night before the morning after Christmas eve, by Wal-
    ter F. Kerr. (2m, 2b) SNAPPY p62-69.
Night club. MACDONALD—CARNIVAL p82-83.
Night clubs
    *At your service
    *Swank night
    Tee Tivoli night club
*Night court. (7m) TAGGART—MEN p59-67.
"Night golf". HUBER—EASY p61-63.

North America, South America and Europe. YOUNG—
GAMES p68-69.

The north pole. CORMACK p35.

Northboro, Southboro. DEPEW p274.

Norwegian
*Fun from Norway

Nose and potato race. DEPEW p316.

"Noses". DRUMMOND—STUNT p86.

Nosey old Lady O'Grady, by Lois M. Lawrence. ROHR-
BOUGH p171-172.

*Not for credit, by Jean Provence. (2) (2m, extras)
BRINGS—MASTER p53-55; (3) PROVENCE—FLASH p60-
62.

*Not for sale. (4f) HUBER—SIX p83-90.

*"Not qualified". (3) PROVENCE—VAUD. p21-23.

*Not so crazy, by Jean Provence. (2) (3m) BRINGS—MAS-
TET p191-192; PROVENCE—LIGHT p49-51.

Not today, Madame. SULLIVAN—MORE p26-29.

*Not wanted. (7m) TOPOLKA p9-18.

*Nothin' but work. (2m) KENT—ONE p92-97.

A novel introduction. BUGBEE—GOOFY p78.

Novelty quartette. BRINGS—MASTER p389.

A novelty telephone stunt. TARBELL—CHALK STUNTS
p91-94.

Now and then program, by Beatrice Plumb. "THAT GOOD"
p54-58.

*"Now we'll play 'East Lynn'!" (3m, 2f) CASEY p61-68.

The noy and the buts. EISENBERG—FUN p58.

The nudist. DRUMMOND—STUNT FUN p14.

Nudists
*Naughty nudist

Number dance. GEISTER—NEW p121-122.

Number men. CROWLEY p18-22.

Number mixer. March music. GEISTER—NEW p16-17.

*Number, please! By Selden M. Loring. (4m, 2f) EASY—
IMPR. p112-116.

Number race. GEISTER—NEW p52.

Number spin. YOUNG—GAMES p11-12.

Numbers. DEPEW p215.

*The numbers game. (5m, 5f, extras) PRESTON—FUN p38-51.

Nurse girls in the park. BRINGS—MASTER p396.

The nursery quartette. DRUMMOND—SPOT p57-58.

Nursery rhyme riddle. DEPEW p366.

Nursery rhymes. *See* Mother Goose

Nursery rhymes. (2) DEPEW p304; FRICK—SUMMER p60.

Nursery rhymes (for adults). CONNOR p60-62.

Nurses
*At the day nursery
*Father and child doing well
The fixit clinic
*How the Red Cross began
*Hurry, doctor (2)
There's one born every minute
*There's one born every minute

Nuts to you, by Alta Toepp. CASEY—PEPPY p104.

O, no, John. PARTIES p26.

*The obedient princess, by Anna Penland. (2-5m, 2-5f) ROHRBOUGH p154-161.

Object hunt. DEPEW p316-317.

O'Brien, Stanley
The love of beauty

Observations. YOUNG—GAMES p174.

Occult
See also Ghosts
*'Arry and 'Arriet
A fake seance
*"The seance"
*The spirit calls
*Spirits on parade

Oculists *See also* Eye
*"Eye trouble"

Odd mathematics. TARBELL—COMEDY p23-25.

Of thee I sing, by Beatrice Plumb. "THAT GOOD" p44.

Off for Alabam'. CANOPY—HIGH p83-85.

Off key. GEISTER—NEW p74.

Off to the races. PRESTON—FUN p105-109.

*Off with their heads! (5b, teacher) BARBEE p18-21.

The ogre of Rashamon, by Catherin Miller Balm. (2)
EISENBERG—HAND. p214-217; MILLER—STUNT
p174-178.

*Oh, Doctor! By Jean Provence. (3) (2m) BRINGS—MASTER
p160-161; (5m) BRINGS—MASTER p165-169; (5m)
PROVENCE—LIGHT p73-74.

Oh, Hamlet, Hamlet. FUNNY p40-45.

*"Oh, marry me". (2m, 2f) DRUMMOND—STUNT p6-10.

*Oh! Miss Dinah. (1m, 1f) "THAT GOOD" p70-72.

Oh—Missus Smith! By Robert N. McGregor. BREEZY p72.

Oh, my darling Clementine. EISENBERG—FUN p196-199.

Oh! To be an actoress! KASER—SURE p102-105.

*Oh, waitress! (3m, 2f) MIKSCH—CURTAIN p57-71.

"Oh, yeah!" By Richard Judd. CASEY—PEPPY p58-60.

O'Hanlon, Edwin
*Ye olde junke shoppe

Old age
How to live long
*One hundred years old
*Taking Maw's advice
*That tired feeling

*"The old and the new". (1m, 1f, 1b) HUBER—THREE
p11-12.

The old bear. CROWLEY p22,24,26.

"Old Black Joe". JOHNSON—BAKER'S p62.

Old bottles. CROWLEY p49,55.

Old clothes antics. DEPEW p327.

Old curiosity shop. CONNOR p11-12.

The old family album. CANOPY—HIGH p99-102,104.

The old family all-bum. TARBELL—FUN p96-106.

An old-fashioned courtship. ENTERTAIN—STUNTS p2-3.

Old-fashioned courtship. PARTIES p22-23.

"An old-fashioned garden"—"Laces and graces"—
"The charmers of long ago and today". FERRIS p70-71.

*The old-fashioned girl. (5f) MALCOLM p19-22.

Old-fashioned literary society. EISENBERG—HAND. p43.

Old favorites. GEISTER—NEW p117-118.

*The old fight. (3) By Selden M. Loring. (8m) EASY—
  IMPR. p30-37; (5m, 1f) HUBER—FOUR p143-147;
  (2m, 2f, 1b, 1g) HUBER—NO SCENE p91-98.
The old flivver ride. DRUMMOND—STUNT FUN p88-89.
*Old fogey. (3m, 2f) HUBER p26-35.
The old gray mare. (2) By Cressy M. Weaver. CASEY—
  PEPPY p63; PARTIES p32.
"The old home town". FERRIS p43.
Old King Cole. (2) EISENBERG—FUN p199-200; PRESTON—
  PANTOM. p198-204.
Old MacDonald's farm, by Harry Githens. GITHENS p66.
*The old maid minstrelettes. (6f) KASER—TOP p43-50.
The old maid's drill, by Walter Ben Hare. SHANNON p74-75.
*The old maid's secret. (3f) BUGBEE—LIVE WIRE p38-39.
Old man Blake. HUBER—PRACT. p18-22.
*Old man river. EASY—ENTERTAIN p67-69.
*The old one room school. (1f, 6g) KENT—ONE p37-46.
*"Old sayings". (2m, 1f) GEORGE—TWELVE p34-38.
The old stage queen. BAKER'S—GAY p38.
Old stuff. WILLIAMS p40-41.
Old time records. FUNNY p6-8.
*The old village school. (4m, 5f) SHELDON p5-19.
The old woman in the wood. FRICK—SUMMER p26-31.
The old woman who lived in a shoe, by Harry Githens.
  GITHENS p71-72.
Olympics
  Burlesque Olympics
On a busy street corner, by Louise Iwan. ROHRBOUGH
  p99-100.
On the board walk. BUGBEE—LIVE WIRE p41.
*On the campground. (4b) BUGBEE—LIVELY p69-72.
*On the good ship Moonbeam. (11m, 2f) KASER—ACTS
  p20-27.
On the Isle of Bombalay (a miniature operetta), by
  Arthur L. Kaser. JOLLY p71-74.
On the line, by Beatrice Plumb. BREEZY p61-62.
*On with the dance. (4b, 4g) BARBEE p13-14.
On with the dance. LEVIS—TEN p37-41.
Once over, lightly. HUBER—GIANT p153-154.
*One a penny, two a penny. (3f) SIX—MORE p17-21.

One among the many. TARBELL—CRAZY p27-29.
*One Arabian night was stunt night: The secret of success.
(7m, 1f) MILLER—LANDS p55-63.
*One conclusion, by Jean Provence. (2m) BRINGS—MASTER
p162-163; PROVENCE—LIGHT p89-90.
One-eyed threading-the-needle contest. DEPEW p305.
One finger keeps moving. DEPEW p260-261.
*"One hundred and forty-four davenports". A study in
purple mystery. (3m, 1f) STAHL—IMPRO. p29-35.
100 conundrums. DEPEW p369-374.
100 head $100. DEPEW p343.
*One hundred years old, by Arthur L. Kaser. (2) BRINGS—
MASTER p271.
The 105-pound bullfrog. BUCHANAN p44-46.
One line stunt. BUCHANAN p47-48.
One man stunts. BRINGS—MASTER p378-388.
*One man's word. (3m, 1f) HUBER—ARENA p5-11.
*One more question. (3m) PROVENCE—LIGHT p77-79.
One only. YOUNG—GAMES p76.
One right and one left. FRICK—FALL p29.
One summer night. PRESTON—FUN p160-163.
*One timetable. (1m, 2f) McCOY SIXTEEN p71-77.
The onion detector. TARBELL—CRAZY p35-37.
Opening and closing numbers. BAKER'S—GAY p58-60.
Opening chorus. KERR p9-15.

"Opening numbers"
The curtain rises
*Revere English (STAHL—AMAT.)
"We thank you"
Opening pantomime chorus. WILLIAMS p10-11.
The opening scene. FERRIS p167-168.
Opening the world series, by Beatrice Plumb. PRESTON p14.

Opera
*Canned opera
Il Advertiso
*Madeline gets analyzed
The opera. EISENBERG—FUN p193-195.
*"Opera", by Robert Lewis Shayon. (2m, 1f) MILLER—
BROADWAY p23-29.

*Opera opens, by Norman L. Zeno, Jr. (2m, 2f) MILLER—
BROADWAY p55-62.
The opera singer. (2) BRINGS—MASTER p378; DRUMMOND
STUNT FUN p49.
Opera singer at home. FUNNY p37-39.
Operatic advertisements, (2) BRIDGE p20; EISENBERG—
FUN p188.
Operatic movie, by Harry W. Githens. GITHENS p109-111.
Operating stunt. ENTERTAIN—STUNT FUN p3.
The operation. DRUMMOND—STUNT—FUN p73.
*"The operation". (1m, 2f) PROVENCE—FLASH p73-75.
The operation stunt. EISENBERG—HAND. p25-26.
Operations
Cutting up
*Operations, by Jean Provence. (2) (4f) BRINGS—MASTER
p189-190; PROVENCE—LIGHT p33-34.
Operettas, Miniature
The missionary and the cannibals
On the Isle of Bombalay
*Opportunity. (3m, 1f) KAUFMAN—HIGHLOWBROW p145-
151.
An opportunity-night program. WILLIAMS p4-5.
Opposite actions. YOUNG—GAMES p36.
Opposites. EISENBERG—FUN p39-40.
Optimism
*The bright world
The optimistic road knight, by Arthur L. Kaser. (2) BRINGS
—MASTER p339-341; KASER—BUSHEL p21-23.
Orange trees in rows. DEPEW p342.
The orator. (2) CORMACK p29; DRUMMOND—STUNT FUN
p10.
*The orator, by Mabel Tuttle Craig. (1m, 1f) "THAT GOOD"
p36-37.
Oratorical contest. DEPEW p180-181.
Orchestra. JOHNSON—BAKER'S p90.
On orchestra without note. EISENBERG—FUN p191.
Orchestras
Band music
The comb orchestra
Comic orchestra

*School circus
When Johnny joined the Army
The world's outstanding sympathy orchestra
Orchestras, Cowboy
A hill-billy orchestra
Orchestras, Kitchen
The home town band
The kitchen band (2)
Kitchen band, or toy orchestra
Kitchen cabinet orchestra
Kitchen orchestra (3)
Orchestras, Pigmy
Pigmy orchestra
Orchestras, Plumber's
Plumbers' orchestra
The ordeal. DEPEW 246.
*Order in the court. (4m) HUBER—No p91-95.
Organ
Human organ (2)
While the organ peeled
Organ grinder man. EISENBERG—FUN p188-189.
Organ-grinders
"See-a-da-monk"
An organization stunt. FERRIS p184-186.
*Organizing a dramatic club at Goose Landing. (5m, 5f)
HOXIE p5-14.
Oriental dance. CORMACK p25.
Orphans
Up from the doorstep
Oscar and his imported dogs. DRUMMOND—STUNT FUN
p68.
Oscar the blockhead. DRUMMOND—STUNT FUN p17-21.
Oshkosh. EISENBERG—HAND. p87.
*Oshkosh land. (4m, 9f) KASER—BUSHEL p40-58.
'Ostler Joe, by George R Sims. BAKER'S—GAY p36-37.
*Oswald Oozelpopper, hoss thief. (8m) KASER—MERRY
p4-14.
Othello. EISEBERG—HAND. p171-177.
Other contests. BUGBEE—NUTTY p83.
Our country. FRICK—FALL p66.

Our Father. JOHNSON—BAKER'S p59.

*Our friend—the books. (3b, 3g) BARBEE p64-66.

*Our miniature fire brigade. (3m, 2f) TOPOLKA p91-94.

Our money. RYAN p96.

"Our president". FERRIS p108.

Our team—The athletic department. LAMKIN & FLORENCE p54-56.

"Our telephone operator whiles away dreary hours"! FERRIS p17.

Our Thanksgiving dinner. FRICK—FALL p66.

Our town. STAHL—MORE p77-80.

"Our treasures". FERRIS p43.

Out for a walk. TARBELL—COMEDY p92-95.

Out in the deep (a shadowgraph). ABELL—STUNTS p87-89.

*Out of the bag. (2f) EISENBERG—FUN p85-86.

Out of the garret, by Agnes Allison. ROHRBOUGH p138-142.

Out of the night. PRESTON—FUN p118-126.

Out of the storm, or Love will triumph. RYAN p38-43.

"Out yonder". (3m) STAHL—HEARTY p14-16.

*The outcome of income. (2m, 2f) HUBER—No p38-43.

Outdoor games. *See* Games, Outdoor

An outing at Coney Island. The Atlantic City board walk. Dreamland and screamland. Hitland and Skitland. FERRIS p127-129.

Over and under. FRICK—FALL p23.

Over one. FRICK—FALL p22.

Over or under two. FRICK—FALL p23.

"Over the hills and far away". FERRIS p67-68.

Over the pavement and through the towns. LLOYD p51-53.

Over the slide. DEPEW p197.

Over the tea-cups. WILLIAMS p18.

Owen, Jerry
   The world series

The owl's tale. TARBELL—SUNDAY p30-39.

Packages. YOUNG—GAMES p73.

Packing for Santa. PRESTON—PANTOM. p232-235.

Pageants
A community pageant
Girls of America
*Movie camera pageant

Pageants, Camp
Alice in wonderland
A camp fire pageant number
How the fire was saved
The law of the camp fire
The old woman in the wood
The picture writing from Hiawatha
When ghosts walk
When you and I were young
Pageants from dramatizations. PARTIES p36-45.
Paid in full. WILLIAMS p28-29.
*Painless dentistry, by Charles George. (2m) BRINGS—
MASTER p227-231.

Painters. *See* Artists
The painter's masterpiece. WILLIAMS p19.

Paintings. *See* Art
A pair of spectacles. TARBELL—FUN p71-73.
Palmistry, by Robert N. McGregor. BREEZY p74.
*(Pan)Dora's box. (4b, 4g) BARBEE p37-41.
Pan pipes a tune. PRESTON—PANTOM. p157-167.
*The pancake divorce case. (5m, 2f, extras) BUGBEE—GOFFY
p67-75.
A pantomime of class work. FERRIS p180-183.

Pantomime songs
The ancient festival
Corn song (harvest)
The first Christmas
Hear the Southland calling
A history song
The land for me
Packing for Santa
Up on the house-top
We've been thinking
Windmills keep turning around

A pantomimed melodrama, by Harry Githens. GITHENS
    p78-80.
Pantomimed proverbs. BREEZY p51-53.
Pantomimes
    See also Burlesque; Pantomime songs; Puppet pantomimes;
        Shadow plays
    After midnight
    Always a gentleman
    The animal pageant
    The answer is "Yes"
    The ant and the grasshopper
    The artist's model
    At the movies (FERRIS; JOHNSON—BAKER'S)
    The automat lunch
    The bachelor's dream
    The bare facts
    "Belle and Bill"
    Bill Tell
    The birth of a nation
    The busy waiter
    Cedric's return (2)
    Cinderella Goldilocks
    Cinderella on the screen
    Cinderella up-to-date
    City adventures! Perils to pedestrians
    Closing pantomime chorus
    Comic valentines (BRINGS—MASTER)
    Cornfield capers
    The courtin'
    The departure
    Doctor's dilemma (HUBER—PRACT.)
    Donald Dare, demon detective
    Drama at KQZ
    Drink
    Driven from home
    The dumb lecturer
    The eclipse (2)
    The elusive fly
    Even as you and I (2)
    An evening with the American girl

"Familiar folks in familiar poses"
The fatal ride
Father Time's art gallery
The football fool
For the lands' sake (2)
Fourth of July celebration—or Fireworks on parade
The gentleman's gentleman
Girl buys an Easter hat
A girl scout number
Grandmother remembers
Grandmother's great grievance or Who purloined the
  bustle?
Group dramatization of life situations
"The Hall of Fame, or, Heroes and heroines from
  bookland"
Hasty Harry (EASY—STUNTS; EISENBERG—FUN)
The haunted house
Heaven protects the working girl
Hiawatha and Mondamin
Hisses and kisses
A hole in one (2)
Hollywood
A hollywood chance
Home run Bill
Honest Ben
The house that Jack built
How the fire was saved
In the land of Schmozz
In the park
In the photograph studio
Indian love songs
Indian pep
Individual pantomimes
Ladies before gents
The laidly worm
The landing of Columbus
The law of the camp fire
Let George do it
The life of a basketball player
Lifelike likenesses: satisfaction guaranteed

Lily of the alley (2)
Little Boy Blue
Little Sally
Love knoweth no bounds, or Where is Joe?
The love of beauty
The midnight ride
"Movies" (FERRIS)
News of the war
Old man Blake
The old woman who lived in a shoe
One summer night
Opening pantomime chorus
The opera
Our town
Out of the garret
Out of the night
Out of the storm, or Love will triumph
Pan pipes a tune
A pantomimed melodrama
Pantomimed proverbs
Paul Revere's ride (SHANNON)
Pick your stunt
Pierrot and Pierrette
Playing solitaire
Pokey hunters
The proud princess (2)
Puppet pantomimes
Pure gold (2)
Putt! Putt!
Pyramus and Thisbe
A quarter to Christmas
The rainstorm
Red Riding Hood (SHELDON)
Rob 'em good
Robot love story
Romance in the moonlight
The romance of little Cinderella
Romeo and Juliet (JOHNSON—BAKER'S)
St. George and the dragon
Same my child

Courtship through the ages
Pantomiming a record
The poets art gallery
Ring out the bells
Spot the song
What do you see in music?
Pantomimes, With dancing
Dame Dimwitty's dolls
Pantomiming a record. EISENBERG—HAND. p134.
Pantomiming occupations. PRESTON p96.
Paper and pencil games. See Word games
Paper and pencil games, by Lettie C. Van Derveer.
GITHENS p125-131.
The paper read aloud. EISENBERG—FUN p113.
Paper sack puppets. EISENBERG—HAND. p23-24.
The parade. CANOPY—HIGH p31-34.
Parade of the nations. CONNOR p65.
Parade of the stars. ABELL—PEP p35-38.
Parades
The bouncing baby
The calabozo
The clown wagon
Columbus
*A grave problem
Hokey-pokey, the trained horse
Just married
Let's join the parade
Oscar and his imported dogs
Rubes in town
The stunt parade
Taxi
Parcher, Emily Seaber
The bathroom door
*Pardon, Madame. (1m, 2f) EASY—STUNTS p20-22.
*"Pardoned". (3m) PROVENCE—FLASH p89-93.
Parent-teacher associations
A clubwoman speaks
Parent's night
The school day
Parent's night. PRESTON p46-48.

Gasoleen mavourneen
Giving
The goat quartet
Good old class
Goodnight, Mollie
Hail! Hail! the meat's all gone
Half through the night
Here comes the groom
Here's to the banquet
Horror song titles
How couldn't thou leave me?
Howdy do, everybody
I arrived at the church
"I don't have a pain no more"
I'd rather have fingers than toes
If you think your church is best
I'm as happy as a donkey
An imperfect day
In the good old wintertime
It's a good time
It's a short, short life
It's good to be a joy-er
It's happening in Daytona
I've got a cold
Jack Horner
"Jingle bells"
"Jingle bells" parody
The joys that once through gullet walls
Just a kiss at twlight
Just before the battle, Maggie
Keep the home tires turning
Kimono
Lady, won't you dance
The last woes of summer
Let me call you Lizzy
Let's be merry
Let's give a cheer
Limburger cheese
Love's old sweet lies
Loyal, loyal to conference

Backgammon
Backward party
A backward party for April Fool's Day
Bumpity, bump, bump, bump
Capsule revelation party
Checkers
Children's entertainment
Chinese writing
Christmas (decorations)
Columbus Day (decorations)
A community Christmas
Constantinople
Continuous story
Crazy questions and answers
Cross-word puzzles
A cupid's tour of the world
Descriptions
Domestic science
Double scrambled names
Easter party (decorations)
Electricity
Empty chair
Ending words
Endless thread
Fake peanut hunt
Finding partners with conundrums
Flag day (decorations)
Geography (DEPEW)
Getting ready for the party
A golden hours party
The graduates' homecoming party (decorations)
Ground hog day (decorations)
Hallowe'en (decorations)
Hallowe'en social or party
Harvest festival
He can do little (DEPEW)
Hot and cold
Hot dogs (DEPEW)
"Howdy neighbor" social
Human jig-saw

Independence day (decorations)
An indoor camping party
Indoor zoo
An informal St. Patrick's party
Jig-saw puzzles
Lincoln's birthday (decorations)
Line introductions
Lucky circles
May day celebrations (decorations)
Memorial day (decorations)
A middling-good party
Mrs. Santa Claus' reception
Murder
Mystic circle
New Year's eve (decorations)
Noisy-peanut hunt
Nursery rhymes (DEPEW)
One-eyed threading-the-needle contest
Peanut polo
Picture-taking
A pink valentine party
Place them
Putting baby to sleep
Quaker wedding
Rabbit (DEPEW)
Safety spots
St. Patrick's day (decorations) (YOUNG—GAMES)
St. Patrick's social or party
(St.)Valentine's day (decorations)
St. Valentine's social or party
Scrambled names
Silhouette show
Snootie
Snow festival (decorations)
Spinach
Spoon pictures
Spooning contest
Spring party (decorations)
Thanksgiving (decorations)
Think of a number

*A tragedy in rhyme
Truth or consequences
Try your balance
Vacation party (decorations)
Washington's birthday (decorations)
Which book?
Parties, Japanese
A night in wonder-wander land, a Japanese party
Parties, Persian
The festival of No-Ruz, a Persian party
*The parting tear, by LeRoy Stahl. (1m, 1f) BRINGS—MASTER p180-182.
"Parting the hair". HUBER—EASY p64-66.
Partner leap frog. FRICK—SUMMER p84.
Partner tunnel. FRICK—SUMMER p83.
*Partners. By Selden M. Loring. (4m) EASY—IMPR. p38-44;
(2) LEVIS—TEN p33-36.
Partners, Choosing. *See* Get-acquainted stunts
Partnership. GEISTER—NEW p51.
Pass it. GEISTER—NEW p103.
Pass the ball. YOUNG—GAMES p82.
Pass the clothes pins. YOUNG—GAMES p78.
Pass the orange, by Beatrice Plumb. BRINGS—MASTER p421.
The passenger aeroplane. CONNOR p39-40.
Passing a dime through a table. DRUMMOND—STUNT p30.
*The passing of Bruno. (2m, 1b) DRUMMOND—THREE p76-78.
Passing of old Doc Knocker. BUGBEE—LIVE WIRE p41.
Passing the balloon. YOUNG—GAMES p10.
Passing the buck. DEPEW p175-176.
Passing the punch bowl. BUGBEE—GOOFY p78-79.
*Passing the turkey. (2m, 2f) MCCOY—HOLIDAY p80-87.
*Past, present and future. (3g) BARBEE p81-83.
Past presidents' chorus. DEPEW p259.
Patience
*A near tragedy
Patients
See also Doctors; Hospitals; Nurses
*Doctor
Dr. Dobbs' assistant

Patriotic
America
America first
America, the beautiful
The flag
A history song
The land for me
The spirit of '76
Truthful Betsey
*Uncle Sam's peace party
Uncle Sam's singing army
What's your state? (2)
"With the colors"
Patriotic spelling bee. WILLIAMS p6.
The Paul Jones. GEISTER—NEW p25-26,117.
Paul Revere relay. DEPEW p333-334.
Paul Revere's ride. TARBELL—FUN p60-61.
Paul Revere's ride, with apologies to the serious-minded.
     By Wilmer Baffle. SHANNON p24-29.
Paul Revide's rear. EISENBERG—FUN p62-64.
*"The pawn shop". (3) PROVENCE—FLASH p79-82.
*The pay off, by Selden M. Loring. (1m, extras) EASY—IMPR.
     p61-63.
The pea little thrigs. EISENBERG—FUN p59-61.
Pea marathon. YOUNG—GAMES p80.

Peace
Armistice Day stunt
*Uncle Sam's peace party
*The peacemaker. (3m, 1f) HUBER—ARENA p47-54.
Peach pie. EISENBERG—FUN p92-94.
Peanut Butter. EISENBERG—FUN p118.
Peanut hunt. GEISTER—NEW p114.
Peanut polo. DEPEW p307.
Peanut punch. DEPEW p318-319.
Peanut relay. DEPEW p318.
Peanut throw. DEPEW p319.
Peanuts! DRUMMOND—STUNT FUN p106-107.
Peanuts and milk bottles. DEPEW p216.
Pease porridge hot. GEISTER—NEW p28-29.

Pebble roll. FRICK—SUMMER p84.
The peculiar Chinese. TARBELL—COMEDY p40.
Peddlers and peddling
  *A practical use for peddlers
Pedestrians
  City adventures! Perils to pedestrians
Pedigree unknown. ABELL—STUNTS p35.
*The pen is mightier than the word, by Arthur L. Kaser.
    (5m, 1f) BAKER'S—GAY p10-11.
*The penalty, by Jean Provence. (3m, 2f) QUICK p53-58.
The penguin family, by Grace Keith Samuelson. BUGBEE—
    NUTTY p100.
Penland, Anna
  *The obedient princess
The penny arcade and the automat. BUGBEE—LIVE WIRE p26.
A penny for your thoughts, by Gladys Lloyd. JOLLY p92.
A "pep expert" livens up an audience. FERRIS p16.
Pep meetings
  See also Cheers and cheer leaders; Letters, Formation of;
    Marching; names of sports, e.g. Football
  Add a man
  And then
  The best joke
  Blind alley
  The bottleneck
  *Canned opera
  *The casual casualty
  Color blindness
  Come to the game
  The crystal gazer (BUGBEE—LIVE WIRE)
  Dixie pep
  Do not open
  Extra! Extra! (ABELL—PEP)
  *Fancy football
  Fatalism
  The fish pond
  *Foiled again
  Follow the arrow
  Follow your impulse
  A football broadcast

Football quiz
A football rally
Formation of letters (2)
The French chef
Funeral of opponent
A German band stirs up pep
*The ghost goes home
Gob chatter
*Grandma's sick
*Great men
Hanging in effigy
*The happy medium
*Hard sledding
High power pep
Hit the nail
A homecoming pep meeting
How do you feel?
The human clock
If football players were bridge players
Impersonations
In proper order
Indian pep
The irate dad
Is that right?
It's impossible
It's in the bag
Jumbled words (HUBER—GIANT)
The jury convicts
Just a balloon
*Just a basketball
The life of a basketball player
Living basketball statuary
Lost and found (HUBER—GIANT)
*Lovers of art
Loyalty test
*Make a note of it
Many a slip
Marked men and women
Meet the team
A message for you

Weighed in the balance
What a melody
What do you know?
What's the word?
*Who's a dummy?
Who's who in basketball
Whose hat is that?
*Willie the weeper
Pep—old and new. ABELL—PEP p98-99.
A pep oration, by Agnes Dubbs Hays. CASEY—PEPPY p62.
Pep squad stunts. FRICK—FALL p28-32.
Pepping up the gang. BUGBEE—GOOFY p87-88.
"The perfect day". FERRIS p106.
"Perfect day" parody. DEPEW p277.
*A perfect gentleman. (3m, 1f) REACH—QUICK p62-69.
The perfect host, by Gail White. JOHNSON—EASY p48-50.
A perfect picnic, by Beatrice Plumb. BRINGS—MASTER p428.
*"The perfect thirty-six". (2m, 1f) STAHL—HEARTY p32-34.
Perry, M. Lee
    A meller dramatic evening at home
*The persecuted maiden, or Curses! Foiled again, A
    syncopated surge of dastardly doings. (3m, 3f) KASER
    —TEN p99-108.
*Persia presents: The bored king and the bandit. (1m, 1f)
    MILLER—LANDS p121-131.

Persian
    The festival of No-Ruz, a Persian party
    *The magic word—Persia
"Personal" readings from the signs of the zodiac. JOLLY
    p78-82.
Personal service to boys. DEPEW p154-158.
*Personality does count. (3m, 5f) TOPOLKA p105-112.
Persuasive pictures. BUCHANAN p77-78.
Pete, the postman. KASER—BUSHEL p9-13.
Peter Rabbit. EISENBERG—FUN p28-29.
*Peter's Christmas tree. (4m, 4f) BUGBEE—CATCHY p61-68.
Peters, John G.
    Columbus discovers America

Peterson, Minnie L.
  *At the ticket office
  The fixer
The Pharisees. TARBELL—SUNDAY p92-98.
Phases of the World War. TARBELL—CHALK TALKS p75-91.
Phelps, Franklin
  *Henry, the model husband
  I have written a play
  *The king's toemain
  *Logical advice
  *Sudden riches
Phelps-Jones, Esther
  Mock marriage in rhyme
*The philosopher. (1m, 2f) REACH—QUICK p97-107.
Phoney calls. (2) ENTERTAIN—STUNTS p4-5; PARTIES
    p29-30.
Phonograph and songs. PARTIES p60.
Photography
  *At the photographer's
  Busted, by gosh
  *Camera study
  In the photograph studio
  Lifelike likenesses; satisfaction guaranteed
  The tragic tintype
  The wise photographer
*"Physical culture". (2m, 2f) HUBER—THREE p83-84.
Physical feat and tricks. EISENBERG—HAND. p228-242.
Piano
  The great Russian maestro
  "The home center: our piano"
  *"Interlude"
  Keeping the wolf away
  Keyboard funnies
  Musical Hungarian goulash
  "Professor Bangthekeyski"
  Sands in the desert (or "The desert symphony")
  When Johnny practices
Piano duet. CANOPY—HIGH p108-109; DEPEW p261.
Piano stool sparring. DRUMMOND—SPOT p73.
Pick up. DEPEW p331.

Pin the tail on the donkey. WILLIAMS p27-28.
The pink persimmon tree—Japan. MILLER—STUNT p85-96.
A pink valentine party. JOHNSON—BAKER'S p79-80.
Pinning the tin cup. EISENBERG—FUN p33.
Pippa's song, by Karin Sundelof-Asbrand. BUGBEE—
    NUTTY p95.
Pirate picnic. FRICK—FALL p16-17.
The pirate's chest. TARBELL—FUN p39-47.
Pirates
    Buried booty
    Sir Ronald the ruthless
    *What's in a name? (DEASON—SKIT)
Piscatorial art. (2) BRINGS—MASTER p385; DRUMMOND
    —STUNT FUN p57.
Place cards. GEISTER—NEW p101.
Place them. DEPEW p294.
Plain efficiency. (2m, 1f) HUBER—FOUR p83-86.
Planets
    See also Stars; Mars; Venus
    The interstellar league
*The planters. (4b, 4g) BUGBEE—LIVELY p114-117.
Plate race. GEISTER—NEW p98-99.
The play's the thing. ABELL—STUNTS p48-50.
*"The play's the thing". (1b, 5g) BARBEE p52-55.
Playful static, by Beatrice Plumb. CASEY—PEPPY p109-110.
Playing a one-string instrument. CANOPY—HIGH p88-89.
Playing cards introduction. DEPEW p193-194.
Playing solitaire. PARTIES p19.
Playing the ponies, by Beatrice Plumb. BREEZY p59-61.
A playlet—The drama department. LAMKIN & FLORENCE
    p52.
Please promise me. FUNNY p28-29.
Pledge stunts. CORMACK p17-18.
"The pledge test". HUBER—EASY p13-16.
Plenty of nothin'. EISENBERG—FUN p94.
Plumb, Beatrice
    All aboard!
    Animals
    Balloon balance
    Beautiful, but dumb

On the line
Opening the world series
Pass the orange
A perfect picnic
Playful static
The prehistoric family album
Rainbow sing-down
Repressions
Say it with bricks
Screen test game
Seeing the funnies
Shut-in's picnic
Sleuthing customs
Smoke screens
Speedy seven up
Spring song
The straw vote
A "striking" stunt
Supposing
Swat the fly
Synchronized spooners
Talloween fortunes
Theatre box
Three little pigs—and the wolf
The treasure box
Twenty questions (BRINGS—MASTER)
A vacation for mom
Watch night stunt
What's wrong with whom?
What's your state? (2)
Where's the youngster?
Your horror-scope
Zoo's zoo

Plumbers and plumbing
 *"Such a hot day"
 *Where is the plumber?
Plumbers' orchestra. DRUMMOND—STUNT FUN p9.
Plumes from a handkerchief. DRUMMOND—STUNT p38.
Plunging. DEPEW p325.

Pocahontas
*Historical hystericals (2)
*How we started
The true story of Capt. John Smith (2)
*"Pocahontas", or "The Indian maiden's
    travail". (3m, 1f) STAHL—IMPR. p5-12.
"The pocket-size minstrel". CASEY p97-107.
Pockets to purses. DRUMMOND—STUNT FUN p105.
Poe, Edgar Allen
*"The purloined letter"
*"Three Sundays in a week"
The poet's art gallery. PRESTON—FUN p168-171.
A poet's romance. JOHNSON—BAKER'S p11-16.
Poetic calisthenics. PARTIES p10.
Poetical
   See also Ballads; Lyrics, Song
   Acting out rhymes
*All ashore
The alphabet is queen
The answer is "Yes"
*Around the world in bed
The bachelor's dream
The banana bandits
The barnyard clock
The Bon Ton Saloon
Brazos Pete
*Carpet rags
Casey at the bat
Casey's revenge
Cave men stuff
Cinderella up-to-date
*Cindy Ella slips
A class poem
College and knowledge; etc.
College revisited
A commercial relay
Curfew must not ring tonight (BAKER'S—GAY)
The curtain rises
Donald Dare, demon detective
The drug store cowboy

The drunkard-maker
*The elopement (SHANNON)
The end of a perfect day
An endurance test
The Eskimo tragedy
An evening with the American girl
The face on the barroom floor
Father Time's art gallery
The fire bug
Four unfortunates
*Fun from Norway
The ghost of mathematics
Ghosts (JOHNSON—BAKER'S)
*The ghosts' minuet
The grumbler
Guilty or not guilty?
Hasty Harry (ROHRBOUGH)
The house that Jack built
How's this for romance?
*"Hurry, doctor" (HUBER—THREE)
Impromptu party
*"In the nick of time" (DRUMMOND—STUNT)
An interrupted recitation
Jazz justice
*"Justice a la rime"
*The knot is tied
*Kupid's kollege
"Lady Clare"
The landing of Columbus
*Landing of Columbus
Last line contest
The little hills—with gestures
*Mademoiselle Tania
*Man versus dog
Missing syllables
Mock marriage in rhyme
*Mother Goose dream
Mother's strike
A mule named Joe and the circus show
The murder of Jabel Jenkins

*"My book"
*Needle, thread and jabber, a sewing circle entertainment
The newsboy's debt
Nursery rhymes (DEPEW)
Old man Blake
The old stage queen
*One Arabian night was stunt night
'Ostler Joe
Othello
Pan pipes a tune
Paul Revere's ride (SHANNON)
Pictured songs
The pink persimmon tree—Japan
*Potluck
Progressive poetry
The proud princess (2)
*A really significant poem
Recitations
Relay poetics
*Rhyme and reason
*"Rhythmatic" (STAHL—AMAT.)
Robot love story
Romance from Pif Pif land
The romance of little Cinderella
Romeo and Juliet (JOHNSON—BAKER'S)
The sad story of Augustus DeLisle
*School days (BRINGS—MASTER)
*The seasons
Shakespearean hash—The English department
She was "somebody's Mother"
The sky ride—class poem
*Some class (MALCOLM)
*The spelling class
The spirit of '76
Sunshine in your heart
Teaching them to drive
*Thank you for coming
*There's going to be a wedding
*Thick and thin
A toast to the banquet

*A tragedy in rhyme
*"The trial of the house council"
 "The true story of Captain John Smith" (2)
*Tunetown gossip or Carol entertains the musical club
 Two benches in the park
 Two sinners
 The week before Christmas
*The welcome
 Welcome
 Welcome, freshmen
*What we'd like to be
 When I was young
 Who am I? New Year's entertainment
 Who's a poet?
*Woman's way
 Womanless wedding (DEPEW)
 Wrong as ever
Poison. GEISTER—NEW p42.
Poison Gulch, by Jack Fuller. JOHNSON—EASY p16-17.
Poison Indian club. DEPEW p328-329.
Poker (game)
 *Bridge and poker
 *The night before the morning after Christmas eve
Pokey hunters. EASY—STUNTS p15-17.
Policemen
 *The big stunt
 *Birds of a feather
 A call for the ambulance
 Calling all cars
 *He always gets his man
 *Here lies a lie
 *The hold-up man
 *In line of duty
 *It's against the law
 *Just like John
 The kops and kitchenmaids
 *Last chance
 *Life
 *The limb of the law
 *A little matter of a motor car

*Make a note of it
*"The masher"
*Night
*Night school
*The pay off
*The peacemaker
*Self-preservation
*"So you won't talk" (STAHL—HEARTY)
*The third degree
*Three o'clock in the morning
*Two cops off duty
*Where's Henry?
*The winning ticket
  Working on the dry squad
*You've got to be tough!
*Polite but firm. (3) (2m, 1f) EASY—BLACKOUTS p29-35;
      by Marion Holbrook. JOHNSON—EASY p35-38; SIX—
      MORE p12-16.
  The political rally. EISENBERG—FUN p161-165.
*The politician. (2) BUGBEE—NUTTY p38-39.
  Politics
    *"Anything to get votes"
    Burlesque campaign parade
    Campaign speeches by presidential candidates
    Fake radio political broadcast
    Meeting the train
    Mock election
    *Mrs. Clarke wins seat in Congress
    Reprocrat rally
    The straw vote
    Vote for me (3)
  Poor blind bat. YOUNG—GAMES p14.
*The poor boob. (3m) DRUMMOND—STUNT FUN p25-26.
  The poor conductor. EISENBERG—HAND. p73-74.
*The poor little dear. (1m, 2f) STAHL—MORE p43-45.
  The poor man's lamb. TARBELL—SUNDAY p81-87.
  Poor me is married. KENT—ONE p84-86.
  Poor old Nag. FUNNY p34.
  The pop bottle. CROWLEY p54-55.
  Pop-bottle relay. DEPEW p333.

*Self-preservation
*The sentimental sap
Privation, by Jeff Gannett. BRINGS—MASTER p402.
Prize fight. (2) CANOPY—HIGH p97-98; MACDONALD—
   CARNIVAL p33-34.
A prize for slang. BRINGS—MASTER p391.
Prizes
  Balloons (DEPEW)
  Bedroom suite
Problems in punctuation. DEPEW p354.
A processional. FERRIS p170-171.
Proctor, Lois
  Shakespearean hash
Production numbers
  The farmer goes to the city
  Good night, Elaine
  Opening chorus
  The stars, the night, the moon
  You-uns and we-uns got religion
Professional encounters. FERRIS p33-34.
Professions. YOUNG—GAMES p53.
*"Professor Bangthekeyski". FERRIS p25-26.
*"Professor Cookoo, crystal gazer". (5m) DRUMMOND—
   IMPRO. p19-24.
Professor Cookoo—crystal gazer, by Harry Githens.
   GITHENS p48-50.
Professor Dauber's art gallery. "THAT GOOD" p8-13.
Professor Quack's quaint quiz, by Lettie C. Van Derveer.
   GITHENS p50-52.
Professor See-All and Know-All. FRICK—FALL p48-49.
Professor Shag's puppet show. BUGBEE—GOOFY p19-24.
Professor ———'s side show. PARTIES p61.
*Professor Sniderschmultze's pupils. (7m, 1f) KASER—
   TOP p3-17.
Professor Stretchem's upsetting exercises. PRESTON p101-102.
Professor Von Ribbenbropper's football kindergarten.
   ABELL—PEP p39-48.
Professors
  *Agatha's errands
  Be kind to insects

*Protection or else. (3m) DRUMMOND—SPOT p17-21.
The proud princess. (2) By Catherine Miller Balm.
    EISENBERG—HAND. p217-221; MILLER—LANDS. p77-87.
A proved salary. TARBELL—CRAZY p61-67.
Provence, Jean
  *About time (2)
  *At the gates
  *Braves, arise
  *Browned biscuits (2)
  *College never changes
  *Corn cure
  *Don't get excited
   Father's quiet evening
  *Fishing
  *His sister
  *Insurance
  *No sale
  *Not for credit (2)
  *Not so crazy (2)
  *Oh, Doctor! (3)
  *Once conclusion (2)
  *Operations (2)
  *The penalty
  *Seeing Father (2)
  *Some dilemma
  *Statistics (2)
  *Stop thief (2)
   Success story (JOHNSON—EASY)
Proverb transformation. DEPEW p358.
Proverbs
  Acting proverbs
  Comparison
  Illustrated proverbs
  Locate your maxim
  Pantomimed proverbs
  Pied proverbs
  Shrieking bromides
  Telldown
  Unfinished proverbs
Proving that a person is not here. EISENBERG—FUN p42.

*Proximity. (1m, 1f, announcer) KAUFMAN—HIGHLOWBROW
   p93-98.
*P.S.—He got the job. (2m, 3f) (REACH—QUICK p50-56.

Psychonalysis
   *Assorted nuts
   Cy the psychiatrist
   *The doctor's dilemma (3)
   Don't brush them on me
   It's my brother
   *Madeline gets analyzed
   Milk language
   *Some fun, son
*Public hero number one. (2m, 3f) McCOY—HOLIDAY
   p70-79.
Public orator. YOUNG—GAMES p35.

Publicity
   *It's colossal! (TAGGART—FIVE)
Publicity stunts. FERRIS p204-205.

Pulitzer prizes
   We present our winners
Pull fingers apart. DEPEW p331.
Pulling in the cow. BRINGS—MASTER p396-397.
*Pulling Sam's tooth. (3b, 2g) BUGBEE—LIVELY p106-109.

Pullmans
   *Let me off at Sapulpa
The pumpkin and the witch. TARBELL—FUN p78-79.
The "punch" bottle. CROWLEY p57-58.

Punctuality
   See also Tardiness
   The barnyard clock

Punctuation
   Problem in punctuation
Punkin pie. CORMACK p31.

Puppet pantomimes
   Fisherman (PRESTON)
   Fourth of July celebration—or Fireworks on parade
   Girl buys an Easter hat
   Little Boy Blue
   Tennis match

Puppet pantomimes. PRESTON p9-11.

A puppet play. EISENBERG—HAND. p24-25.

Puppets
See also Puppet pantomimes
Dance of the races
Fist puppets
Paper sack puppets
Potato puppets
Prof. Shag's puppet show

Puppets, Human
*The bride of the dragon king—China
Human marionettes
Live puppets

Puppets. FRICK—FALL p67-71.

*The Purdy's Christmas package. (2m, 2f, 1b, 1g) BUGBY—
—CATCHY p61-75.

Pure gold, by Arthur L. Kaser. (2) BRINGS—MASTER p287.
292; KASER—AMATEUR's p35-39.

Pure water. EISENBERG—HAND. p91.

*"The purloined letter". (3m) PROVENCE—EASY p36-47.

The purple pen. STARR—JR. p33-37.

*The pursuers. (3m, 1f) HUBER—FOUR p53-56.

Push button tuning. EISENBERG—HAND. p168-171.

Pussy and Fido. YOUNG—GAMES p40.

Put it to music. ENTERTAIN—STUNTS p1.

"Put on your old grey bonnet". FERRIS p106-107.

Putt! Putt! By LeRoy Stahl. EASY—SKITS p19-21.

Putting baby to sleep. DEPEW p296.

Putting out a fire. FERRIS p134-135.

Puzzlers
See also Conundrums; Quizzes
A blank old lady
Dous
Ergro
Hidden words
Vowels
Word golf

*Pygmalion and Galatea. (2m, 1f) LAUFE—EASY p5-23.

Pyramus and Thisbe. PRESTON—PANTOM. p62-72.

Qt, Mt. Eisenberg—Fun p41.

Quacks

Dr. Killemquick's medicine show, or the friendly quack

*The medicine man (Stahl—More)

*"Sure cure" (Provence—Flash)

Quadrilles

Freak quadrille

Opening and closing numbers

The quadruped race. Drummond—Stunt—Fun p.106.

Quaker wedding. Depew p297-298.

The quarter in the yarn ball. Drummond—Stunt p26-27.

A quarter to Christmas. Preston—Pantom. p134-143.

Quartets

*"At the country drugstore"

*Audition

Baby quartet

Bachelors' quartet

The base quartet

Bass quartet (2)

*Bustin' up the old quartet

Comic quartet

*Cowboys from Brooklyn

*"The darktown strutters' quartet"

Death-dealing quartette

The disappearing quartet (2)

Discordant encore

Dumb quartet

Eleven ideas for quartet singing

*Emergency broadcast

Farmer quartet

The farmers' quartet

*The gay nineties barber shop

The goat quartet

*"Harmony a la hobo"

*The harmony laundry

High power pep

*In the music shop

Lather harmony

Mills Sisters' quartette

*"Mixed voices"

*Nobody knows
The nonsense school
Novelty quartette
Off key
Old man river
Pictured songs
*Pops tonsorial parlor
Queer quartets
Scarecrow quartet (2)
Sheet music
Telling the world
*The tonsorial quartette
The trades quartette
Turnabout quartet
Two-faced quartet
Two-faced quartette
Upside down
Upside-down quartet
The vanishing quartette
Volstead quartette
*The walkie-talkie juke box
The war in song
*The woman's hour

The quitting party. LLOYD p14-16.

Quib ball, by Gladys George. JOLLY p92.

Quiz, please. BARBEE p41-43.

Quiz program. (2) GEISTER—NEW p61-62; By Grace
Keith Samuelson. "THAT GOOD" p49-50.

Quiz steeplechase. SHELDON—GIANT QUIZ p20-27.

Quizzes
Around the world quiz
Ask and ye shall know
*Ask me another
A billion
*He knew all the answers
Inconsequential journeys
Intelligence test (CASEY—PEPPY)
Is it true or false
*The jackpot
*Miss Information, please
Prof. Quack's quaint quiz
*A series of queries
True or false
"Twenty questions" (BARBEE)
What's in a name? (CASEY—PEPPY)
Who wrote it?
*Who wrote it?
Win-O-spin
Your screen test

Quizzes, Athletics
Batter up! A sports quiz show
Football quiz

Quizzes, Biblical
A biblical quiz
A biblical tug-o'-war

Quizzes, Biographical
The famous men quiz

Quizzes, Country life
The barnyard quiz

Quizzes, February
Quotation quiz for February

Quizzes, Mother Goose
Mother Goose guesses

Quizzes, Moving pictures
  The stardust trail
Quizzes, Musical
  Musical answers
  A musical quiz
Quizzes, Mystery
  Whodunit?
Quotation quiz for February, by Mabel Tuttle Craig.
  Casey—Peppy p118.
Quotations
  Finish-them stunt
  *"Old sayings"
  Your fortunes told

Rabbit. (2) Depew p297; Eisenberg—Fun p42.
The rabbit in the hat. Tarbell—Fun p51-52,55.
The race. Eisenberg—Hand. p186-189.
The race for the bacon. Abell—Pep p124.
The race is run. Huber—Giant p140-141.
Races
  See also Contests; Relays; Swimming races
  Athletic meeting
  Back to back race
  Bell pass
  Blindfold race
  Blowing race
  Chair pass
  Chariot race
  Easter bonnet
  Folding chair race
  Giddy-ep! Whoa! Back up!
  A horse race (Depew)
  Ice cream race
  Kiddie car race
  Leapfrog race
  Marshmallow race
  Nipple race
  Nose and potato race
  "Noses"

The quadrupled race
The race is run
Relays and races
A rooster race
Suit case race
Three-legged race
Three-legged swimming race
*Traffic trouble
Tub race
Turtle race
Water balloon race
Water candle race
Wheelbarrow race
The racing bug, by Robert N. McGregor. BREEZY p67-68.

Radio

See also Amateur hours; News commentators; Quizzes;
Television; etc.
*Advice to students
*The ambulance always
*"And they get paid"
Ask and ye shall know
At the broadcasting station
*Atomic energy
*A backward march of time
*Birds and blood
*Blood red roses
*Books! Books! Books!
*Boys' glee club fantasy
A broadcasting fantasy
*Bunny Bargain Bloom is on the air (2)
*Bus ride
*A candle burns tonight
*Captain Paul
*Caroline bakes a cake
*Celebrity day
*Christmas carols
Christmas highjinks
*Clubs and friends
Combing the air waves
*Coming clean

*Community fund play
*Courtesy in the halls
*The crime club
*Danger, fate at work
*A decision must be made
*Diamond ring
*Direful doin's
*Emergency broadcast
*Farewell to Easter
*The fateful bargain
 A football broadcast
*Football rally
*Getting a job
*The girl next door
*Girls' glee club fantasy
*Glass of poison
*Goodbye, students
*Granger helps Kate
*Green hat and yellow feather
*Hallowe'en (STARR—RADIO)
*The ham what I am
*He knew all the answers
*History versus geology
*How can I be popular?
*I'll be home Thanksgiving
 In a radio studio
*"In the radio store"
*Industrial progress
*The interview
*Interview with Santa
*Invitation to a wiener roast
*Is it worth the sacrifice?
*The jackpot
*Join the hiking club
 The Jones store buys a radio
 Just a voice on the radio
*Keep your engine oiled
*Let's deny it
*Listening in on Joe's new radio
 Local broadcast

*To whom it may concern
*Twelve skulls mean death
*Unwarranted speed
*Vice versa
*Wanted: young office assistant
*Weather—or—not
*Welcome, students
  "What a game! What a game!"
*What price carelessness?
*Who wrote it?
  The whole 'fam damily
*Woman of Hilltop House
*The woman's hour
*You can't try an insane man
Radio act. CANOPY—HIGH p89-90.
Radio auditions. CASEY—PEPPY p42-43.
A radio interview. ABELL—STUNTS p23-25.
Radio jumble. EISENBERG—HAND. p62-64.
Radio or television broadcast. PARTIES p61.
*A radio program. (4b, 4g) EDGERTON p126-129.
*Radio recipes, by Ora L. Smith. (1m, 2f) ROHRBOUGH
    p107.
Radio rumpus. (7m, 2f) HUBER p31-39.
A radio-show program. WILLIAMS p5-6.
Rag dolls. DRUMMOND—STUNT FUN p116.
"Rags and tags". FERRIS p85.
Railroads. *See* Railway stations; Trains
Railway stations
  *Afternoon at Central Station
  *At a railway station
  *At Eagle Bend
  *At the ticket office
  At the union station
  The berth of an upper or howareya?
  *"Follow the leader"
  *The idol worshippers
  *Man of many miens
  *The sentimental sap
  Stations
  Ticket, please

*The train to Mauro
*Waiting for the stump hollow train
*When is the train due?
Rain. EISENBERG—FUN p86-87.
Rainbow sing-down, by Beatrice Plumb. BREEZY p63-64.
The rainstorm. PARTIES p19.
Rallies. *See* Pep meetings
Ramble on, by Richard Drummond. BRINGS—MASTER
    p347-348.
The rambling ring. DRUMMOND—STUNT p36-37.
Raspberries. WILLIAMS p12-13.
Rastus and the ventriloquist. ABELL—STUNTS p36-38.
Rattle boxing. DEPEW p322.
The raw recruits. BUGBEE—LIVE WIRE p16-17.
*Razzberry. (2m, 2f) EASY—BLACKOUTS p49-54.
Reach behind you. EISENBERG—FUN p43.
Read 'em and weep. CONNOR p55-57.
Read it and weep. BUGBEE—NUTTY p23.
*"Reader of lips". (2m, 1f) HUBER—THREE p70-71.
Real estate
    *Fire!
    *Fountains of youth
*A really significant poem. (3g) DEASON—SKIT p57-64.
*"Reason enough". (4f) PROVENCE—FLASH p57-59.
Receiving line. GEISTER—NEW p110-111.
Receiving lines
    Continuous receiving line
Reception marches. BUGBEE—CATCHY p8-9.
Recitations. *See* Monologs
Recitations. LYONS p33-47.
Red Cross
    *Enroll in the Red Cross
    *How the Red Cross began
Red ear. FRICK—FALL p61.
The red rabbit. TARBELL—FUN p71,74.
Red Riding Hood
    A modern romance
*Red Riding Hood. (3m, 3f) PRESTON p38-41.
Red Riding Hood. SHELDON p20-25.
Red tape, by Gladys Lloyd. JOLLY p98.

Red, white and blue chorus. WILLIAMS p6.

Reddisch Riden Hood. EISENBERG—FUN p64-65.

Reducing. *See* Dieting

Reformers
  "Miss Swat-the-fly: an ardent reformer"

Refreshment stands
  *There is always a way

Refreshments. YOUNG—GAMES p91-97.

Regatta. GEISTER—NEW p54.

The rehearsal. (2) ENTERTAIN—STUNTS p5; PARTIES p29.

*The rehearsal. (3m, 1f) HUBER—FOUR p35-38.

Relationship. DEPEW p351.

Relay poetics, by Gladys Lloyd. JOLLY p96-97.

Relays
  All fours relay
  Angleworm relay
  The bag relay
  Banana relay
  Barrel-hoop relay
  Bean-passing delay
  Carry relay
  Clothesline relay
  Coat and vest relay
  Cracker relay
  Crazy relay
  Double relay
  Dressing relay
  Four-footed relay
  Four-legged relay
  Golden chair
  Good morning!
  Heel and toe relay
  Horseback
  Kangaroo relay
  Laughing relay
  Leap frog relay
  Light relay
  Mamma and baby relay
  The milky way (WILLIAMS)
  Name relay

Newspaper advertisement relay
Newspaper relay
Over and under
Over one
Over or under two
Partner leap frog
Partner tunnel
Paul Revere relay
Peanut relay
Pebble roll
Pillow case relay
Pop-bottle relay
Relays and races
Running relay with stunt
Simple running relay
Singing relay
Skin the snake (FRICK—SUMMER)
Stunt relay
Try your balance
Tunnel leap frog
Tunnel relay
Under one
Weaver's relay
Wheel barrow
Wheelbarrow relay
Relays and races. KEMMERER—GAMES p47-54.
Religion
You-uns and we-uns got religion
The remedy. EISENBERG—FUN p92.
Remove the dime. EISENBERG—FUN p33.
Removing a shirt. DEPEW p173-174.
The report of the stunt committee. DEPEW p202.
Report of the Board. EISENBERG—FUN p188.
Reporters
Hot news
*Taking Maw's advice
Repressions, by Beatrice Plumb. BRINGS—MASTER p418.
Reprocat rally. ABELL—STUNTS p39-40.
*"Required: one man". (4f) DRUMMOND—FUNNY p14-23.
A resolution. DEPEW p202-203.

*Resolutions for two. (1m, 3f) McCoy—HOLIDAY p3-9.
Resolved, That banana oil is a greater benefit to mankind
　　than apple sauce. CANOPY—BURL. p79-91.
Resolved, That halitosis is a greater menace to our
　　country than dandruff. CANOPY—BURL. p39-54.
Resolved, That Sarah Brum is a more important girl than
　　Sarah Bellum. CANOPY—BURL. p93-105.
Resolved, That the calendar should have thirteen months
　　instead of twelve. CANOPY—BURL. p55-78.
Resolved, That the oyster is a more intellectual animal
　　than the sponge. CANOPY—BURL. p107-117.
Resolved, That there is more nourishment in the hole of a
　　doughnut than in the fragrance of limburger cheese.
　　CANOPY—BURL. p9-38.

Restaurants
　*A la carte
　*"Big business"
　*Carrot topped
　*"Chop suey"
　*"Fish business"
　*Here's a hair
　*In Paris
　*Let's eat
　*P.S.—He got the job
　*Up from the depths or The rise of Tillie Tureen
　*Your order, please
The retro-moviescope, by Willis N. Bugbee. JOLLY p26-33.
"Reuben and Rachel". RYAN p95.
"Reuben, Reuben" parody. DEPEW p279.
*The revenge and repentance of grandpa. (3m, 2f) PAR-
　　SONS p69-75.
Revere, Paul
　The midnight ride
　Paul Revere relay
　Paul Revere's ride (2)
　Paul Revide's rear
Reveries
　Her reverie
　His reverie
　The sailor's reverie

*Reversal in rehearsal. (4m, 1f) HUBER—No p5-11.
*Reverse English. (2) (many char.) STAHL—AMAT. p57-63;
  (4m) TAGGART—MEN p18-24.
Reverse spelling. YOUNG—GAMES p71.
Revivals, Negro
  You-uns and we-uns got religion
Revolutionary tea. WILLIAMS p6-8.
*"The reward". (2m, extra) PROVENCE—VAUD. p89-90;
  (3f) QUICK p48-52.
*Rhyme and reason. (2m, 3f) HUBER—SIX p90-98.
"The rhythm band travesty". DRUMMOND—STUNT p71-72.
"Rhythmatic". STAHL—AMAT. p106-109.
*"Rhythmatic". (6 students, prof.) STAHL—AMAT. p85-88.
Rhythmic spelling. EISENBERG—FUN p40-41.
Rice, Arthur L.
  *The boss of the king
  *Woman's way
Riddles. See Conundrums
Rideout, George M.
  *Chip off the old block
Riders, Famous
  See also Revere, Paul
  Famous riders of history
The ridiculous handkerchief. JOHNSON—BAKER'S p97.
Right and wrong reception. DEPEW p230-233.
Right-eyed or left-eyed? EISENBERG—HAND. p51.
Ring out the bells. PRESTON—FUN p163-168.
Ring the bell. YOUNG—GAMES p79-80.
Ring the cat's tail. FRICK—FALL p46.
Ring the witch's hat. FRICK—FALL p46.
Ring toss. FRICK—SUMMER p19.
Rip! DRUMMOND—STUNT FUN p13-14.
The rising card. TARBELL—FUN p31-35.
The rising king, by H. H. Gross. ROHRBOUGH p125-128.
*The rising style. (1m, 2f) STAHL—MORE p33-36.
The rising sun. TARBELL—FUN p57,58,61.
*The rivals, by Charles George. (2m) BRINGS—MASTER
  p235-236.
River boat minstrels. KASER—AMATEURS' p61-66.
Roadside cribbage. FRICK—SUMMER p9.

Rob 'em good, by Ruth Putnam Kimball. GITHENS p80-83.

*"The robbery of 'Dell Manor' "! (3m, 2f) STAHL—
HEARTY p81-83.

Robin Hood
*The sheriff of Nottingham's nephew

*Robin Hood, by Olga E. Gunkle. (20 players) ROHR-
BOUGH p47-48.

Robinson Crusoe way. FRICK—SUMMER p71-72.

Robot love story. HUBER—PRACT. p28-31.

*The robot rebels. (4m, 3f) HUBER—SIX p61-69.

Rock a-bye baby. BUGBEE—LIVE WIRE p53.

The rogue's gallery. BUGBEE—LIVE WIRE p29-30.

Rolling the wheelbarrow. DEPEW p247.

Roman art. TARBELL—CHALK STUNTS p55-61.

Roman football game. DEPEW p38-40.

Roman mob. PARTIES p14.

Romance. *See* Engaged; Honeymoon; Love; Marriage;
Proposals

*Romance. (2m) EASY—BLACKOUTS p87-91.

*Romance á la mode. (2m, 2f, announcer) STAHL—MORE
p29-32.

Romance from Pif Pif land. EISENBERG—FUN p99-102.

Romance in the moonlight. PRESTON—PANTOM. p168-175.

The romance of little Cinderella. MILLER—STUNT p72-82.

Romantic. PRESTON—PANTOM. p250-252.

Romantic notes. EISENBERG—HAND. p133.

Rome, Ancient
Roman art
Roman football game

Romeo and Juliet. (2) FERRIS p108; JOHNSON—BAKER'S
p17-19.

*Romeo and Juliet and their papas. (3m, 1f) DEASON—
SKIT p16-21.

Romeo and Juliet up-to-date. BUGBEE—LIVE WIRE p76-77.

*Room service. (3m, 2f) HUBER—TV p99-106.

*Room 213. (7m, 1f) KASER—BUSHEL p28-40.

Roommates
*What price roommate?

Rooster fight. DEPEW p319.

A rooster race. DEPEW p183-184.

The roosters sing. ABELL—PEP p105-106.
Rope boxing. DEPEW p322-323.

Rope stunts
  At both ends of a rope
The R.O.S. initiation. BUGBEE—GOOFY p15-19.
"The rosary". JOHNSON—BAKER'S p61.
The rose vs. the lemon. JOHNSON—BAKER'S p94.

Rotary clubs
  Half-minute speeches
  Ima Rotarian
Rotary friend X. DEPEW p208.
"Round and round". HUBER—EASY p20-22.
Round table luncheon. DEPEW p243.
The royal bumper. CORMACK p29-30.
Royce, Bob
  *The backward helper
  *Bill, the matchmaker (BRINGS—MASTER)
  Death-dealing quartette
  Me and Smitty
  *Thank you for coming
R.S.V.P. YOUNG—GAMES p42.
Rubber. EISENBERG—FUN p114.
The rubber arm. EISENBERG—FUN p27-28.
The rubberneck twins. BUGBEE—LIVE WIRE p14-15.

Rubes. *See* Dialect, Country
Rubes in town. DRUMMOND—STUNT FUN p69.
The rubetown cabaret. BUGBEE—LIVE WIRE p44-45.
The rules of the game. ABELL—PEP p70-71.
Rumblings from wrecks. ABELL—STUNTS p41-43.
Running relay with stunt. FRICK—FALL p21.
Runs her own life. EISENBERG—FUN p95.
Ruopp, Julia Phillips
  Spring salad

Rural life. *See* Country life
Rural minstrels. FERRIS p125.
Rural symphony. YOUNG—GAMES p14.

Russians
  The great Russian maestro
  *Ivan Vosco, sanitary inspector is jailed

Sack boxing. DEPEW p322.

The sacred stone. CORMACK p27-28.

The sad story of Augustus DeLisle. PRESTON—PANTOM.
p193-197.

Safety
See also Accidents; Automobile accidents
*The ambulance always
*Danger, fate at work
*Is it worth the sacrifice?
*(Pan)Dora's box
Rumbling from wrecks
*Strike for safe driving
*Unwarranted speed
*What price carelessness?
*Safety first. (2) (3m) PROVENCE—FLASH p52-53; (2f)
PROVENCE—LIGHT p14-15.
Safety first. TARBELL—CRAZY p39-41.
Safety spots. DEPEW p293.
The saga of the farmyard. YOUNG—GAMES p19.

Sailors
*Captain Paul
*Fit as a fiddle
Gob chatter
Merry middy minstrels
*This brave new world
A tub on the ocean wave
Sailor's pep. ABELL—PEP p49-52.
The sailor's reverie. FERRIS p110.
*A sailor's technique, by Paul S. McCoy. (2m, announcer)
SNAPPY p110-117.
St. George and the dragon. MILLER—STUNT p147-154.
St. Patrick minstrels. FERRIS p124.

St. Patrick's Day
"Cheer in Erin"
The game of Ireland
*Green candles
An informal St. Patrick's party
*St. Patrick's day (2m, 1f) BUGBEE—CATCHY p89-92.
St. Patrick's day (decorations). YOUNG—GAMES p105.

St. Patrick's day (games and stunts). KEMMERER—GAMES
   p15-16.
St. Patrick's social or party. BUGBEE—CATCHY p39-40.
Saint Richard, by Robert N. McGregor. BREEZY p70.
St. Valentine's Day. *See* Valentine Day
(St.) Valentine's Day (decorations) YOUNG—GAMES
   p104-105.
St. Valentine's social or party. BUGBEE—CATCHY p38-39.
The salesman. PARTIES p20.
Salesmen and Salesmanship
   See also Department stores; Grocery stores;
      Peddlers and peddling
   *Balm of life
   *The book agent
   *Close deal
   *"The customer is right" (2)
   *Dunk that doughnut!
   Echo
   Fresh!
   *Getting rid of an agent
   "He works his way"
   *High pressure (2)
   *Honorable mention
   "I'll tell the world"
   *I'm not here
   *"In the radio store"
   *Matilda's beau
   *Nerve on display
   *Nice cream
   *No sale
   *Polite but firm (JOHNSON—EASY)
   *Rhyme and reason
   *"Something important"
   *Super salesman
   The tune the salesman played (EASY—ENTERTAIN)
   *Was his face red!
   *We want your business
   *What a classroom
   *What all housewives know
   *What are you selling?

Sanders, Emily
   *A mono-word play
Sands in the desert (or "The desert symphony") FERRIS
   p22-24.
*Sandy, defunct, by Jay Tobias. (3m, 1f, announcer)
   SNAPPY p34-37.
Santa Claus
   *"The death of Santa Claus"
   *Interview with Santa
   Mrs. Santa Claus' reception
   *The night before the morning after Christmas eve
   Packing for Santa
   "Santa Claus land". FERRIS p77.
   "Santa Claus serenade". FERRIS p108.
*Sarah Perkins' hat shop. (8f) KASER—TEN p41-54.
Sardine. GEISTER—NEW p99.
Satires
   See also Radio; Television
   Our town
   *Strained interlude
Save my child. HUBER—PRACT. p35-38.
*Saved by the hero, by Arthur LeRoy Kaser. (4m, 1f)
   JOLLY p68-70.
*Saved in the nick of time. (2m, 2f) DRUMMOND—SPOT
   p91-94.
*Saved, or love's dilemma, by Arthur LeRoy Kaser. (2m, 1f)
   BUGBEE—LIVE WIRE p132-134.
The saving of Capt. John Smith. BUGBEE—GOOFY p93-96.
Sawing a man in half. DRUMMOND—STUNT FUN p14.
*Say, Dad, by Harry W. Githens. (1m, 1b) GITHENS p93-95.
Say it with bricks, by Beatrice Plumb. BREEZY p64-67.
"Say it with flowers"—"The flowers he sends her". FERRIS
   p70.
The scales. MACDONALD—CARNIVAL p80.
*The scandal. (5f) KELLEY p18-26.
Scarecrow quartet. (2) EASY—STUNTS p6; PARTIES p33.
Scat! YOUNG—GAMES p33.
Scene at the art gallery, by Victor Hoag. ROHRBOUGH p129.
A scene at troop headquarters. FERRIS p169-170.

Scene from William Tell. CANOPY—HIGH p92,93-97.

Scenes from daily life. EISENBERG—HAND. p28-29.

*Scenes of the sixties. (6 scenes with various no. of b. & g.)
    BUGBEE—LIVELY p65-75.

The scenic ride. MACDONALD—CARNIVAL p82.

The Schlitz murder case, by Richard Judd. CASEY—PEPPY
    p68-69.

Schmikel hair tonic. EISENBERG—FUN p143-144.

School
    See also Attendance; College students; Freshmen; High
        school students; Seniors; Teachers; etc.
    *Accuracy
    *Almost the last day of school
    As it used to be
    *A class in geography
    Commencement exercises, or schoolroom burlesque
    The country school
    *Daffydill school
    *"The district school at Carrot Corners"
    Education don't pay
    *Getting acquainted
    *"The glacier"
    *In the class room"
    The kindergarten kids
    *Learning to say yes
    Maisie goes to school
    *The old one room school
    *The old village school
    *Professor Sniderschmultze's pupils
    Professor Von Ribbenbropper's football kindergarten
    *Sleepy Hollow school
    *Some class (2)
    *"The ultra-modern school"
    *Water, water (PROVENCE—LIGHT)
    What? No vacation?

School annuals
    *Who buys?

*School bazaar (various no. of voices) STARR—RADIO p13-14.

*The school bell. (1 speaker) STARR—RADIO p9-10.

The school bell and the professor. CROWLEY p79,81.
*School circus (1 speaker, band) STARR—RADIO p115-116.
School dances
  *On with the dance (BARBEE)
  The school day. FRICK—FALL p8-9.
  School day minstrels. FERRIS p124.
*School days. (2) By Arthur L. Kaser. (1f, 3b, 2g)
    BRINGS—MASTER p141-143; CHAPLIN p31-48.
  School days. (4) FERRIS p54; FERRIS p77; GEISTER—NEW
    p42-43; GEISTER—NEW p43.
*School days at Porcupine Junction. (5m, 5f) KASER—
    AMATEUR'S p15-21.
  School daze. ABELL—PEP p100-101.
*School daze minstrels. (teacher & 4 endmen) HUBER—NO
    p24-31.
School lunches
  Sue's lunch
School papers
  *Coming clean
  *My kingdom for an aspirin
  *Tomorrow at ten
School songs
  Suggested school songs
  School spirit. (1m, 2f) TOPOLKA p73-77.
*Science is wonderful. (3m, 3f) MIKSCH—CURTAIN p88-103.
  Science of today, by Arthur L. Kaser. BRINGS—MASTER
    p337-339.
Scientists
  *Atomic energy
  The scissors grinder, by Richard Judd. CASEY—PEPPY p62.
  Scooping the scoop, by Alta Toepp. CASEY—PEPPY p101-102.
  Score stunt. FRICK—FALL p32.
Scotch
  See also Dialect, Scotch
  *"Not qualified"
  *Your change
  The Scotchman's greeting card. TARBELL—FUN p76-77.
  The Scotchman's hat. TARBELL—FUN p75-77.
  Scott, Sir Walter
  *"The tapestried chamber"

*Scourge of the desert. (3m) PROVENCE—KNOCKOUT p24-25.
Scouts. *See* Boy Scouts; Girl Scouts
*"Scrambled dates". (4m) STAHL—AMAT. p68-73.
The scrambled egg. CORMACK p29.
Scrambled names. DEPEW p298.
Scrambled states. ABELL—STUNTS p12.
Screen stars. YOUNG—GAMES p66.
Screen test game, by Beatrice Plumb. BRINGS—MASTER p429.
Scribner, Edwin
 *A hit with papa
 *A wronged husband
Scripture spelling match, by Mabel Tuttle Craig. JOLLY p90.
Seaman, Abel
 *The swing
A seance. BUGBEE—NUTTY p27-28.
*"The seance". (1m, 1f, voice) PROVENCE—VAUD. p67-70.
Seances. *See* Occult
The search is ended. HUBER—GIANT p133-134.
Seachlight scenes. BUGBEE—CATCHY p12-13.
*The seasons. (4g) EDGERTON p91-93.
The secret cavern. PRESTON p97-99.
*The secret of success. *See* *One Arabian night was stunt
  night
"Secret pals"
 *Anybody's gift
 Capsule friends
Secretaries
 *A backward march of time
 *Plain efficiency
*"The secretary". (1m, 2f) HUBER—THREE p17-18.
"See-a-da-monk". FERRIS p74-75.
See-saw, by Gladys Lloyd. JOLLY p98-99.
See the weenie. EISENBERG—HAND. p55.
See the winkle bird. TARBELL—COMEDY p68-73.
*Seeing father. (2) By Jean Provence (1m, 1b, 1g)
    BRINGS—MASTER p193-195; PROVENCE—LIGHT p117-
    119.
*Seeing stars. (2m) BUGBEE—NUTTY p25-26.
Seeing the funnies, by Beatrice Plumb. JOLLY p48-50.
Seeing things. TARBELL—SUNDAY p62-67.

Seeing things at night—class prophecy. LAMKIN & FLORENCE
    p43-48.
"See-saw". FERRIS p68.
Sees all-knows all. DEPEW p209.
Self-expression style show. WILLIAMS p11-12.
Self-introduction. (3) DEPEW p153; DEPEW p115-216;
    GEISTER—NEW p112.
*"Self preservation. (5m) HUBER—ARENA p39-46.
"Selina Sue sees the show". FERRIS p21-22.
The senate clock. WILLIAMS p9-10.
*The senator says. (3m, voice) HUBER—GIANT p66-69.
*The senator's visit. (1m, 4f) ROGERS—PLAYS p81-83.
Seniors
    Burying the seniors
Senior Limburgio, strong man. RYAN p98-99.
Sense of hearing. DEPEW p185.
Sense of sight. DEPEW p185.
Sense of smell. DEPEW p185.
Sentence me. YOUNG—GAMES p73.
*The sentimental sap. (1m, 2f) HUBER p45-52.
Serenades
    "Our President"
    "Romeo and Juliet" (FERRIS)
    "Santa Claus serenade"
    "Seventeen —by the pale moonlight"
*A serenading party. (4f) IRISH—CATCHY p32-35.
*A series of queries. (3m, 2f) HUBER—VAUD. p21-29.
Serpentine. GEISTER—NEW p123-124.
Servants
    *A capable servant
    *"Crossed wires"
    "Help wanted"
    *Interviewing servant girls
    *The logical guess
    *The new maid
    *Not for sale
    *The sick maid
    *Too busy
*Service. (2m) KAUFMAN—HIGHLOWBROW p59-66.
Service for others. DEPEW p278.

*"Serviceable". (1m, 2f) GEORGE—TWELVE p54-57.
Serving the summonses. BUGBEE—NUTTY p23-24.
The seven ages of man's education. BRIDGE p15-16.
"The seven ages of woman". FERRIS p107.
*Seven is the perfect number. (4b, 3g) BARBEE p9-10.
Seven-league boots, by Glayds Lloyd. JOLLY p93.
Seven thirteens. DEPEW p350.
Sevens always. TARBELL—COMEDY p56.
"Seventeen—by the pale moonlight". FERRIS p108-109.
Sewing
   *Needle, thread and jabber, a sewing circle entertainment
The sewing bee. BUGBEE—GOOFY p84.
*"The sewing club meets". (5m) MACDONALD p5-15.
Sewing fingers together. EISENBERG—HAND. p56.
*The sewing society. (1b, 6g) IRISH—CHILDREN'S p33-37.
Sextets
   The Flora Dora sextet
Sh! DRUMMOND—STUNT FUN p77-78.
Sh! A pantomime by Jeff Gannett. BRINGS—MASTER p309.
A shadow graph for the commercial department. ABELL—
      STUNTS p79-81.
Shadow guessing. YOUNG—GAMES p22.
The shadow of the cross. TARBELL—SUNDAY p53-57.
Shadow picture possibilities. BRIDGE p22-23.
Shadow pictures
   Additional shadow picture ideas
   Greenpath shadowalker
   Searchlight scenes
Shadow pictures. ENTERTAIN—STUNTS p2.
Shadow plays
   Androcles and the lion. (PRESTON—PANTOM.)
   At home with the range
   Canoe song
   Cutting up
   The dentist
   The delectable ballad of the Waller lot
   Fat man and lean man
   The fatal scream
   The floating man
   Going native

Shakespearean hash, by Lois Proctor. ROHRBOUGH p173-178.

Shakespearean hash—The English department. LAMKIN & FLORENCE p51,56-57.

Shakespearean scraps. ABELL—STUNTS p13-14.

Shall we show you how as ladies? ("The Farmer"). LLOYD p23-25.

The shampoo. CORMACK p30.

*The Shantytown scandal. (6f) SIX—MORE p5-11.

Sharps and flats. BARBEE p74-75.

*"The sharpshooter". (3m) HUBER—THREE p42-43.

Shaughnessy's ball, by Willis N. Bugbee. BREEZY p76-78.

Shayon, Robert Lewis
  *The candy shop
  *"Opera"

She was "somebody's Mother", by Mary D. Brine. BAKER'S —GAY p32.

*Shes a beauty, by Anne Martens. (2m, 2f) QUICK—COM. p75-85.

*"She's from Holloywood". (10f) DRUMMOND—FUNNY p40-48.

She's lovely. EISENBERG—FUN p33.

Sheet music. DRUMMOND—STUNT FUN p87.

The shepherd's hut. TARBELL—SUNDAY p99-106.

*The sheriff of Nottingham's nephew. (7m) DEASON— SKIT p40-52.

Sherman, Charles
  *The insomniac
  *We want your business

Sherman, Robert L.
  *All one-sided
  *Hospitality
  *Naughty nudist
  *Parsing a sentence

Shimmy shakers. CORMACK p27.

*Shining example. (4m) PROVENCE—LIGHT p93-95.

Shinkle, M. Lue
  Let George do it

*The ship-shape show. (6m, 6f) KASER—FUNNY p73-82.

*Shipmates. (1m, 2f) TAGGART—LIVE p57-62.

Ships

> *See also* Sailors; Shipwrecks
> *All ashore
> *On the good ship Moonbeam
> *The ship-shape show

Shipwreck today; or, Robinson Crusoe up to date.
PRESTON—FUN p116-117.

Shipwrecks

> *Farewell to Easter

*The shirt's off. (3m, 2f) HUBER—ALL p45-51.

*Shocked beyond words". HUBER—EASY p36-38.

Shoe hunt. DEPEW p319-320.

The shoeman. CROWLEY p28,30.

The shog and his dadow. EISENBERG—HAND. p49.

*Shoot! By LeRoy Stahl. (3m) EASY—SKITS p61-67.

The shooting gallery. MACDONALD—CARNIVAL p77.

The shooting of Dan McGrew. CANOPY—HIGH p87-89.

Shoppers. YOUNG—GAMES p57.

Shopping

> *See also* Department stores, Grocery stores; Salesmen
>   and Salesmanship
> "Do your shopping early" or "A shopper's dream"
> The man who shops for his wife
> "3.98"
> *Window shopping

Shopping. JOHNSON—BAKER'S p93.

*The shortest play in the world. (6m) KAUFMAN—HIGHLOW-
    BROW p133-139.

Shot put. DEPEW p314.

The show freaks. MACDONALD—CARNIVAL p62-71.

A shower for baby. EISENBERG—FUN p95.

Shrieking bromides. YOUNG—GAMES p18-19.

Shut-in's picnic, by Beatrice Plumb. BREEZY p58.

Siamese national anthem. YOUNG—GAMES p13.

Siamese singing. DEPEW p259-260.

Siamese twins. CONNOR p40.

*The sick maid, by J. C. McMullen. (2m, 2f) QUICK p90-93.

*A sick pupil. (4b, 3g) IRISH—CHILDREN'S p81-86.

The sidelines. ABELL—PEP p53-57.

Sideshow and freak tent. JOHNSON—BAKER'S p88-89.

*"Sideshow". (2m, 2f) Huber—Three p59-60.
Side-shows
  *Ballyhoo
  Circus sideshow
  Down below where all is woe
  The faculty graveyard
  For men only (2)
  For women only
  Fortune-telling booth
  Gallery of famous pictures
  Get your picture taken
  The house of terrors
  The jewelry shop
  The monkey cage
  The most popular person in town
  The musem
  The music box revue
  Popular ballroom dances
  Special side show
  Special stunt
  A trip around the world
  Up above where all is love
  Vanity fair
  The variety store
  The whip
  Wild animals and birds
  Witches' den
Siege. Geister—New p49.
The siege of limburger. Bugbee—Live Wire p68-69.
The sifter. Depew p361.
Sight. *See* Eye
The sight seeing bus. Bugbee—Live Wire p95-96.
Sight seeing in a wheelbarrow. Bugbee—Goofy p27-29.
Sign language. Geister—New p109.
*The sign on the door, (4m, 1f, extras) Preston—Fun
    p76-80.
The sign painter, by Beatrice M. Casey. Casey—Peppy
    p24-26.
*"Sign up". (2m, 1b) Huber—Three p50-51.
Signing the declaration. Bugbee—Live Wire p69-70.

The banana bandits
The bathing beauty
Beauty parade
*"Befo' de wah"
*Bewildering popularity
*"The botany hike"
*Bunny Bargain Bloom is on the air (2)
The calendar (JOHNSON—BAKER'S)
*The carol singers
Carry on the song
Clash and clatter band
Community songs
*A coon concert
Cradle to grave in song
Cunning Junior
A cupid's tour of the world
Daisies won't tell
Dixie pep
*Do they?
Down on de old plantation
*The evening paper
The flag
*"Flowers and weeds"
Funiculi, funicula
Gay nineties minstrel
The gimmes
Girls of America
Giving
A golden hours party
The Gossip Hollow ladies' minstrels
Got the grip
*Harold meets the cowboys
*Hattie's singing lesson
*"Hoboes en route for Hoboken"
Human xylophone (4)
*Ill-treated Trovatore
I'm forever blowing bubbles
*In Grandma Perkins' store
*"In the class room"
*In the garden"

Indian love call
Indian love songs
The inharmonious choir
*"Joining the whole truth club"
The joke
The joking singers
Keep the song going
*The lady known as Lou
Laughing song
Limelight limericks
*The love lyrics of letters
"Mee-ow-ooooo"
Meet the team
A melodrama sing
Melody mixer
*Minstrel maids
*The modernist
*Mother Goose dream
Mother Goose grand opera (2)
Mouthophonic phonograph
*"Musical dreams"
*Musical eggs
Musical neighbors
A musical voyage
The musical wand
Of thee I sing
Off for Alabam'
Old King Cole (EISENBERG—FUN)
*The old maid minstrelettes
The old maid's drill
Our Father
Out in the deep
"The pocket-size minstrel"
Popular pets: a revival of old-time favorites
*Potluck
*A promenade
Rainbow sing-down
Reprocrat rally
*"Rhythmatic"
Rip!

The rising king
River boat minstrels
The rooters sing
*A serenading party
Siamese national anthem
Sir Cyril Semaphore's singers
*Sissy football
Smoke rings
*So this is Paris
*Some class (MALCOLM)
Song of the dish towel
The song of the shoes
Spring salad
A stereopticon sing
*The sunflowers' wooing
Sweet music
Sweethearts on parade
Tableaux of songs
Telling the world
*Ten barrooms in one night
A toast to ———— high school
A tub on the ocean wave
Two in one
Two marionettes
*Up from the depths or The rise of Tillie Tureen
Upside down
*"Valley View minstrelettes"
The wail of the Christmas ties
When Molly was a baby
Where's the collar button
Whiteface minstrels
*Women's way
The xylophone
The Yowell club
Singing commercials. EISENBERG—HAND. p130.
Singing contest. DEPEW p258.
The singing hen. (1m, 3f) ROGERS—PLAYS p84-85.
Singing lesson. FUNNY p60-64.
Singing relay. FRICK—SUMMER p85.
Singing scarecrows. EISENBERG—FUN p195-196.

Singing school at Cyclone Junction, by Harry W.
   Githens. GITHENS p112.
Singing stars. EASY—ENTERTAIN p37-49.
Singing stunt. DEPEW p198.
Singing waiters. EISENBERG—HAND. p134-135.
Single file marching. FRICK—FALL p28.
Sink the ship. DEPEW p311-312.
Sir Cyril Semaphore's singers. PRESTON—FUN p112.
Sir Ronald the ruthless, by Marjorie Higbee. ROHR-
   BOUGH p143.
*Sissy football. (3) ROHRBOUGH p49-53.
Sisters
  *Entertaining sister's beau
  *Entertaining sister's beaux (2)
  *That's love
  *Two hats for Easter
Sister's beau. GODDARD—CHILDREN'S p29-31.
*Sit still, Mother! (2m, 2f) McCoy—HOLIDAY p45-52.
*Sitting tonight. (2m, 2f) MIKSCH—TEEN p23-31.
Six on a side. DEPEW p360.
Sixteenth century
  *"Direct from the 16th century"
Sixty dollars a week. EISENBERG—HAND. p82-83.
Sixty jokes for stunts. EISENBERG—HAND. p105-117.
Skaters. GEISTER—NEW p119-120.
"Skaters of skill and fame". FERRIS p69.
Skid. YOUNG—GAMES p60.
Skidoo, germs. BUGBEE—LIVE WIRE p26-27.
Skiing
  The joy of winter sports
Skill game. KEMMERER—GAMES p115-125.
Skin the snake. (2) DEPEW p330; FRICK—SUMMER p82-83.
"Skipping skippers". FERRIS p80.
The sky line—class will. LAMKIN & FLORENCE p48-49.
The sky ride—class poem. LAMKIN & FLORENCE p43.
Skyrocket express leaving. STARR—JR. p37-42.
Slang
  A prize for slang
  *Society for the suppression of slang
Slang. (2) DEPEW p170; JOHNSON—BAKER'S p95.

Sleep
   *That tired feeling
*Sleep softly. (2m, 3f) HUBER—FOUR p113-117.
"Sleeping Beauty"
   *The truth about Sleeping Beauty
*Sleepy Hollow school, by Harry W. Githens. (6b, 6g)
      PRESTON p73-79.
Sleight of hand. FRICK—FALL p38.
*Sleight-of-hand, by Avis Crocker. (3m) ROHRBOUGH p117.
Sleuthing customs (for Thanksgiving, Christmas or New
      Year), by Beatrice Plumb. CASEY—PEPPY p112-113.
The slide for life. DRUMMOND—STUNT FUN p12-13.
*Slightly exaggerated. (6f) REACH—QUICK p24-31.
Slipper hunt. GEISTER—NEW p94.
The slippery penny. DRUMMOND—STUNT p29.
Slogan contest, by Mabel Tuttle Craig. JOLLY p91.
Slogans
   Advertising slogans
Slogans or mottoes. CORMACK p8-9.
*Small sale. (2m, 3f) HUBER—TV p47-54.
Smell
   Blindfold test
   How's your smeller?
   Sense of smell
   A swell smell
Smile a second—after dinner stories. LYONS p21-31.
Smile a smile, everybody. DEPEW p282.
*Smile awhile. (7m) HUBER—GIANT p118-123.
Smith, Captain John
   *Historical hystericals (2)
   *How we started
   The saving of Capt. John Smith
   The true story of Captain John Smith (2)
Smith, Ora L.
   *Radio recipes
Smoke rings. RYAN p9-10.
Smoke screens, by Beatrice Plumb. PRESTON p29.
Smudge boxing. DEPEW p323.
Snail. March music. GEISTER—NEW p17-18.
*"Snakes". (2m, 1f) HUBER—THREE p92-93.

Snap shots of busy men. BUGBEE—GOOFY p85-86.

Snappy answers. YOUNG—GAMES p56.

*Snapshot album. (3f, misc. char.) PARTIES p58-60.

Snatch. GEISTER—NEW p98.

Sneezing
 The free clinic
 Giant sneeze (2)

Snipe-hunting
 *Waitin' for de snipes

Snootie. DEPEW p299.

Snow festival (decorations). YOUNG—GAMES p103.

Snow-white and her dwarfs, by Harry Githens. GITHENS p72.

*Snow White and the seven giants. (7b, 1g) BARBEE p55-56.

Snow, white snow. FUNNY p29.

Snyder, Marian Ogden
 Majoress Bow-Wow's amateur hour

*So this is love. (1m, 1f) EASY—STUNTS p25-27.

*So this is Paris. (9m, 7f, group) MILLER—LANDS p15-39.

*So you won't talk! (3) By Charles George (1m, 2f)
 BRINGS—MASTER p98-101; (1m, 2f) GEORGE—
 TWELVE p45-48; (4m) STAHL—HEARTY p64-66.

Sobs and tears. (2) BRINGS—MASTER p382; DRUMMOND—
 STUNT FUN p53.

*Social climbing. (1m, 2f) McCOY—SIXTEEN p53-56.

*Social difficulties. (1m, 4f) IRISH—CATCHY p18-22.

The social order of the onion. CORMACK p80-83.

Society
 *The pride of the Van Smythes
 *Social climbing
 *Sudden riches
 *The thinkers

*Society for the suppression of slang. (6f) IRISH—CATCHY
 p36-40.

"Sock savers". HUBER—EASY p23-25.

Soda fountains
 *Nerve on display
 *Razzberry

The soda jerk. CROWLEY p76,78,81.

*Sofapillio. (2m, 3f) EISENBERG—HAND. p164-167;
 ROHRBOUGH p55-61.

*Some people are goofy, by Willis N. Bugbee. (MC, contestants) BREEZY p10-14.
*"Some story". (1m, 2f) HUBER—THREE p90-91.
Somebody told me. HUBER—GIANT p129-130.
*Something free. (4m, 3f) HUBER—FOUR p135-138.
Something has been disturbed. YOUNG—GAMES p75.
*"Something important". (3m, 1f) HUBER—THREE p5-6.
*Something loose. (2) KASER—SURE p35-41.
*Somewhat divorcified. (5m, 2f) KASER—MERRY p23-29.
The song grinder. JOLLY p85.
Song lyrics. LYONS p59-69.
Song matching, by Alta Toepp. CASEY—PEPPY p96.
Song of the dish towel. ROGERS—PLAYS p90-91.
The song of the shores, by Patricia and Peleg Glynn.
     ROHRBOUGH p101-104.
Song parodies, by Karin Asbrand. GITHENS p113-123.
Song programs. FRICK—SUMMER p55-56.
Song stories. FRICK—SUMMER p54-55.
Song stunts. CASEY—PEPPY p70.
Song titles
　　Carmen
　　Comedy song titles
Songs
　　See also Ballads; Lullabies; Lyrics, Song; Parodies;
　　　School songs; Serenades; Singing; Tableaux, Singing
　　The cannibal king
　　Comin' round the mountain
　　The cooking of the prunes
　　Living songs
　　More neighborly songs
　　Neighborly songs
　　O, no, John
　　Stunt songs (2)
Songs for group singing and musical games. KEMMERER—
　　GAMES p82-106.
Songs, Illustrated
　　See also Tableaux, Singing
　　"Just a love nest"
　　"Kentucky babe"
　　"Last rose of summer"

"Love's old sweet song" (JOHNSON—BAKER'S)
"Mother Machree"
"Old Black Joe"
Pictured songs
"The Rosary"
"Sweet and low"
"Tramp! Tramp! Tramp!"
Songs in tableaux. DEPEW p261-262.
Songs in fashion. ABELL—STUNTS p69-70.
Songs of the nineties. BAKER'S GAY p24-27.
Songs, parodies, etc. CORMACK p15-16.
The sound detectors. YOUNG—GAMES p51.
Sound effects
  *The crime club
  Long, long ago
  Mr. Totten takes a rest
  The whole 'fam damily
*"Sound effects man. (4m, 2f) HUBER—ALL p25-31.
Soup. KASER—SURE p93-95.
"Soup to nuts". HUBER—EASY p48-50.
South
  See also Dialect, Southern
  *"Befo' the wah"
  *Chiseling on chivalry
  Down on de old plantation
  Hear the Southland calling
  *Turkey
South America
  Going to South America
South Dakota
  *Vacation
Southern melodies. MACDONALD—CARNIVAL p34-37.
Spaghetti
  The battle of spaghetti
Spain
  A day in Seville
The spark of love, by Beatrice M. Casey. CASEY—PEPPY
  p27-31.
Sparkler drill. WILLIAMS p9.
Speak swiftly. YOUNG—GAMES p72-73.

Speakers and speaking
Armistice, 1918
Candidates for congress
Extra Extra! (DEPEW)
Half-minute speeches
The orator (2)
Oratorical contest
The prominent citizen addressing the graduating class
Public orator
Self-introduction (DEPEW)
Speaking from notes
A speaking marathon
*The speech of acceptance
Talk-fest
A talk on athletics
Talk on business or profession
Talk on hobbies
Talks on attendance
Talks on travel
Triple oration
A walkout
Speaking from notes. DEPEW p174.
A speaking marathon. DEPEW p182.
Spear 'em alive. DRUMMOND—STUNT FUN p107.
Special games and ideas. BRIDGE p10-12.
Special recognition. DEPEW p245.
Special side show. CANOPY—HIGH p57-58.
Special stunt. FRICK—FALL p45.
Spectator games. *See* Games, Spectator
*The speech of acceptance. (1m, 1f, 1b) DRUMMOND—THREE
    p21-24.
*Speech through wires. (7m) STAHL—LAND. p123-136.
The speed kids vs. The lightning flashes. FERRIS p36-37.
Speeding up the housework. DRUMMOND—STUNT FUN
    p110-111.
Speedy seven up, by Beatrice Plumb. BRINGS—MASTER p425.
Spell it. YOUNG—GAMES p8.
Spelling
Ghosts (BRINGS—MASTER)
Jumbled words (HUBER—GIANT)

Lucky words
Reverse spelling
Rhythmic spelling
Scripture spelling match
Spelling bee. DEPEW p169.
*The spelling class. (3b, 3g) EDGERTON p130-133.
A spelling contest. JOHNSON—BAKER's p94-95.
Speling in reverse. YOUNG—GAMES p58.
*The spelling lesson. (5b, 5g) IRISH—CHILDREN's p22-25.
Spelling test. DEPEW p109.
Spies
 *A perfect gentleman
 A spy story
Spinach. DEPEW p301.
Spinning on a stick. DEPEW p315.
Spiral marching. FRICK—FALL p29.
The spirit cabinet. DEPEW p81-85.
*The spirit calls. (5f) HUBER—SIX p76-83.
*The spirit is willing. (2m, 2f) REACH—QUICK p14-18.
*The spirit of 4-H clubs. (7b) ROGERS—PLAYS p5-9.
*The spirit of Montague manor. (3m, 1f) WEATHERS—
    MYSTERIES p80-90.
*Spirit of peace. (3m, 4f) HOPE p43-48.
The spirit of St. Louis. CANOPY—HIGH p96-97.
The spirit of '76. PRESTON—PANTOM. p150-157.
Spirit reading. DEPEW p94-96.
Spirit television. BUGBEE—LIVE WIRE p51.
*Spirit world. (1m, 2f) PROVENCE—KNOCKOUT p34-35.
*Spirits on parade. (3m, 1f) MCCOY—SIXTEEN p43-52.
Spiritualism. *See* Occult
The spool game. GEISTER—NEW p96-97.
Spoon pass, by Alta Toepp. CASEY—PEPPY p87.
Spoon pictures. DEPEW p296.
A spoonful of fun. JOHNSON—BAKER's p89-90.
Spooning. DRUMMOND—STUNT FUN p86.
Spooning contest. DEPEW p298-299.
Sportlight minstrels. FERRIS p122.
Sports and games. *See* Athletics; names of individual sports
    and games
The sports announcer. ABELL—PEP p90.

Statues, Living
From Eve on down
Living basketball statuary
Silent statues
*Story and statue"
Statuesque de silly, by Conny Hill. (3m, 3f) SHANNON
p66-73.
*Stay awake. (6m) HUBER—CHAR. p79-88.
Stealing sticks. FRICK—FALL p19.
"Stealthy Steve the sleuth". FERRIS p20.
Steed, Rev. G. Hubert
Sunday a.m. in the average home
Steel, Sidney
Comic valentines (BRINGS—MASTER)
*The first rehearsal (BRINGS—MASTER)
Hats
*Have a good time
I'll call the doctor
*I'll fix it, Mom
*It's her or the car
Late again (BRINGS—MASTER)
*Leave it to mother (BRINGS—MASTER)

Stenographers
See also Secretaries
*Kitty Dawn, stennygrapher
"Wanted: capable stenographer"
Stephens, Margerie G.
The eclipse (2)
A stereopticon sing. FERRIS p102-103.
Stevenson, Robert Louis
*"Markheim"
Stick out tongue, touch nose. EISENBERG—FUN p41.
The still in the night. SHELDON p90-94.
Stocking faces. EISENBERG—HAND. p119.
*Stop—look—listen, by Helen C. Hodgkins. (2m, 1f)
SHANNON p59-61.
*Stop thief, by Jean Provence. (2) (1m, 1f, 1b) BRINGS—
MASTER p195-196; PROVENCE—LIGHT p29-30.

Stores
> *See also* Department stores; Grocery stores; Shopping;
>   etc.
> *Fun in the general store
> The Jones store buys a radio
> *Keeping store

Stork tag. DEPEW p317.

A story about a cat. YOUNG—GAMES p56.

*"Story and statue". (5m) DRUMMOND—STUNT p41-43.

The story of Ruth and Naomi. TARBELL—SUNDAY p123-131.

Story-telling. FERRIS p166-167.

The stox and the Fork. EISENBERG—FUN p57-58.

*Strained interlude. (3m, 1f) STAHL—MORE p64-67.

Strange animal. DEPEW p344.

The straw vote, by Beatrice Plumb. PRESTON p13-14.

Strawberry blonde and mom. BUCKANAN p33-34.

Streamline de luxe model of 1941. BARBEE p29-30.

*The street broadcast. (announcer, several char.) "THAT
   GOOD" p68-70.

Strength test. CORMACK p31-32.

The strike ends. BUGBEE—NUTTY p50.

*Strike for safe driving. (6g) BARBEE p83-85.

A "striking" stunt (for Hallowe'en) by Beatrice Plumb.
   CASEY—PEPPY p106-107.

*Stringing along. (2m, 1f) STAHL—MORE p74-76.

Stringing them. KASER—BUSHEL p13-16.

*"Stripes". (3m) HUBER—THREE p40-41.

The strong man (2). DEPEW p361; DRUMMOND—SPOT p72.

Strong man act. CANOPY—HIGH p103,105,107.

"A student of nature". FERRIS p19.

Students
> *See also* College students; High school students
> *Celebrity day
> *The interview
> *"The world's full of crooks"

*Students are good citizens, I, II, III (3b, 3g) STARR—RADIO
   p69-70,91-92, 111-113.

*A student's complaint. (announcer, several char.) STARR—
   RADIO p43-46.

*Studio stooge. (2m) HUBER—NO SCENE p40-46.

A study in transformation. TARBELL—FUN p86-89.

Studying

*How girls study

*Stung again. (3m) "THAT GOOD" p80-83.

The stunt parade. DRUMMOND—STUNT FUN p67.

Stunt relay. FRICK—SUMMER p85.

Stunt songs. (2) BUGBEE—CATCHY p5-7; BUGBEE—GOOFY p110-117.

Stunts for a May basket party, by Mabel Tuttle Craig. BREEZY p45-48.

Stuttering

*"Reader of lips"

*The sure cure (HUBER—FOUR)

Style. *See* Fashion

Style show. (4) CANOPY—HIGH p109-110; DEPEW p105; LAMKIN & FLORENCE p68-70. MACDONALD—CARNIVAL p55-58.

*Style show à la masculine. (6m, 3f) DRUMMOND—SPOT p67-71.

Style show for men. DRUMMOND—STUNT FUN p73.

Styles. FUNNY p55-56.

Styles of a century. CONNOR p57-59.

The styles of other days. PRESTON—FUN p147-148.

A stylish gentleman. TARBELL—FUN p22,23,25.

Subject for class orations. LAMKIN & FLORENCE p65.

The submarine club. DEPEW p187-188.

*Subscribe now. (2m, 1f) MIKSCH—TEEN p15-21.

*"The substitute bride". (4m, 3f, 4-6g) DRUMMOND—IMPRO. p69-75.

Subtraction. DEPEW p341.

*Success story. (2) By Jean Provence. (2m) JOHNSON—EASY p39-41; By Harlan Hayford. (3) QUICK p22-28.

*"Such a hot day". (2m, 1f) DRUMMOND—STUNT p82-83.

*Such a mix-up. (3m, 3f) KASER—BUSHEL p87-97.

Such a life. TARBELL—CRAZY p75-80.

Suckers. DEPEW p185.

*A sudden discovery. (2m, 1f) BUGBEE—LIVELY p78-81.

*Sudden richess, by Franklin Phelps. (2m, 2f) BRINGS— MASTER p60-64.

Sued for non-support. WILLIAMS p35-36.

Sue's lunch. ROGERS—PLAYS p90-93.

Sue's message, by Jane D. Silver. ROHRBOUGH p165-166.

"Suez you", by Richard Judd. CASEY—PEPPY p66.

Suffragettes. GEISTER—NEW p118.

Suggested school songs. ABELL—PEP p121-123.

*The suicide. (2) LEVIS—TEN p11-13.

Suit case race. DEPEW p174.

*Sulphur Crik. (6b, 5g) GODDARD—CHILDREN'S p109-120.

Summer camp. GODDARD—CHILDREN'S p33-35.

Summer (girl) minstrels. FERRIS p120.

*Summer holidays. (2m, 3f) HOPE p31-33.

"Summer resort specialties"—"Those alluring summer
    girls"—"On the board walk". FERRIS p66-67.

Sunday a.m. in the average home. DEPEW p78-80.

Sunday-school
  A prize for slang
  *"Reason enough
  Sunday a.m. in the average home

The Sunday school youngsters sing. BRINGS—MASTER p396.

Sundays
  *Each Sunday morn
  Sunday a.m. in the average home

Sundelof-Asbrand, Karin
  Godiva
  Hail, Horatius
  Pippa's song

Sundown-sunup-breakfast! By Alta Toepp. CASEY—PEPPY
    p105.

*The sunflowers' wooing. (6m, 6f) VAN DERVEER—ANY
    p70-75.

Sunshine in your heart. STARR—JR. p50-51.

*Super salesman. (4m) HUBER—FOUR p21-25.

Superstition
  *Don't spill the salt

Supposing, by Beatrice Plumb. BRINGS—MASTER p421.

*A sure bettor. (3) DRUMMOND—STUNT FUN p37-38.

*The sure cure. (4) (4m, 1f) HUBER—FOUR p39-43; (3m,
    1f) PROVENCE—FLASH p36-38; (2f) PROVENCE—
    KNOCKOUT p28-29; (2m) PROVENCE—LIGHT p60-61.

Sure cure for falsehoods. (2) EASY—STUNTS p4; PARTIES
p31.
*The surgery. (3m, 4f, 1b) HOPE p53-55.
Surgical operation. BRIDGE p26.
The surprise camera. BUGBEE—LIVE WIRE p54.
Surprise games
Are you an Elk?
Barnyard melody
Blind man's journey
The church choir
Corpse
Detective
Electrification
Feed the animals
Magic animals
Mahatma Gandhi (YOUNG—GAMES)
Mexican prisoner
Tell my age
The touch of the ghost
Watch your step
What is it? (2)
The wise photographer
Surveyors
*"Along the straight and narrow"
*Swank night. (2m, 3f) MIKSCH—TEEN p124-134.
Swat! DRUMMOND—STUNT FUN p16-17.
Swat the fly, by Beatrice Plumb. PRESTON p14.
*Sweater girls. (2m, 5f) MIKSCH—CURTAIN p46-55.
Sweden
See also Dialect, Swedish
*The squire's bride—Sweden
Sweepstakes
*The winning ticket
"Sweet and low". JOHNSON—BAKER'S p60.
Sweet music. EISENBERG—FUN p190.
Sweet mystery. EISENBERG—FUN p113-114.
Sweetest story ever told. GEISTER—NEW p60.
Sweethearts of mine. EASY—ENTERTAIN p56-66.
*The sweethearts of the gay nineties. *See* *The gay nineties
convention

Sweethearts on parade. ABELL—STUNTS p71-74.

A swell smell. HUBER—GIANT p156-157.

Swell solo. DEPEW p256.

Swim under water. DEPEW p326.

Swimming
  Greased water pole
  No swimming allowed
  Preparedness
  Water baseball
  Water basketball

Swimming races
  Three-legged swimming race
  Turtle race
  Water balloon race
  Water candle race

*The swing, by Abel Seaman. (1m, 2f) QUICK p29-32.

"Swing high—swing low". FERRIS p68.

*Swing low, sweet Juliet. (2m, 3f, child) LAUFE—EASY
    p45-59.

The swing orchestra. MACDONALD—CARNIVAL p37-41.

Syllogisms. DEPEW p356.

Symbolic pictures. BUCHANAN p80-81.

Symbols
  This and that

The sympathetic milk machine. CANOPY—HIGH p80-81.

Synchronized spooners, by Beatrice Plumb. BRINGS—MAS-
    TER p417.

Synthetic celebrities. YOUNG—GRACE p71.

"T" is for Texas, by Richard Drummond. BRINGS—MASTER
    p358-359.

The table. DEPEW p311.

Table scavenger hunt. EISENBERG—HAND. p54-55.

Tableaux
  America
  As it used to be
  Athletic tableaux
  Chalk talks, or Tableaux—The art department

"Don't be a goop"
*The evening paper
"The family album" (FERRIS)
Fashion tableaux
Father Time's art gallery
A girl scout number
The glorious Fourth
"The good club member"
"The Hall of fame, or Heroes and heroines from book-
    land"

Humorous tableaux
"It's out"
"I've got it now"
Living pictures (DEPEW)
Mother and daughter dress parade
Mother Goose tableaux
Our Father
The popular picture gallery
The prehistoric family album
"That one, Doctor"
The two messages
Wha' dat wattahmilyun gone?
When you and I were young
The witches' incantation
Tableaux in a frame. FERRIS p55-56.
Tableaux of songs. DRUMMOND—STUNT FUN p88.

Tableaux, Singing
"Carry me back to Ol' Virginny"
"Comin' thro' the rye"
Famous lovers
"My little grey home in the West"
"The perfect day"
"Put on your old grey bonnet"
"The seven ages of woman"
Songs in tableaux
*The tables turned. (1b, 5g) BUGBEE—LIVELY p51-55.
Taboo. YOUNG—GAMES p41.
Tag of the free. LLOYD p32-33.

Taggart, Tom
  *The letter
Take it away. YOUNG—GAMES p83.
"Take me out to the ball game". FERRIS p68-69.
Take-off on a mind-reading act. (2) BRINGS—MASTER
      p380; DRUMMOND—STUNT FUN p52.
Take-offs
  See also Impersonations
  "Betsy speaks a piece for the caller"
  Boxing match (RYAN)
  "The colyumist"
  A community song-leader
  A drill take-off
  Getting ready for the party
  "Her first piece"
  "Hermione"
  "Household hints by Aunt Matilda"
  The man who shops for his wife
  "Maria Hayseed visits New York"
  "Miss Swat-the-fly: an ardent reformer"
  "Our telephone operator whiles away dreary hours!"
  A "pep expert" livens up an audience
  The prominent citizen addressing the graduating class
  "Selina Sues sees the show"
  The speed kids vs. The lightning flashes
  "Stealthy Steve the sleuth"
  "A student of nature"
  "Tony"
*Taking Maw's advice, by Jay Tobias. (2m, 1f) SNAPPY
      p38-41.
Talk-fest. FERRIS p36.
"Talk of the town." FERRIS p42.
A talk on athletics. DEPEW p204-206.
Talk on business or profession. DEPEW p181.
Talk on hobbies. DEPEW p181.
Talking business. ABELL—STUNTS p44-45.
The talking mail box. ABELL—STUNTS p51-55.
Talks on attendance. DEPEW p243-244.
Talks on travel. DEPEW p181.

Talky-talk. *See* Stage chatter

Tall story club. DEPEW p220-224.

Talloween fortunes (for Hallowe'en) by Beatrice Plumb.
CASEY—PEPPY p107-109.

Tall circles. GEISTER—NEW p11-12.

Tandem. GEISTER—NEW p53.

The tantalizing tune. FUNNY p22-23.

*"The tapestries chamber" (from the story by Sir Walter
Scott) (3m, 1f) PROVENCE—EASY p77-87.

Tardiness
Excuses for being late
Late again (2)
Over the slide
Singing stunt
Why Jack was late

The tattoo shop. CONNOR p40.

Tax assessors
*"The census talker" (HUBER—THREE)
*A farm for sale
*"West wind"

Taxation
Income tax advice

Taxi. DRUMMOND—STUNT FUN p69.

Taxicabs
Back-seat driving (3)

Taxidermy
*Two shorts, one long

The tea kettle. CROWLEY p49,52.

Teachers
*Let the punishment fit the crime

Teaching them to drive. EISENBERG—FUN p136-137.

Teapot. JOHNSON—BAKER's p90-91.

"Tearing time". HUBER—EASY p70-72.

The tea room minstrelettes. KASER—TEN p9-20.

Tearooms
The Elberta: a peach of a tea room in Georgia

"Teen-ager" plays
See also High school
*Afternoon at Central Station

*Anybody's gift
*Blind date
*Camp Crowhill here we come
*The craftsman
*Day of departure
*End of the line
*Entertainment committee
*Evening bells
*Help wanted—badly
*Holiday homecoming
*House quest
*The idol worshippers
*It's no picnic
*Keep smiling
*Life is so dull
*Oh, waitress!
*Science is wonderful
*Sitting tonight
*Star dust
*Subscribe now
*Swank night
*Sweater girls
*Telegram. (2m, 1f) PROVENCE—LIGHT p5-7.
Telegram from the district governor. DEPEW p210-211.
Telegrams
   Zoological garden
Telegrams. DEPEW p178.
The telenews machine. DRUMMOND—STUNT—FUN p93-96.
Telepathy. GEISTER—NEW p83-85.
Telephoning
   The berth of an Upper or Howareya?
   Betty at the telephone
  *Cards on the table
  *Crossed wires
  *Excuse it, please (2)
   Long distance
  *"No joke"
  *Number, please!
   "Our telephone operator whiles away dreary hours!"

Phoney calls (2)
*Speech through wires
Telephone booth. EISENBERG—HAND. p72-73.
Telephone conversation. PARTIES p60.
*Telephone tactics. (2f) STARR—JR. p56-60.
Television
  *The black sheep
  *Blank check
  *The bright world
  *A date with Kate
  *Fan mail
  The fixit clinic
  The flimflam television
  *Happy birthday
  Historical 4-D television
  *Just plain efficiency
  *Last chance
  *No fight tonight
  Radio or television broadcast
  *Room service
  *Small sale
  Spirit television
  A star is born
  *Tenting tonight
  *Tick tock
  *Too many types
  *Virus V
  The woman's night television program
*"Television". (19 or more char.) MACDONALD p17-25.
Tell, William
  Bill Tell
Tell my age. YOUNG—GAMES p31.
*Tell no tales. (3m, 2f) HUBER—CHAR. p89-98.
Telldown, by Gladys Lloyd. CASEY—PEPPY p81-82.
Telling fortunes. BRIDGE p72-74.
Telling right from left. EISENBERG—FUN p43-44.
*Telling the truth. (4b) IRISH—CHILDREN'S p59-62.
Telling the world, by Harry W. Githens. PRESTON p79-87.
Tempus fugit, by Gladys Lloyd. JOLLY p93.

*Ten barrooms in one night, by Charles George. (4m, 2f) BAKER'S—GAY p18-22.

Ten beans. DEPEW p214.

*Ten-minute egg, by Grace Keith Samuelson. (2m) CASEY—PEPPY p67.

*A ten-minute whiteface minstrel show. (12m & f) PRESTON —FUN p87-91.

Ten nails. DEPEW p317.

Tennis match. PRESTON p10.

"Tennis teasers—love all!" FERRIS p67.

The tense moment, by Arthur L. Kaser. BRINGS—MASTER p285-286.

*Tenting tonight. (1m, 1f, 4b) HUBER—TV p39-46.

Terminal tag. GEISTER—NEW p50-51.

A terrible ghost story. THREE—STUNTS p2-3.

*A terrible mistake. (2b) PROVENCE—LIGHT p80-82.

The test of fire. CORMACK p33-34.

*The tethered viciousness. (2b, 2g) RYAN p75-77.

Texas
  "Across the plains"—"The Texas rangers"
  Deep in the heart of Texas
  "T" is for Texas

Thackeray, William Makepeace—"Vanity Fair"
  Becky Sharp

Thank you, by Alta Toepp. CASEY—PEPPY p83.

*Thank you for coming, by Bob Royce. (2f) BRINGS— MASTER p279-280.

Thanksgiving
  See also Pilgrims
  The ancient festival
  *Aunty Hodge's Thanksgiving dinner
  Cornfield capers
  Fun leaves
  The idea of Thangsgiving through the ages
  *I'll be home Thanksgiving
  Our country
  Our Thanksgiving dinner
  *Passing the turkey
  *Pilgrim material

Burying Jacksonville
Burying the seniors
The case of John Imbecile
Chicago
*Curtain time (2)
A day in Seville
Double quartet
The Elberta; a peach of a tea room in Georgia
Ellis Island
The employment office
An evening with the American girl
Grandmaw and grandpaw at the railroad track
Heaven's gate
Hickville comes to conference
Identifying articles blindfolded
Indian medicine
The jig-saw puzzle
King for a day
Kitchen cabinet orchestra
Living pictures (DEPEW)
Long distance
Mars views the earth
*The matinee
Memories
Napoleon's farewell to his grandmother
The President's dream
The questionable well
*Rehearsal
Roman football game
"Selina Sue sees the show"
The spirit cabinet
Spirit reading
Style show (DEPEW)
Sunday a.m. in the average home
*'Tis and tisn't
United by love
What it takes to make a man
The whopper club
Womanless wedding

Theatre box, by Beatrice Plumb. CASEY—PEPPY p70.

*Their first play, by Arthur L. Kaser. (3m, 2f) BRINGS—
MASTER p138-140.

*Their golden wedding anniversary. (1m, 2f) DRUMMOND—
THREE p58-60.

*Then—and now. (teacher, 8g) BARBEE p34-35.

*There are badges and badges. (2m, 1f) DRUMMOND—
THREE p54-57.

There are crows that make us grumpy. DEPEW p281.

There are eats that make us happy. DEPEW p277.

*There are life guards and life guards. (3m, 2f)
DRUMMOND p5-8.

*There is a reason. (2m) PROVENCE—LIGHT p91-92.

*There is always a way. (3m) PROVENCE—LIGHT p86-88.

There were three young maids of Lee. ENTERTAIN—
STUNTS p2.

There's a conference place. DEPEW p282.

*There's a sandburr in gran-pa's stocking, by Arthur L.
Kaser. (5f) SHANNON p16-33.

*There's going to be a wedding, by Arthur L. Kaser.
4m, 2f, 3 or 4g) BRINGS—MASTER p148-152.

There's Maizie on the air. LLOYD p13.

*There's one born every minute. (1m, 5f) EASY—BLACKOUTS
p65-70.

There's one born every minute, by William Milligan. JOHN-
SON—EASY p9-11.

These United States. CROWLEY p71-76.

They total 80. DEPEW p349.

*Thick and thin. (1m, 2f) JOHNSON—BAKER's p7-10.

*A thief in the house. (3m, 3f) KASER—AMATEURS' p58-54.

Thieves. *See* Burglars and burglary

Thieves. YOUNG—GAMES p79.

*Thieves in the night. (2m, 1f) LYONS p139-142.

Thimble tap. CASEY—PEPPY p87.

Think of a number. DEPEW p295-296.

*The thinkers. (6f) HUBER p53-61.

*The third degree, by Selden M. Loring. (6) EASY—IMPR.
p22-29.

The thirst. CORMACK p36.

*The thirteenth trump. (2m, 1f) KELLEY p62-67.

This and that, by Alta Toepp. CASEY—PEPPY p83.

*This brave new world. (8m) STAHL—LAND. p29-60.

This is a movie. EASY—STUNTS p9-10.

*"This is Station PUNK". (2m, 2f) DRUMMOND—FOOT 9-14.

*This is the night. (2m, 1f) HUBER—VAUD. p47-51.

This one, that one. GEISTER—NEW p87-88.

Those evening belles. LLOYD p28.

Thought transference. DRUMMOND—SPOT p26.

Thought transmission cards. DRUMMOND—STUNT FUN p64-66.

Thought waves. EISENBERG—FUN p112-113.

The three bears. EISENBERG—HAND. p60-62.

*Three birthdays. (4b, 2g) BUGBEE—LIVELY p56-59.

Three braw Janes. LLOYD p75.

The three disgraces. BRIDGE p27.

*Three in one, by Ray Christie. (1m, 1f, 3 radio speakers). GITKENS p54-57.

Three-legged race. DEPEW p319.

Three-legged swimming race. DEPEW 327.

Three little pigs — and the wolf, by Beatrice Plumb. BRINGS —MASTER p430-431.

Three men on chairs. DEPEW p172.

The three modern bears. SHELDON p26-29.

The three musketeers. BUGBEE—LIVE WIRE p74-76.

"3.98", by Beaulah Tillotson. (1m, 1f) ROHRBOUGH p150.

*Three o'clock in the morning, by Charles F. Wells. (3m) JOHNSON—EASY p44-45.

The three R's. GEISTER—NEW p43.

*"Three Romeos". (4m, 1f) STAHL—HEARTY p60-63.

*Three strikes. (1m, 2f) HUBER—FOUR p131-134.

*Three strokes too many. (2m) PROVENCE—LIGHT p110-112.

*"Three Sundays in a week". (From the story by Edgar Allen Poe). (4m, 1f) PROVENCE—EASY p24-31.

Three times 7 equals 20. DEPEW p348.

*The three unfortunates. (3m) "THAT GOOD" p83-85.

*Time's up. (2m, 1f) DRUMMOND—SPOT p50.

Tipperary. GEISTER—NEW p12.

Tippo's horse. DRUMMOND—SPOT p59-61.

Tires for defense. BUCHANAN p45-47.

*Tis and tisn't. (2m, 1f) KAUFMAN—HIGHLOWBROW
    p105-119.

'Tis here, 'tis gone. DRUMMOND—STUNT p29.

*Tit for tat, by Richard Drummond. (2m) BRINGS—MASTER
    p163-164.

Titles of songs. *See* Song titles

The Tivoli night club. ABELL—STUNTS p76-77.

TNT. WILLIAMS p13.

*To Ellen from Dad. (2m, 2f) McCOY—HOLIDAY p96-104.

*To meet the Duke. (1m, 3f) KELLEY p14-17.

To start the party, by Mabel Tuttle Craig. JOLLY p89.

*To the ends of the earth. (2m, 1f, officer) PROVENCE—
    LIGHT p26-28.

"To the swift". HUBER—EASY p58-60.

*To whom it may concern. (2m, 4f) WEATHERS p83-100.

Toad in a hole. FRICK—SUMMER p19.

A toast to —— high school. ABELL—PEP p102-103.

A toast to the banquet. DEPEW p146-147.

Toasts

  Banquet toasts

  A few toasts

Toasts. (3) BUGBEE—GOOFY p108-109; JOLLY p100-101;
    "THAT GOOD" p87-89.

Toasts for the class banquet. LAMKIN & FLORENCE p58-61.

"Tobacco Road"

  *Giving you the jeeters

Tobias, Jay

  *Atavism or women are so brave

  *Baby's first word

  *Design for dueling

  *Sambo am a dangerous man

  *Sandy, defunct

  *Taking Maw's advice

  *Triangle (EASY—IMPR.)

  *What's going on?

Toepp, Alta
  Ad writing
  Crazy speeches
  Diaries of the distinguished
  Finding the stars
  Gazook touch
  Hat arguments
  Indoor meet
  Nuts to you
  Scooping the scoop
  Shake!
  Sing down
  Sing song
  Song matching
  Spoon pass
  Sundown-sunup—breakfast!
  Thank you
  This and that
  Time! (for party or picnic)
  Wink! Wink!
*"Tom goes sissy". (3m, 3f) DRUMMOND—STUNT p51-54.
*Tom Tit Tot. (2m, 2f) FRICK—FALL p72-79.
Tomb-stones. WILLIAMS p12-13.
*Tomorrow at ten. (2b, 3g) BARBEE p57-60.
Tongue twisters. DEPEW p361.
Tongue twisters
  "Betsey speaks a piece for the caller"
  Sally Snodgrass's sad story
  The sifter
  Stringing them
  The woodchuck
Tongue twisters. BREEZY p55.
*The tonsorial quartette. (4m) BAKER'S—GAY p27-28.
"Tony". FERRIS p21.
Tony and his monk. DRUMMOND—SPOT p80.
*Too busy. (1m, 2f) QUICK p65-68.
*Too late. (2m, 1f) PROVENCE—LIGHT p35-39.
Too many cooks. EISENBERG—FUN p94-95.
*Too many teeth. (5m, 1f) HUBER—FOUR p156-159.

*Too many types. (2m, 2f) HUBER—TV p23-30.

"Too smart". HUBER—EASY p79-81.

Too wise. DEPEW p354.

Tools of the trade, by Mabel Tuttle Craig. JOLLY p90.

Toothbrush. EISENBERG—HAND. p82.

Toothpicks
   Handkerchief and toothpick

Topsy turvy concerts. (2) ENTERTAIN—STUNTS p1;
     PARTIES p34.

The torture chamber. HUBER—GIANT p130-131.

Total 20. DEPEW p349.

Touch and go. March music. GEISTER—NEW p15-16.

The touch of the ghost. YOUNG—GAMES p24-25.

Touches of home. EISENBERG—FUN p79-80.

Tourists
  *The prevaricator
   Sightseeing in a wheelbarrow

The tournament. ABELL—PEP p72-77.

The town crier. ABELL—PEP p116-117.

The tox without a fail. EISENBERG—HAND. p49-50.

Tra la la. FUNNY p30.

Track
  *Here's the track team!

Trades
   Tools of the trade

The trades quartette. JOLLY p86-87.

A traffic jam. BUGBEE—GOOFY p24.

*Traffic trouble. By Effa E. Preston. (2m, 2f) PRESTON
    p48-50.

Tragedy! DRUMMOND—STUNT FUN p40-41.

*A tragedy in rhyme. (1m, 2f) McCOY—SIXTEEN p34-39.

The tragedy of Squirrel Bait Kingdom. BRIDGE p24-26.

*Tragedy of the sea. (3m, 4f) KASER—AMATEUR's p40-47.

Tragic news. DRUMMOND—STUNT FUN p21-22.

The tragic tintype, by Beatrice M. Casey. CASEY—PEPPY
    p35-36.

Trail lists. FRICK—SUMMER p9.

Trailers
   Keep the home tires turning
*The train to Loontown. (6m, 3f) IRISH—CATCHY p94-99.
*The train to Mauro, by S. A. Frost. (2m, 2f) JOHNSON—
      EASY p58-64.
   Trained animals. FRICK—FALL p38-39.
   The trained dog. CORMACK p30.
   The trained horse, Battle-axe, by J. Hal Connor. BUGBEE
      —LIVE WIRE p18-20.
*The training camp, by Norman L. Zeno, Jr. (5m, extras)
      MILLER—BROADWAY p15-22.

Trains
   See also Porters; Pullmans; Railway stations
   Fresh!
   Grandmaw and grandpaw at the railroad track
   *Hiram and Mirandy
   *A maiden in distress
   *Stop—look—listen
   *The train to Loontown
   *The wasted tip
*The traitor. (3m) PROVENCE—LIGHT p56-59.
   "Tramp! Tramp! Tramp! (3) JOHNSON—BAKER'S p60.

Tramps
   *An April Fool joke
   *Cream puffs
   *Dr. Dobbs' assistant
   *Gratitude
   *"Harmony a la hobo"
   Hobo day
   A hobo fight
   *Hobo minstrels
   Hungry spooks
   *In giving thanks
   *Long live the king
   Marching through Georgia
   The optimistic road knight (2)
   *Success story (QUICK)

A trip to the moon. CORMACK p28.

Triple oration. DRUMMOND—STUNT FUN p10.

Triple somersault. CASEY—PEPPY p68.

Triplets. GEISTER—NEW p80.

Trouble
Burdens

*Trouble in Paradise, by Albert G. Miller. (3m, extras)
MILLER—BROADWAY p31-40.

Truck lines, by Gladys Lloyd. JOLLY p94-95.

True or false. SHELDON—GIANT QUIZ p87-91.

The true story of Captain John Smith, by Richard Drummond. BRINGS—MASTER p295-300; DRUMMOND—IMPR. p30-36.

The true story of George and the cherry tree. DRUMMOND—STUNT FUN p39-40.

Trump, Trump, Trump. LLOYD p58-60.

Truth
See also Lie detectors; Untruth
*"Joining the whole truth club"
*Telling the truth

*The truth about Sleeping Beauty. (more than 13 char.)
MILLER—STUNT p61-71.

Truth or consequences. DEPEW p308.

Truthful Betsey. PRESTON—PANTOM. p144-150.

Try your balance. DEPEW p293.

A tub on the ocean wave. ABELL—STUNTS p26-27.

Tub race. DEPEW p327.

Tug-of-war
Human tug of war
Tug of war. (2) CORMACK p35; DEPEW p328.
Tumbling. FRICK—FALL p39.

Tumbling
Breaking into print
Circus parade tumblers
Pickininnies
Rag dolls
Whoa, Nancy!

The tune the salesman played. (2) EASY—ENTERTAIN p83-96;
By Ken Kelly and R. Paul Fiscus. JOHNSON—EASY
p107-110.
*Tunetown gossip or Carol entertains the musical club, by
Mary H. Derby. (8f) JOHNSON—BAKER'S
p26-31.
Tuning in on the past. FUNNY p56-58.
Tunnel leap frog. FRICK—SUMMER p84.
Tunnel relay. FRICK—FALL p23.
*Turkey. (4m) KAUFMAN—HIGHLOWBROW p121-126.
Turkey in the straw. DRUMMOND—STUNTS FUN p11.
Turn your back. HUBER—GIANT p145-146.
Turnabout quartet. EISENBERG—FUN p193.
*Turning tail. (2m, 4f) HOPE p37-39.
*Turning the fables on Aesop. (2m, 2w, narrator); PRESTON
—FUN p83-87.
Turning the tables. (2) CANOPY—HIGH; DRUMMOND—
STUNT FUN p109-110.
Turtle race. DEPEW p326.
Tuttle, Mabel
Guess who (CASEY—PEPPY)
Twelve parts of the body. YOUNG—GAMES p42-43.
*Twelve skulls mean death. (4m, 2f) WEATHER—MYSTERIES
p54-65.
A twenty cent trick. DRUMMOND—STUNT p25-26.
*Twenty-first century. (2m, 1f) PROVENCE—LIGHT p18-22.
Twenty questions. (2) BARBEE p15-16; By Beatrice Plumb.
BRINGS—MASTER p422.
Twenty-six sheep. DEPEW p341.
Twins
The rubberneck twins
*Some dilemma
Two benches in the park, by Beatrice M. Casey. CASEY—
—PEPPY p17-20.
*Two boys meet girl. (2m, 1f) TAGGART—FIVE p17-24.
Two canaries. DEPEW p365.
Two cats and a mouse. YOUNG—GAMES p81-82.
Two chances. EISENBERG—FUN p87.
*Two cops off duty. (2) KASER—BUTTON p100-104.

Two crooks. EISENBERG—FUN p28.

Two-faced quartet. (2) DEPEW p256; DRUMMOND—STUNT FUN p109-113.

The two farmers. DEPEW p340.

*Two hats for Easter. (3) McCOY—HOLIDAY p38-44.

Two in one. PRESTON—FUN p193.

Two marionettes, by Arthur Law and Edith Cook. ROHR-BOUGH p130-135.

Two men and a girl. GEISTER—NEW p75-76.

The two messages. JOHNSON—BAKER's p54.

Two noses. EISENBERG—HAND. p51-52.

*Two shorts, one long. by LeRoy Stahl. (2m, 1f) EASY—SKITS p7-11.

Two sinners, by Ella Wheeler Wilcox. BAKER's—GAY p37-38.

Tying them up. DEPEW p196-197.

Tyler, Jocelyn W.
  Haunts of the jungle
  When Julius Ceasar

Tyler, Mel
  *Father and child doing well
  *Forget met not!
  *Honorable mention
  *Mountain magic

Typewriters
  *Closed deal

*"The ultra-modern school". (4m, 4f) MACDONALD p47-56.

*The Um-brellah sisters. (2f) JOHNSON—EASY p98-101.

*Uncle Cy at the talkies. (2m, 1f) GEORGE—TEN p5-9.

Uncle George. GODDARD—CHILDREN's p27-28.

*Uncle Jimmy's Thanksgiving. (3m, 3f) BUGBEE—CATCHY p54-60.

Uncle Sam. CROWLEY p49,53.

*Uncle Sam's May party. (1m, 1f) BUGBEE—CATCHY p96-99.

*Uncle Sam's peace party. (2b, 2g) BUGBEE—LIVELY p118-127.

Uncle Sam's singing army. FERRIS p124.

*Uncle Sam's Thanksgiving. (1m, 1f, 7 extras) BUGBEE—CATCHY p51-54.

*Uncle Tom's nabbin' or The Effervescent evaporation of
  Eva, by Don Fitzwater. (2m, 1f) BAKER'S—GAY
  p22-23.

Uncles
  *Old fogy
Under one. FRICK—FALL p22.
Under the hanging mistletoe. EISENBERG—HAND. p126.
Under the spreading chestnut tree. DRUMMOND—STUNT FUN
  p110.
*Under the spreading chestnut tree, by Harry W. Githens,
  (4m, 2f) GITHENS p96-100.
Undressing act. CANOPY—HIGH p106-107.

Unemployed
  *Let's end it all
*The unemployed. (1m, 1f) PROVENCE—KNOCKOUT p9-11.
An unexpected vanishing. TARBELL—CRAZY p94,95-96.
Unfinished business. GEISTER—NEW p66-67.
Unfinished proverbs. BREEZY p53-55.

Unions
  *Local number ten
A unique plank carrier. TARBELL—CRAZY p32-33.
United by love. DEPEW p60-65.

United States—Armed Forces
  See also Sailors; Soldiers
  Advice to draftees
  The firing squad
  *The G.I. minstrels
  *Going somewhere
  *He knew his strength
  *Heroes
  *It's only propaganda
  *Keep your dignity
  *Salute
  Uncle Sam's singing army
  War is not well

United States—History
  See also Civil War; etc.
  *America begins
  *The magic wand

Unlucky 1930. DEPEW p348.

Unlucky number. BRINGS—MASTER p391.

The unpaid chorus in action. WILL.AMS p48.

Untruth

See also Lie detectors

*A-fishing I have been

*The awful fate of a fibber (2)

*The liar's club (2)

Liars' convention

Maybe you did, but I doubt it

A sure cure for falsehoods (2)

Tall story club

*A thrill from Japan

The whopper club

Unusual questions. YOUNG—GAMES p75.

*Unwarranted speed. (3m, 3f) TOPOLKA p79-86.

Up above where all is love. FRICK—FALL p43-44.

Up and down the scale. JOHNSON—BAKER'S p101-102.

*Up from the depths or The rise of Tilly Tureen. (2m, 2f)
PARSONS p7-16.

Up from the doorstep. EISENBERG—FUN p167-176.

Up on the house-top (Christmas). PRESTON—PANTOM.
p235-237.

An up-to-date shell game. (2m) TARBELL—CRAZY p23-26.

Up, up, up. HUBER—GIANT p158-159.

Uplift. GEISTER—NEW p74.

Upside down. JOHNSON—BAKER'S p100-101.

Upside-down quartet. DEPEW p256.

Upside down stunt. TARBELL—CHALK STUNTS p61.

U.R. next. BUGBEE—LIVE WIRE p49-50.

*Uranium or bust, by Richard Drummond. (2m) BRINGS—
MASTER p272-276.

*Use the book. (2m, 2f) HUBER—CHAR. p49-58.

*Use this book. (2m, 2f) HUBER—CHAR. p49-58.

A useless clean-up. TARBELL—COMEDY p29.

The usual way, by Frederic E. Weatherby. ABELL—STUNTS
p56-58.

*Vacation. (3m, 3f) LAMKIN & FLORENCE p85-104.

A vacation from mom, by Beatrice Plumb. BREEZY p55-56.

Vacation party (decorations). YOUNG—GAMES p109.

Vacations *See also* Travel
  *Day of departure
  *Oh, waitress!
  *Summer holidays

Vaccination
  *The fight against disease
The vacuum virtuoso. KASER—FUNNY p118-120.
The valedictorian. LAMKIN & FLORENCE p16-17.
The valedictory. LAMKIN & FLORENCE p18-19.
Valentine. (2) ABELL—STUNTS p92-93; CROWLEY p38-39.

Valentine Day
  *Aunt Mehitable's beaux
  Best spring romances
  Comic valentines (3)
  *Cupid on a rampage
  A cupid's tour of the world
  Great "heartists"
  *The lover's errand (JOHNSON—EASY)
  A pink valentine party
  *"Sam Weller's valentine"
  *Writing valentines
Valentine day (games and stunts). KEMMERER—GAMES
    p14-15.
*"Valley View minstrelettes". (5f, chorus). DRUMMOND—
    FUNNY p70-80.
Van Derveer, Lettie C.
  Finish-them stunt
  How's this for romance?
  If-I-weren't-myself stunt
  Jiffy plays or charades
  Lucky words (spelling contest)
  Mother Goose guesses
  Paper and pencil games
  Prof. Quack's quaint quiz
  A pronounce-down bee
  Quick reading contest
Vandersall, Bernice
  Hisses and kisses
The vanishing line. TARBELL—FUN p18,20-23.

The vanishing quartette. (4m) DRUMMOND—STUNT FUN p9.
The vanishing spinach. TARBELL—COMEDY p47-54.
The vanishing table. TARBELL—COMEDY p12.
Vanity bags. GEISTER—NEW p76-77.
Vanity fair. CANOPY—HIGH p57.
"Vanquishing vamps". FERRIS p84.
The variety store. CANOPY—HIGH p55,57.

Vaudeville
   See also Amateur hours
   Amateur night
   "Booking for vaudeville"
   Departmental vaudeville
   *"The mail-order dragon"
   *"One hundred and forty-four davenports"
   *"Pocahontas", or "The Indian maiden's travail"
   *"The prince and the sleeping beauty"
   *Quiet, please
   *The watch on the Rhine
   *"With General Wow in darkest Africa"
   *Ye olde time vaudeville
*"The vaudeville agency". (6m, 5f) MacDONALD p79-90.
*Vaudeville skit. (1m, 1f) CONNOR p49-53.
Vaulting the horses. BUGBEE—GOOFY p79-80.
Vegetable soup, by Mabel Tuttle Craig. CASEY—PEPPY p96.

Vegetables
   Popular garden pets
The ventriloquist. DEPEW p212-213.
*The ventriloquist. (1f, 1b, 1g) EISENBERG—HAND. p103-104.
*Ventriloquist and his boy, by Arthur L. Kaser. (3m)
      BRINGS—MASTER p392-394.
A ventriloquist stunt. BUGBEE—LIVE WIRE p34-37.

Ventriloquists
   Geometry for moderns
   The great ventriloquist (2)
   The house of horrors
   Jim and Jerry
   Oscar the blockhead
   Rastus and the ventriloquist
   *Who s a dummy?

Venus
Citizens of Venus and Mars
*The Venus beauty factory. (14f or less) KASER—TOP
p73-83.
Verse. *See* Poetical
*A very good reason. (2m) REACH—QUICK p84-87.
Very short shorts, by Richard Drummond. BRINGS—MASTER
p398-401.
*Veteran veterinaries. (3m, 1f) KASER—SURE p83-92.

Veterinarians
*The poor little dear
*Veteran veterinarians
Vicarious dramatics. GEISTER—NEW p74-75.
*Vice versa. (1m, 1f, announcer) KAUFMAN—HIGHLOWBROW
p87-92.
Victory for our team. STARR—JR. p96-100.
Victrola musical. DEPEW p260.
*"The village band rehearses". (5) DRUMMOND—FOOT
p58-61.
*The village concert. (3m, 2f) HOPE p14-17.
*The villain still pursued her. (2m, 2f) REACH—QUICK
p44-49.

Villains. *See* Melodramas
The vintage of 1880. ENTERTAIN—STUNTS p2.
Violin solo. (3) BRINGS—MASTER p383; DRUMMOND—
STUNT—FUN p51; JOHNSON—BAKER'S p86-87.

Violinists
The acrobatic violinist
Stringing them
The vacuum virtuoso

Virginia
*America begins

Virginia Reel
Couple Virginia reel
Virtue triumphant, by Charles F. Wells. JOHNSON—EASY
p30-34.
*Virus V. (12m, 8f) PRESTON—FUN p51-62.
Visiting cheerleaders. ABELL—PEP p87.

Visitors
   *Entertaining sister's beau
   *Entertaining sister's beaux (2)
   *Morning callers
   *Tillie's arrival
*Vocational style show. (1f, 1g, extras) BARBEE p45-47.

Vocations
   See also Professions; Trades
      Professions
   *Vocational style show
   Your future is at stake
*Voices from the void. (1m, 1f) HUBER—GIANT p33-41.
Volstead quartette. JOHNSON—BAKER'S p103.
Vote for me. (3) By Vance Clifford. BRINGS—MASTER
      p349-351; By Arthur L. Kaser. BRINGS—MASTER
      p363-364; KASER—FUNNY p92-94.

Voting
   *When Abner played possum
Vowels. GEISTER—NEW p68,90.
The vulture and the tough. CROWLEY p67-68.

The wail of the Christmas ties. FERRIS p94-95.
Waiter fight. DEPEW p209-210.
Waiter stunt. DEPEW p171-172.
*The waiter who waited. HUBER—No p32-37.

Waiters and waitresses
   *At your service
   The busy waiter
   *Oh, waitress!
   *Up from the depths or The rise of Tillie Tureen
   *Your order, please
*Waitin for de snipes. (3m) RYAN p63-69.
*Waiting for the stump hollow train. (10f) KASER—TEN
      p69-80.
*"Wait'll you sees *Mah* man!" (2m, 2f) CASEY p53-59.
"Walk of death". HUBER—EASY p93-95.
Walker, Kent
   The nonsense school

*The walkie-talkie juke box. (4m) KENT—ONE p54-61.
"The walking lesson". HUBER—EASY p32-35.
Walking on eggs. BUGBEE—LIVE WIRE p54.
Walking, talking, singing and dancing dolls. CONNOR p20-23.
Walking the tight rope. CANOPY—HIGH p87.
A walkout. DEPEW p210.
Wand race. GEISTER—NEW p52.
Wandering Willie Willie. KASER—BUTTON p111-112.
Want a band? TARBELL—COMEDY p12-15.
*"Wanted. capable stenographer". (2m, 4f) CASEY p87-95.
*Wanted: young office assistant. (2b) STARR—RADIO p65.

War
    See also Historical; U.S.—History; names of wars
    *Heroes
    The war in song. CONNOR p36-38.
*"War is ——!" (3m) STAHL—HEARTY p23-24.
    War is not well. HUBER—PRACT. p58-63.
*"War scare". (4m) STAHL—HEARTY p11-13.
    "Warming up" games. *See* "Get acquainted" stunts;
        Mixers
*Was his face red! By J. C. McMullen. (1m, 1f) JOHNSON—
    EASY p28-29.

Washing
    *Turning the fables on Aesop

Washington, George
    Cherry tree stunts
    *Double tribute
    *God's country
    I did it with my little hatchet
    *In the secret drawer
    Meet George and Martha Washington
    *The prevaricator
    Profile stunt
    *The stars and stripes
    *Telling the truth
    *Three birthdays
    The true story of George and the cherry tree
    Who stole the cigars?
Washington crosses the Delaware. BUGBEE—GOOFY
    p98-101.

*Washington or Lincoln. (3b) EDGERTON p87-88.
*A Washington reception. (7m, 2f) BUGBEE—CATCHY
    p78-83.
Washington's birthday. *See* Washington, George
Washington's birthday (decorations). YOUNG—GAMES p105.
Washington's birthday (games and stunts). KEMMERER—
    GAMES p11-14.
Washington's farewell address. (2) BRINGS—MASTER p378;
    DRUMMOND—STUNT FUN p49.

Washington, D.C.
    *All aboard for Washington!
*The wasted tip, by Nancy Beach. (3m) ROHRBOUGH p9-11.
The watch fob minstrels. KASER—GAY p9-14.
Watch night stunt, by Beatrice Plumb. "THAT GOOD" p38-39.
*The watch on the Rhine. (2m, extras) STAHL—MORE p11-17.
Watch our smoke! By Robert N. McGregor. BREEZY p71.
*Watch this. (2m, 1f) HUBER—FOUR p65-68.
A watch trick. DRUMMOND—STUNT p39-40.
Watch your step. YOUNG—GAMES p30-31.

Watchmen
    *There's is a reason
Water balloon race. DEPEW p325.
Water baseball. DEPEW p325.
Water basketball. DEPEW p325.
Water candle race. DEPEW p327.
A water carnival. ABELL—STUNTS p82-85.
Water stunts. FRICK—SUMMER p63-64.
Water uphill. DEPEW p345.
Water, water! EISENBERG—FUN p111.
*Water, water. (2f, extras) PROVENCE—LIGHT p31-32.

Watermelons
    The great watermelon uprising
Wax figures up-to-date. BUGBEE—LIVE WIRE p43-44.

Wax works
    Manager's chamber of horrors

W.C.T.U.
    *The Brewer's great white horses or Life with Fodder
Way down yonder. EISENBERG—HAND. p57.
*We agree. (3m) HUBER—SIX p26-32.

We always stress harmony—The music department.
      LAMKIN & FLORENCE p52.
We don't like coffee. YOUNG—GAMES p58-59.
*We fix it. (3b, 8g) GODDARD—CHILDREN's p53-61.
We introduce, with pride. EISENBERG—FUN p165-166.
We present our winners. BARBEE p91-93.
"We thank you" (a greeting). KASER—FUNNY p4.
*We want your business, by Charles Sherman. (2m) MILLER
      BROADWAY p69-76.
We won't go home until morning. GEISTER—NEW p32-33.

Weather
   Here comes the weatherman
   *A hot day
   Rainbow sing-down
*Weather-or not, by Carl Webster Pierce. (3m, 1f) EASY—
      SKITS p33-41.
Weatherby, Ferderic E.
   The usual way
Weaver, Cressy M.
   Hand me down a quart of corn
   Just a voice on the radio
   The old gray mare (CASEY—PEPPY)
The weaver. GEISTER—NEW p49-50.
Weaver's relay. DEPEW p331.
*Wedded bliss. (3m, 1f) PROVENCE—KNOCKOUT p45-47.
*Wedding bells and belles. (5m, 7f) KASER—MERRY p83-95.
*Wedding bells for Hepsidie. (4m, 7f) KASER—MERRY p58-78.
Wedding of Augustus Peabean and Perlina Eggplant, by
      Chester Willis. BUGBEE—LIVE WIRE p106.

Weddings
   See also Mock weddings
   *"The bridegroom cometh"
   *The fatal wedding
   *Here comes the bride (2)
   *Woman's way

Weddings, Golden
   *Golden wedding
   *Their golden wedding anniversary
The weed in the eye. TARBELL—COMEDY p54-56.

The week before Christmas. EISENBERG—HAND. p149-150.
Weighed in the balance. ABELL—STUNTS p59-60.

Weight
    Gold or feathers?
    Senior Limburgio, strong man
    Strong man act
*The welcome. (2g) BRINGS—MASTER p280.
Welcome. DRUMMOND—STUNT p7.
Welcome and good-bye. (7g) CANOPY—HIGH p113-115.
Welcome, freshmen. STARR—JR. p12.
A welcome sentence. KASER—MERRY p30-42.
*Welcome, students. (2 students, 7 voices, glee clubs)
      STARR—RADIO p5-8.

Welcomes. *See* Introductions
We'll be going. DEPEW p285.
*Well qualified. (2) PROVENCE—LIGHT p54-55.
Wells, Charles F.
  *Do you believe in signs?
  Her souvenirs (SIX—NEW)
  How's your golf?
  The movie mystery
  No
  *Three o'clock in the morning
  Virtue triumphant
"We're as crazy as can be". DRUMMOND—STUNT p48-50.
We're forever boosting C.E. DEPEW p279.
We're glad this week has come. DEPEW p278.

West
    See also Cowboys; Texas; etc.
    "Across the plains"—"The Texas rangers"
    At home with the range.
    *The boots-and-saddle gang
    *Poison Gulch
    *Sulphur Crik
    *When the West was young
*"West wind". (2m, 1f) STAHL—HEARTY p20-22.
Weve been thinking. PRESTON—PANTOM. p219-222.
Wha' dat wattahmilyun gone? JOHNSON—BAKER'S p55-56.
What a breath! EISENBERG—HAND. p89.

"What's the matter with father", parody. Depew p280.

What's the word? Huber—Giant p144-145.

What's this. Young—Games p17.

What's wrong with this? Eisenberg—Hand. p124-125.

What's wrong with whom? By Beatrice Plumb. Brings
—Master p422-423.

What's your state? By Beatrice Plumb. (2) Brings—Master p430; "That Good" p43.

The whatzit bird. Crowley p34,36.

Wheel marching. Frick—Fall p30-31.

Wheel barrow. Frick—Summer p85.

Wheelbarrow race. Depew p329.

Wheelbarrow relay. Frick—Fall p22.

When a sleuth sleuths. Kaser—Bushel p5-9.

*When Abner played possum. (1m, 2f) Hoxie p45-51.

"When artists frolic"—"Mind-the-paint girls". Ferris p81-82.

*When David woke up. (2m, 4f) Hoxie p37-44.

When do we eat? Depew p283.

When ghosts walk. Frick—Summer p42-45.

When I was young. Rohrbough p151-153.

*When is the train due? By Arthur L. Kaser. (2m, 1f)
Brings—Master p390-391.

"When it's apple-blossom time in Normandy". Ferris p70.

When it's ten o'clock on Sunday. Depew p275.

When Johnny joined the army, by Karin Asbrand. "That
Good" p13-18.

When Johnny practices. Funny p19-20.

When Julius Caesar, by Jocelyn Wallace Tyler. Bugbee—
Live Wire p120-121.

When Molly was a baby. Parties p12.

"When the cows come home". Ferris p72.

*When the West was young. (4m, 5f) Kaser—Funny p62-70.

When we came in. Depew p281.

When you and I were young, by Lucile Crites. Breezy
p91-100.

"When you look in the heart of a rose" by Leo Feist;
"Mighty lak a rose" by E. Nevin (J. Church). Ferris
p70.

When you're right, you're wrong. Funny p8-9.

Where am I? By Gladys Lloyd. Casey—Peppy p8.

Where did you meet him? DEPEW p152.

Where is the plumber? (1m, 2f) PROVENCE—LIGHT p113-116.

Where the ocean breeze is blowing. DEPEW p274.

Where to find sympathy. EISENBERG—FUN p27.

Where's Gran'paw? By Arthur L. Kaser. (2) BRINGS—
MASTER p324; KASER—FUNNY p71-72.

*Where's Henry? (4m, 3f) KASER—BUSHEL p76-87.

*Where's my cake? (2b, 4g) IRISH—CHILDREN'S p48-51.

"Where's my sock?" DRUMMOND—STUNT FUN p15.

Where's the baby? (2) By Jeff Gannett. (2m, 2f) BRINGS—
—MASTER—p42-45; (2m, 2f) KASER—FUNNY p57-61.

Where's the collar button? YOUNG—GAMES p11.

Where's the youngster? By Beatrice Plumb. BRINGS—MAS-
TER p414.

Which book? DEPEW p300.

Which travels fastest? DEPEW p347.

While the organ peeled. EISENBERG—HAND. p135-136.

The whip. CANOPY—HIGH p55-56.

Whip tag. DEPEW p329.

Whistler's farewell to his mother. BRINGS—MASTER p386.

Whistles
   The three bears

Whistling magic. YOUNG—GAMES p41.

Whistling marathon. DEPEW p335.

White, Gail
   Going native
  *Just another one
   The perfect host
   Some like them thin

White, Kate Alice
   Driven from home

"White elephants"
   Exchanging white elephants

Whiteface minstrels, By Harry W. Githens. PRESTON p60-68.

Who am I? FRICK—FALL p4.

Who am I? New Year's entertainment. JOHNSON—BAKER'S
p51-53.

*Who buys? (speaker, 1b, voices) BARBEE p21-23.

Who hit me? JOHNSON—BAKER'S p98.

Who is my neighbor? JOHNSON—BAKER'S
   p91.
Who is so smart? EISENBERG—FUN p28.
Who reads the ads? YOUNG—GAMES p68.
Who stole the cigars? BUGBEE—LIVE WIRE p51-52.
*Who stole the world? (14m) KASER—MERRY p49-58.
Who was who? By Effa E. Preston. BRINGS—MASTER p411.
*Who wears the laurel crown? (2b, 2g, extras) BARBEE
   p51-52.
Who were they? DEPEW p350.
Who wrote it? BARBEE p60-64.
Who wrote it? (2m, 3f) TOPOLKA p55-59.
Whoa, Nancy! DRUMMOND—STUNT FUN p115.
Whodunit? SHELDON—GIANT QUIZ p71-79.
*The whole 'fam damily. (6m, 1f) SHELDON p76-80.
*The whole truth. (1m, 1f) REACH—QUICK p77-83.
*Wholesale jealousy". (10f) DRUMMOND—FUNNY p5-13.
The whopper club. DEPEW p115.
*Who's a dummy? (3m) HUBER—GIANT p26-32.
*Who's a hick? (3m, 1f) DRUMMOND—THREE p45-49.
Who's a poet? RYAN p100-101.
Who's crazy now? BUGBEE—GOOFY p35-37.
Who's who in basketball. ABELL—PEP p126-127.
Who's who? or The rougue's gallery, By Willis N. Bugbee.
   BREEZY p50-51.
*Who's your butler? (1m, 2f) HUBER—ARENA p76-83.
Whose hat is that? HUBER—GIANT p141-142.
Why Jack was late. DEPEW p206-208.
*Widow more than once. (2m, 1f) WEATHERS—MYSTERIES
   103-115.
Wiener roasts
   *Invitation to a wiener roast
"Wig-wag"—"All's well". FERRIS p76.
Wilcox, Ella Wheeler
   Two sinners
The wild and wooly cowboy. BUGBEE—NUTTY p14.
Wild animals and birds. CANOPY—HIGH p57.
The wild man from Borneo (a variation). CONNOR p26-30.
*The will and the way. (1m, 2f) STAHL—MORE p18-21.
William Tell. DRUMMOND—STUNT FUN p11-12.

William the Conqueror
    *"Scrambled dates"
Williams, Pearl
    * Do they?
*Willie the weeper. (1m, 3f) HUBER—GIANT p14-18.
Willis, Chester
    Wedding of Augustus Peabean and Perlina Eggplant
*Willoughby's widow. (5m, 10 extra f) PRESTON—FUN p68-72.

Wills
    *"Con Cregan's legacy"
    *The will and the way
Wilson, James
    Casey's revenge
Wilson, Marriott
    *Father and child doing well
    *Forget-me-not!
    *Honorable mention
    *Mountain magic
The wind gauge. BUGBEE—LIVE WIRE p56.
Windmills keep turning around. PRESTON—PANTOM.
    p237-240.
The window. DEPEW p361.
The window of Charvel. PRESTON—PANTOM p127-133.

Window shopping. *See* Shopping
*Window shopping. (2m, 1f) HUBER—ARENA p89-94.

Window-trimming
    *Willoughby's window
Wink! FUNNY p33-34.
Wink! Wink! By Alta Toepp. CASEY—PEPPY p90.
Winning that candy bar. DRUMMOND—STUNT FUN p59.
*The winning ticket, by Walter F. Kerr. (4m, 1f, announcer)
    SNAPPY p77-87.
Win-O-spin. SHELDON—GIANT QUIZ p52-60.
Winter adventure. EISENBERG—FUN p70-71.
*Winter carnival. (misc. char.) STARR—JR. p75-79.
Wiping up water. DEPEW p324.
*Wise and otherwise. (2m) KASER—BUTTON p80-85.
The wise photographer. YOUNG—GAMES p29.

Witches
  Ghosts (JOHNSON—BAKER'S)
  The witches' cauldron. FRICK—FALL p34.
  Witches' den. FRICK—FALL p42-43.
  The witches' incantation. JOHNSON—BAKER'S p54-55.
*With complications, by Marion Holbrook. (3m) SIX—NEW
      p29-32.
*"With General Wow in darkest Africa". (3m, 1f) STAHL—
      IMPRO. p21-28.
  "With the colors". FERRIS p76.
*Without benefit of license, by Arthur DeRoy Kaser.
      (3m) QUICK—COM. p97-100.
  Wittemore, Ruth H.
  The banana bandits

Wives
  *"The new invention"
  *Stringing along
  *"Wholesale jealousy"

"Wizard of Oz"
  In the land of Schmozz

Wolves
  Keeping the wolf away
*Woman of Hilltop House. (3m, 5f) WEATHERS p101-126.
  Womanless wedding. (2) DEPEW p117-121; JOHNSON—
      BAKER'S p103-104.
*The woman's hour. (12f) KENT—ONE p147-53.
  The woman's night television program. BUGBEE—NUTTY
      p55-59.
  Woman's way, by Arthur L. Rice. (3m, 2f) ROHRBOUGH
      p1-8.

Women *See also* Brides; Wives; etc.
  *The African explorer
  *Atavism, or women are so brave
  *First!
  *"The seven ages of woman"
  Women drivers. (2) By Arthur L. Kaser. BRINGS—MASTER
      p307; By Grace Keith Samuelson. "THAT GOOD" p47-48.

Women's clubs
  *Bewildering popularity

*Days gone by
*Potluck

Women's rights
  *Vice versa
  The wonder cornet. CONNOR p35-36.
*"Won't grandpa be surprised". (3m) DRUMMOND—STUNT
    p16-18.
  Wood, Mabel Travis
  *The matinee
  Woodward, Mary Jane
    Deep in the heart of Texas
  The woodchuck. DEPEW p360.
  Woodcraft league "movies". FERRIS p183-184.
  A woodcraft league number for boys. FERRIS p164-165.
  Wooden soldiers. DRUMMOND—STUNT FUN p10.
  Word acrobats. YOUNG—GAMES p50-51.
  Word contest. YOUNG—GAMES p82-83.

Word games
  See also Spelling
  Ad writing
  Adding adjectives
  Adjectives
  An alarming time
  Biography
  Bird competition
  A blank old lady
  Building words
  Cablegrams
  Can you read this letter?
  Catchy verses
  Character sketch
  Concealed jewels
  Consequences
  Constantinople
  Cross questions and crooked answers
  Crossword puzzle
  Diaries of the distinguished
  Domestic science
  Double scrambled names

Three words
The tree competition
Twelve parts of the body
Unusual questions
Vegetable soup
Vowels
Where's the youngster?
Who's a poet?
Word acrobats
Word golf
Word mathematics
Words and letters
Word golf. GEISTER—NEW p69-70.
Word mathematics. DEPEW p357-358.
*The word theory. (2m, 1f) HUBER—VAUD. p85-91.
Wordless solo. BRIDGE p21.
Words
> *See also* Adjectives; Word games
> Alliterative applications
Words and letters. YOUNG—GAMES p71-72.
Working on the dry squad. BUGBEE—LIVE WIRE p115.
The world series, by Jerry Owen. JOHNSON—EASY p115-117.
World's champion swimmer and high diver. CANOPY—HIGH
   p90-93.
*"The world's full of crooks". (3m) DRUMMOND—FOOT
   p91-96.
The world's outstanding sympathy orchestra. EISENBERG—
   FUN p191-192.
"The worm". HUBER—EASY p90-92.
*Worming around. (2m) DEASON—SKIT p52-57.
Wrap at the door. EISENBERG—FUN p32-33.
A (w)ringing welcome, by Grace Keith Samuelson.
   BUGBEE—NUTTY p8.
Writin' home. KASER—BUSHEL p18-19.
*Writing valentines. (3f) BUGBEE—LIVELY p75-78.
Wrong as ever. HUBER—PRACT. p5-8.
The wrong cup. EISENBERG—HAND. p89.
Wrong pronoun. GEISTER—NEW p88.
*A wronged husband, by Edwin Scribner. (3m, 1f) SNAPPY
   p95-100.

Wyatt, Rev. C. E.
   The case of John Imbecile
Wynken, Blynken and Nod. ABELL—STUNTS p89-90.

X-ray eyes, by Robert N. McGregor. BREEZY p71-72.
The xylophone. DRUMMOND—STUNT FUN p104.

Yancy Coogan. LLOYD p66-69.
A Yankee Doodle kitchen. BRIDGE p21.
Yardstick balance. DEPEW p170-171.
Yawning in the morning. DEPEW p286.
*Ye olde junke shoppe, by Edwin O'Hanlon. (1m, 2f)
      EASY—IMPR. p117-122.
Ye olde medicine show. RYAN p22-26.
*Ye olde time vaudeville, by Arthur L. Kaser. (3m)
      BRINGS—MASTER p144-147.
Yeah, by Arthur LeRoy Kaser. JOHNSON—EASY p118-120.
Yells, cheers, etc. CORMACK p13-14, 85-90.
Yes and no taboo. EISENBERG—HAND. p122.
Yes, we're having our banquet. DEPEW p272.
You ain't goin' to eat no more. DEPEW p274.
You can't go to heaven. DEPEW p262-265.
*You can't try an insane man. (4m) BERLE p55-60.
You have eleven fingers! EISENBERG—HAND. p53.
You never say it before, will never see it again. EISENBERG—
      HAND. p52.
*You said it, Doc. (2m, 1f) HUBER—FOUR p9-12.
You will please stand. DRUMMOND—STUNT FUN p16.
You won't stay away from me. KERR p66-67.
Your boy—the farm's best product. BUCHANAN p79.
*Your change. (3m) PROVENCE—KNOCKOUT p12-13.
Your dream interpreted. EISENBERG—FUN p44-46.
Your fortunes told. LAMKIN & FLORENCE p30-34.
Your future is at stake. STARR—JR. p51-55.
Your Horror-scope, by Beatrice Plumb. JOLLY p77-78.
*Your order, please, a nonsensical sketch, by Kurtz Gordon.
      (2m, 2f) SHANNON p5-15.
Your screen test. SHELDON p43-48.

*You're just the man. (2m, 1f) STAHL—MORE p46-48.

Youth and beauty machine. DRUMMOND—STUNT FUN p89-90.

*The youth and the North wind. *See* *Fun from Norway

You-uns and we-uns got religion. KERR p33-37.

*You've got to be tough, by Selden M. Loring. (4m) EASY—IMPR. p68-75.

The Yowell club. DEPEW p255-256.

Zeno, Norman L. Jr.
  *As the Byrd flies
  *Ivan Vosco, sanitary inspector is jailed
  *Mrs. Clarke wins seat in Congress
  *Opera opens
  *The training camp
Zig zag bean bag. YOUNG—GAMES p78-79.
Zoological garden. YOUNG—GAMES p7-8.
Zoos
  *At the zoo (2)
  Katie goes to the zoo
Zoo's zoo, by Beatrice Plumb. BRINGS—MASTER p418.
Zulu Zu. TARBELL—FUN p65,68.